What Readers Are Saying About P31 Devotionals

"With these devotionals and my Bible, I'm understanding my place in this world."

"I learn new ways of praying every time I read one of your devotions."

"Every day Jesus speaks to me in a new way through your devotions. It often amazes me how timely the messages are or how deeply they penetrate my heart. I think they have changed me beyond belief!"

"I just wanted to let you know that every day, and I do mean every day, your devotions say exactly what I need to hear. I am amazed at how each one speaks directly to whatever I am facing that day. Also, sometimes, I don't get to read it in the morning, and if I happen to have a bad day, I have found that when I do read it, I wish I had read it in the morning because it applied to what was going on that day and would have made a difference. I just wanted to say thank you for making a difference in my ʾe and my walk with God."

ʾnted to tell you how much I've enjoyed your daily devotions. I started ʾg them a couple of weeks ago, and now they are the first thing I go ʾe morning. They are making such a difference in my life."

awesome and REAL! Looking forward to more devotions from

for today's devotional. It touched my soul and made me fall ʾ feet. Please continue writing devotionals that destroy the valls we put up before others and before God."

ng so transparent and authentic in today's devotion. I bet o do. What a great model you're being for the rest of us."

peaking Christian girl and I read your devotion each me a lot to not only comprehend the love of God for go nearer and nearer to the One I love so much."

"I truly enjoy these daily devotions. They are so uplifting, encouraging, and heartfelt."

"The devotions have been such a blessing to me. Proverbs 31 Ministries has changed my life. It has helped me be disciplined with my morning devotions, and it has helped me be a better mom. Never in my life have I been more like a sponge, just soaking up God's Word!"

"I read these devotions daily and they are a great source of practical application."

"I thank you for sending me your encouragement from Proverbs 31 today. It really spoke to me."

"I look forward to the devotional each day, but the one for today left me in tears. Thank you so much! I am the proud mother of a two-year-old princess, and I needed every word of this devotional today."

"I am also a wife and a mother, and your devotions give me lots of Christian values that I have used to better our relationship and children throug the Word of God."

"I have been a Christian most of my life and know I desperately nee at all times! Especially now that I am getting older and supposedl God wants me to depend on Him like a child. He uses your team and these devotions to reach out to so many people like my been in different Bible studies, but I truly appreciate this teac have for women."

God's Purpose for Every Woman

Lysa TerKeurst

Rachel Olsen

HARVEST HOUSE PUBLISHERS

EUGENE, OREGON

Cover by Garborg Design Works, Savage, Minnesota

Cover photos © iStockphoto

GOD'S PURPOSE FOR EVERY WOMAN
Copyright © 2007 by Proverbs 31 Ministries
Published by Harvest House Publishers
Eugene, Oregon 97402
www.harvesthousepublishers.com

Library of Congress Cataloging-in-Publication Data
   God's purpose for every woman / Lysa TerKeurst and Rachel Olsen, general editors.
       p. cm.
   ISBN-13: 978-0-7369-2064-3 (pbk.)
   ISBN-10: 0-7369-2064-1
   1. Christian women—Religious life. 2. Christian women—Prayers and devotions. I.
TerKeurst, Lysa. II. Olsen, Rachel, 1970-
   BV4527.G63 2007
   248.8'43—dc22

                                                                    2007002493

Printed in the United States of America

       07 08 09 10 11 12 13 14 15 / VP-SK / 12 11 10 9 8 7 6 5 4 3 2

To the more than 150,000 women around the globe who have joined us daily for our online devotions, Encouragement for Today. Together we seek the heart of God and His peace, perspective, and purpose for our lives.

You are the reason these words are published.

Acknowledgments

This book would not exist without the team at Proverbs 31 Ministries. I am continually blessed by the authenticity and insight of our writers as I read these devotions. Thanks to each of you who have put pink and ink to the stories of your life and the longings in your heart: Charlene, Glynnis, Luann, Lysa, Marybeth, Melissa, Micca, Renee, Shari, Sharon, Susanne, Van, Wendy, and Zoë. I'm thankful to work with this amazing group of women!

Extra thanks to Micca and Susanne for their help with this project. Micca, your passion, dedication, and time week in and week out have paved the way for tens of thousands of women to be blessed through P31's devotions. I thank God for you. Susanne, your editorial help has been invaluable to me the past few years, just as your friendship has. Thank you both for serving alongside me.

Special thanks to LeAnn and Renee for cracking the whip at times, shouldering the burden at times, and administrating us all with excellence and grace. You two inspire me to go the extra mile without grumbling. Thanks also to the P31 staff—Barb, Laurie, Leah, Melissa, Teri, and Wendy—for your behind-the-scenes service to this team.

Last but certainly not least, thank you, Lysa—not just for effective leadership, not just for inspiring messages, but for your God-centered life lived out with us. You keep it real, and I treasure you for that.

Finally, I extend heartfelt appreciation to Harvest House Publishers for their vision for this project. Many thanks, Terry, for seeing the potential in the writings of this little band of women. Kim, thank you for sharpening our words, just as iron sharpens iron. The whole group at Harvest House has been a pleasure to know and work with.

—Rachel

Real Women—Real Issues—Real God

We imagine you are standing at the book rack looking for some encouragement. Something about this book intrigued you, so you picked it up and started flipping through the pages. Maybe you've already noticed it's written by a group of women from Proverbs 31 Ministries. Before you start rolling your eyes while images of perfect women flash through your head, let us put your mind to rest.

We are very ordinary women with the same everyday struggles you probably face. We have days where balance or organization eludes us. We have PMS days where attitudes are bad, tempers flare, and emotions run a little wild. Some of us struggle with our weight and a dislike of exercise. Others of us feel financial pressures. Some of us have prodigal children. Some of us have been prodigal children. All of us realize that despite our many shortcomings, we can find hope for today and tomorrow in God.

Perhaps it's because we are real women willing to be real with our struggles and our need for God that our online devotions have touched so many. Since launching a daily devotion in 2003 from our website (www.proverbs31.org), more than 150,000 women have subscribed. One woman wrote us to comment, "Do you have a secret recorder or little camera in my home? Everyday when I read my e-mail devotional, it speaks right to me about what I'm going through! All the time!! This ministry really has its finger on the pulse of Christian women and what they are going through."

We do understand what women go through, because we go through it too.

Jeremiah 29:11-13 says, "'For I know the plans I have for you,' declares the LORD, 'plans to prosper you and not to harm you, plans to give you hope and a future. Then you will call upon me and come and pray to me, and I will listen to you. You will seek me and find me when you seek me with all your heart.'"

God has good plans for every woman. He has plans to prosper us, not to harm us. When we cry out to Him, He will listen. When we make Him a priority, He'll act on our behalf in the most amazing ways. To understand and live by this truth is God's purpose for every woman. It's why we wrote this book.

At the back of the book you'll find an index listing each devotion by topic. In the pages within we'll share how we've found God, how He's changed our everyday lives, and how you can find Him too. Our desire is that long after you've forgotten our names and the stories of our lives in these pages, you'll remember God's unchanging faithfulness—and you'll have stories to tell of how He's touched your heart and changed your life as well. It's our hope that you'll discover your purpose in Him.

Sincerely,

Lysa TerKeurst,
President of Proverbs 31 Ministries

Rachel Olsen,
Senior Editor of Devotions

We are God's masterpiece.
He has created us anew in Christ Jesus,
so that we can do the good things
he planned for us long ago.

Ephesians 2:10 NLT

1 Be There

Lysa TerKeurst

*She watches over the affairs of her household and
does not eat the bread of idleness. Her children arise and
call her blessed; her husband also, and he praises her.*

PROVERBS 31:27-28

I always chuckle at speaking engagements when I hear the event
coordinator introduce me as an award-winning author and nationally
known speaker...blah, blah, blah. To those who know me best, I'm
simply a carpooling mom of five kids whose husband rises to call me
blessed if I can manage one monumental task...having clean under-
wear in his drawer every morning.

My life is not much different from that of any other woman. To
be honest, some days when I think about all that needs to be done,
I start feeling overwhelmed. I do laundry, pay bills, answer e-mails
or phone calls, return library books, shop for groceries, pack lunches,
make dinner, help with school projects, write thank-you notes, buy
birthday gifts, wash the car, and take the dog to the vet. Whew! No
wonder we keepers of the home have become masters at doing many
things at once.

Now, I'm all for multitasking, but sometimes it can get me into
trouble. Recently, while filling up at the gas station, I was trying to
do so many things at once that I almost pulled away with the nozzle
still attached to my car!

Multitasking helps me cross more things off my never-ending to-do
list, but I've found it's not good practice when I'm with my family. A
wise friend once told me, "Lysa, when you're with those you love—be
there." In other words, let the legacy you are creating with your family
be one of love and attention, not a completed task list. The jobs still
need to get done, but maybe we can learn to prioritize our to-do list,

complete what we can, and let other things wait. That way we can make sure we are being what God designed women to be, the heart of the home.

Simple things can speak volumes of love and attest to our priorities with our families. When my husband comes home from work, I get off the phone. When I pick up my kids from school, I give them my full attention as they share a myriad of details from their day. And each morning I take time to read the Bible and talk to God first, even before throwing a load of laundry in the washer or checking my e-mail. Then I can say with confidence to those I love, "I'm really here for you."

Dear Lord, I dreamed my whole life of being a keeper of my home. I want to do this job in a way that honors You and showers love on those closest to me. Sometimes it's hard having so many constant demands, but I know You can help me prioritize and complete my tasks. Will You help me know what needs to be done and what can be put off until later? Will You speak to my heart when I'm too wrapped up in my tasks and not attentive enough to my family? Help me create a legacy of truly being there for my family. In Jesus' name. Amen.

Application Steps

Take an honest look at your to-do list today. Prioritize your list into three categories: Must Do, Want to Do, Can Wait if Necessary. Then make an honest assessment of the time you'll be with your family and purpose to fully *be there*.

2 Competition or Mission?

Rachel Olsen

For we are God's masterpiece. He has created us anew in Christ Jesus, so that we can do the good things he planned for us long ago.

Ephesians 2:10 NLT

Do you ever look at other women and compare yourself to them—compare what you have to what they have, or what you do to what they accomplish? I know I sometimes do, and every time I make that comparison I come up short. Either I'm not as pretty or not as smart, not as rich or not as popular, not as energetic or not as organized, not as creative or not as productive.

If you can relate, if you too often feel inadequate, then let me let you in on a freeing truth. God didn't create us to live someone else's life. He gave us each our own mission, and He's gifted us uniquely for it.

When I keep my eyes on the Lord and His plans for my life, what others are doing or how well they are doing it becomes irrelevant. I don't have to compete because there is no competition for the role of Rachel Olsen on this earth or in the Father's heart.

There is no true competition for your role, either. You were specifically knitted together in your mother's womb by God Himself with purpose and care (see Psalm 139:13). No one else has the exact same combination of personality traits, spiritual gifts, and life experiences as you. You are a one of a kind, and you have a mission only you can fulfill. Ephesians 2:10 says it this way: "We are God's masterpiece. He has created us anew in Christ Jesus, so that we can do the good things he planned for us long ago" (NLT).

I can say with confidence that no one else can be your parents' daughter or your siblings' sister. No one else can be your husband's wife or your children's mother. I believe there are specific roles for you to play in your church and in your community. You were destined for these roles—nobody can fill them like you!

While I don't know the specific designs God has on your life, I know they are good and worth pursuing wholeheartedly. But you won't discover them by envying other women or accepting their mission in place of your own. Ignore the competition. Better yet, be happy for their success! They are no threat to you. Just keep your eyes on the Lord and keep asking Him to bring about His good plans for you.

> *Dear Lord, I believe You have satisfying plans for my life and You've gifted me to accomplish them. I ask You to reveal them to me and bring them closer to completion. Convict me, Holy Spirit, when I begin to experience envy or feel the need to compete. Remind me not to compete with others, but to love them. In Jesus' name. Amen.*

Application Steps

Next time you find yourself feeling competitive or envious of another woman, march right up to her and compliment her with all the gracious sincerity you can gather. When you walk away, whisper thanks to God that you don't have to compete with anyone to have or be all that He intends for you.

3 Whosoever

Micca Campbell

*For God so loved the world, that he gave
his only begotten Son, that whosoever believeth
in him should not perish, but have everlasting life.*

JOHN 3:16 KJV

As a little girl, I remember gazing at a picture of the crucifixion hanging on the wall in my Sunday school class. Christ's body was thin and hung limply to one side. His head bowed low. Blood trickled down His face from the crown of thorns atop his head. Nails pierced His hands and feet.

As an adult I read about the crucifixion in the Word of God. The Bible painted a different picture of Christ's death than the one I had seen as a child:

> Yet many shall be amazed when they see him—yes, even far-off foreign nations and their kings; they shall stand dumbfounded, speechless in his presence. For they shall see and understand what they had not been told before. They shall see my Servant beaten and bloodied, so disfigured one would scarcely know it was a person standing there (Isaiah 52:14-15 TLB).

Suddenly, I realized they had not simply nailed Christ to a cross, placed a crown of thorns upon His head, gashed His side with a spear, spit in His face, gave Him vinegar to drink, gambled for His clothes, and beat Him with a whip, but they beat Him until He became unrecognizable flesh hanging on the cross.

My mind flashed back to the first time I walked into the hospital room after my husband had been burned in a house fire. His skin was completely black, his head was swollen twice the normal size, and the skin on his arms was gone. He was utterly unrecognizable.

If Porter had been told ahead of time that working in that house would result in a fiery death, I'm sure he would have chosen not to go. Christ knew the horror of what would happen to Him on the cross, and yet He chose to go. He laid aside His royal crown, took off His righteous robe, and left His holy Father and His heavenly home to come to the dark land of sin to die for us. This King of all kings, innocent of wrong, was willing to pay our debts.

Christ didn't deserve death. He had never lied, stolen anything, or hurt anyone. Christ never disobeyed, harbored hatred, or judged and rejected others. He never gambled or yearned for His neighbor's wife. Christ never cheated on His taxes or betrayed a friend. No, Jesus Christ didn't do any of this, but we do.

Suddenly, I realized I was the guilty one. His death was for my past, present, and future sins. It wasn't man's will or nails of iron that held Jesus on the cross. It was the obedience of a Son and the love of a Father for me.

Today's verse says Christ died for "whosoever"! Whosoever you are… a teenager, a wife, a mother, a grandmother…a runaway, an addict, an adulteress, a murderer…will you receive His gift of forgiveness today? If so, your life will never be the same.

Dear Lord, forgive me of all my sins. Take my life and make me Your own. Thank You for dying on the cross to save me. In Jesus' name. Amen.

Application Steps

Pray the above prayer and invite Jesus Christ to be Lord of your life.

4 Mentoring—Moments or Meetings?

Renee Swope

They urged him to stay with them, and he stayed two days.

John 4:40

Don't you just hate the feeling you get when you think you've let someone down? I had that gnawing sense of regret one day after I met with a friend who had asked me to mentor her. I wanted to say no when Leslie asked because I felt inadequate. Now I was certain I wasn't cut out for the job.

Surely Leslie was disappointed in my lack of spiritual depth that day. *I should have brought up God more,* I thought. Instead, we talked about how hard it is to balance being a wife and mom. I mostly listened. I wished I had said something more profound to help her. Just listening didn't seem like a good way to mentor someone.

As I pondered my failure, I felt God gently remove the mentoring-effectiveness measuring stick from my hand and whisper, "Renee, it's a relationship. It's about being together." I knew it was God's Spirit speaking to me because it matched Jesus' way of life. He spent much of His time just being with people, talking and listening. Even when Jesus had somewhere to go, He would change His plans to spend time with someone.

One day while Jesus was on His way back to His hometown, He met a woman from Samaria. When they finished talking, she ran to tell her friends about Jesus. They wanted to meet Him too. In fact, "they urged him to stay with them, and he stayed two days. And because of his words many more became believers" (John 4:40-41). Their lives were changed because they were with Jesus. He hadn't planned to stay.

It wasn't really a scheduled meeting. Jesus simply mentored people in everyday moments that became chalkboards for life lessons.

Mentoring is part of God's purpose for *every* woman. Talking about spiritual truths and praying together is an important part of that role, but the effectiveness of our mentoring won't be based on how spiritual our time is or how much godly advice we give. It will be based on how well we get to know the woman God called us to befriend, and how well we let her get to know us—and Christ in us.

Leslie has grown into a beautiful wife, mother, and child of God. I saw her recently and wondered if our times together made a difference. She walked up with tears in her eyes and said, "I don't think I ever thanked you. You'll never know what a difference you made in my life."

Leslie needed a friend who would listen, a heart that would pray, a life she could watch, and a shoulder she could lean on. Isn't that what every woman needs? Could God be calling you to be that for someone today?

> *Dear Lord, is there a woman in my life who needs a friend and mentor? Is there someone who wants to go where I am headed, who is willing to follow along, whom I can lead toward the place You are calling her to? If so, please show me who she is and how You want me to share my life with her. In Jesus' name. Amen.*

Application Steps

Read Titus 2:3-4. Reflect on God's calling for women to mentor women. List three women you know who are at earlier stages in their journeys than you are. Pray for their relationships with God, their husbands, their kids, their ministries, and their careers. Ask God for moments to be an encouragement to them.

5 My Septic Heart

Wendy Pope

Out of the overflow of the heart the mouth speaks.
MATTHEW 12:34

"All you do is yell at the kids." Those are not encouraging words to hear from your husband. Like nails piercing the deepest part of my being, his words challenged my fitness as a mother. I became defensive immediately. Inside I was yelling back all the excuses I could muster up for why I had to yell. Then I heard the small whispering voice of the Holy Spirit convicting me. I realized my husband was right.

Why did I always yell? After all, I had Jesus in my heart. Why wasn't His love flowing from me? I began to pray and soon came to understand that the yelling was just a symptom of a deeply rooted problem: a septic heart. The heart and mouth are closely related. If I want to stop yelling at my kids and start expressing God's love to them, it's necessary for me to begin filling my heart with godly thoughts.

The word "septic," according to Webster's Dictionary, means "to make rotten" or "having the nature of sepsis." The word "sepsis" means "the presence of disease-causing organisms or toxins in the blood." My heart was unclean. Anger was a toxin in my spirit, which was a side-effect of unresolved issues in my heart. I'd been carrying many unresolved issues for years.

If you are like me, you may have a tough time taming your tongue or controlling your temper. We have to realize that our heart may be poisoned by the toxins of anger, resentment, unmet expectations, unforgiveness, bitterness, and unfulfilled dreams.

I've discovered four simple truths that jump-started my cleansing process. The toxins are not completely gone, but I take the antioxidant of God's Word daily to combat their effects. Try it! And you don't need a spoonful of sugar to help this medicine go down.

1. Renew your heart every morning (Isaiah 50:4-5). We have a whole day of living to do, and we need to set our mind on Him and receive His guidance.

2. Repent daily (Psalm 51:10). We can't carry the burden and conviction of our sin from day to day. Lighten your load.

3. Rend your heart often (Joel 2:12-13). Examine your heart honestly and ask God to help you identify those things that are not of Him.

4. Rest your heart when needed (Psalm 127:2). Though not always practical, sometimes lying down for a quick nap is just what the heart and soul need.

Dear Lord, You are slow to anger. Make that my desire. Help me submit totally to Your control so I can be a reflection of Your love to my family and those who cross my path. I realize love does not flow from a septic heart, full of past hurts and sins. I want to surrender the things in my heart that are not like You. In Jesus' name. Amen.

Application Steps

Ask God to help you to be slow to anger. Ask your family to forgive you for your behavior and to pray for you. Stop, leave the room, and pray before you yell. If you can't leave, still stop and pray. Ask a friend to hold you accountable for your temper.

6 Pass It On

Susanne Scheppmann

He said to them, "Go into all the world and preach the good news to all creation."

MARK 16:15

"Welcome! What can I get for you today?"

"A large Americano."

"Room for cream?"

"Nope."

"That will be $3.85 at the window."

The car ahead of me pulled out and turned the corner. I let my foot off the brake and crept toward the drive-through window. I fumbled for the exact change and then waited expectantly.

The window opened. A young brunette grinned and handed me the cup. I stretched out my hand to offer her the money. She said, "You don't have to pay. The car ahead of you bought your drink."

I jerked my head to see who might have been in the car ahead of me, but it was long gone. I asked, "Who was it?"

"You probably don't know them. The last eleven cars have all paid for the order behind them. It's been so fun to watch."

Amazed, I was about to pass on the blessing to the next vehicle. Then this thought went through my mind, *What if the order is for a whole office staff? What if it's $38.50 and not just $3.85?*

However, the blessing had to be passed on! I said, "Okay, I'll buy the order behind me." It turned out to be $4.95 and was worth the smile on the young worker's face. She giggled and turned to her coworkers. "Hey, it's number twelve now! Isn't this incredible?"

I drove off wishing I could have seen the face of the next coffee aficionado who was about to be pleasantly surprised. As I pondered this incident the rest of the day, I felt God teaching me a valuable lesson.

Do I pass on the blessing of Jesus to others, or do I fear what it could cost me? I might face rejection and ridicule. I could embarrass myself by not having all the right answers.

I recalled sitting around a smoky campfire with my youth group. We sang with gusto, "That's how it is with God's love...You want to pass it on." It seemed so easy to sing for lost souls when there wasn't one in sight.

So now, how often do I pass on the gospel of Jesus Christ? Unfortunately, not as often as I could. Jesus stated, "The harvest is plentiful, but the laborers are few; therefore beseech the Lord of the harvest to send out laborers into His harvest" (Luke 10:2 NASB).

We are His laborers sent to spread the good news of eternal salvation through the Lord Jesus Christ. Today's verse states for us to "go into all the world and preach the good news." Today my world may be my family, neighbors, coworkers, or a chance meeting in a store. I want to pass on the good news, no matter the cost.

Who in your world needs more than a cup of free coffee? Let's agree together to pass on the love of God to a harvest of hurting people.

Dear Lord, teach me how to pass on Your good news. Give me the courage when I feel timid to share my faith. In Jesus' name. Amen.

Application Steps

Today pass on a small blessing to someone else. Buy someone's coffee. Treat a child to some ice cream. Offer to babysit. Next, pass on the message of the gospel. Ask God to reveal a creative way to share the message of salvation with someone who needs eternal life.

7 The Difference a Faith-full Woman Can Make

Marybeth Whalen

They said to Joshua, "The LORD has surely given the whole land into our hands; all the people are melting in fear because of us."

JOSHUA 2:24

Perhaps you have heard the story of Rahab, the prostitute in Jericho who housed two spies and asked to be spared when Israel overtook Jericho. If not, read about her in the second chapter of the book of Joshua. While you might be familiar with the story of her bravery and the scarlet cord hung as a sign to spare her household, have you ever stopped to consider what could have happened to Israel if there had been no Rahab? When I began to consider this, I realized that the first time that Israel sent spies into the land, there was no Rahab. And things turned out very differently indeed.

The first time Israel spied out the land, 12 men (in Numbers 13) did not find any Rahabs to give them information about the inhabitants. There was no faith-full woman willing to help them, to give them shelter, or, most importantly, to tell them that their enemies were afraid of their God. So out of those original 12 spies, 10 came home in defeat—all but Caleb and Joshua. Ten men forgot that the God of the universe had already guaranteed their victory.

It seems that Rahab's offer of hospitality and hope gave the second set of spies just the dose of encouragement they needed to go home and say, "Let's go for it, guys! We've got God on our side!" (paraphrase of Joshua 2:24).

As I pondered these two separate-but-linked episodes in Israel's history, I realized that Rahab was a woman who impacted an entire nation for generations to come. Her faith in God was bigger than her fear of man, and she was not afraid to act. Because of her willingness, this highly unlikely heroine found her way into Jesus' lineage as the mother of Boaz (Matthew 1:5) and the "Faith Hall of Fame" (Hebrews 11:31).

God used Rahab to bolster His beloved people as they prepared to finally take possession of the land He had promised them. Rahab responded to God's call and became an active, courageous participant in His plan.

As I thought about this faith-full woman, I began to think about myself. I asked some tough questions about my own faith and obedience. I wondered, *If there were no me, would it make a difference? Can I name a specific time when God has invited me to join Him, and I have done it willingly and boldly, without first counting the cost?* As I realized how differently Israel's two missions turned out, I thanked God for using a woman who was probably a lot like me—unqualified, unprepared, and unworthy. Her example encouraged me that my active involvement in God's plans can make a difference far beyond what I can see from this side of eternity.

Dear Lord, thank You for the example of Rahab. Thank You for using unlikely people to make a difference for Your kingdom. Help me to be a faith-full woman as she was, and to step out boldly for You. In Jesus' name. Amen.

Application Steps

Journal your reactions to the two set of spies and Rahab. Has God brought to mind something that you could do to make a difference? Write these things down and pray about how you can become a faith-full woman for Him.

8　If Only
Luann Prater

He told me everything I ever did.
John 4:39

Have you read about the woman at the well in the fourth chapter of the book of John? Look her up in the dictionary, and you'll find a picture of me! We all have labels we dislike: addict, unfit, shy, stuck-up, party girl, fat, arrogant, stupid, unproductive, quitter, alcoholic, cheapskate, unworthy. Mine was "the woman at the well."

Who was this woman? If you are not familiar with her story, take a few moments to read John 4:1-30. What was her background? We don't have details, but we can be sure that her misdirected life didn't happen all at once. It was achieved by believing and acting on one lie at a time. This woman was on a desperate journey to find herself and her worth through men.

Her encounter at a well with Jesus brought two lives together and changed one forever. Through Jesus she found the love and worth she desperately desired—just as I did. Her story delivers hope when divorce is claiming more than two million victims each year, leaving broken lives and aching hearts in its wake.

I suspect this woman had been suffering from the "If Only" disease. You may be familiar with it: the questioning of her life that caused her "dis" (the absence or reversal of) "ease" (freedom). *"If only I hadn't made that wrong decision." "If only I had married a man who found value in me." "If only my children would show me respect." "If only my parents were different."* If only...if only...if only.

Last week I spoke to a group of 100 women. Ninety of them told me they felt unworthy, unloved, and unimportant in the scheme of life. It breaks my heart to hear this because I once felt that way too. I tried to find my worth in love—love from a man, love from my children, love from my friends—not realizing the love of God was freely offered and would satisfy me.

Life can be a monotonous pattern of doing the same thing over and over, hoping for some satisfaction. Though we may find temporary satisfaction, we will soon be thirsty again. We will keep trying to quench our thirst with a different man, a better job, a bigger house, another drink.

We live in a hurting world. Haunting choices from the past linger in our lives and prevent us from being all that God intends for us to be. Baggage doesn't have to be a reality in your life. God longs to give you an abundant life *if only* you will accept His life-giving water and leave your drought in the dust.

> *Dear Lord, I pray for every woman who has been touched by the pain of divorce, whether as a wife or daughter. I ask that You would allow them to see their worth through Your eyes. You, Lord, saw value in the woman at the well and, without a doubt, You see it in each one of Your children. Teach us to drink from Your life-giving water each day and live the abundant life You provide. In Jesus' name. Amen.*

Application Steps

It was the flawed people in the Bible who called Jesus a friend. He never sought perfect people, only people willing to follow a perfect Savior. Promise yourself that you will never use the words "if only" again. Drop a coin in a jar every time you slip and begin to linger in past mistakes. See how poor you can become in the jar and how rich you can grow in the Lord.

9 The Ministry of Interruptions

Glynnis Whitwer

While he was saying this, a ruler came and knelt
before him and said, "My daughter has just died.
But come and put your hand on her, and she will live."
Jesus got up and went with him, and so did his disciples.

MATTHEW 9:18-19

"I know how busy you are, and I'm so sorry to bother you," began my friend. Her request was simple, and I was glad she asked. But afterward I was pierced by her apology for "bothering" me.

Her comment haunted me. Why did she feel bad about asking for my help? Obviously I must give off the impression that I'm too busy to be bothered. As I pondered this idea, God brought my own words to mind. Sadly, I realized that for many years my standard answer to "How are you?" was "I'm busy."

This caused me to not only evaluate my words, but also my body language and schedule. Did my words and lifestyle welcome the interruption of a friend in need or put up a stop sign? I wondered how many opportunities to help a friend had been missed by my hectic life and don't-bother-me approach to interruptions. While I'd been checking items off *my* to-do list, had I missed something on *God's* to-do list?

Jesus had a different approach to interruptions—He welcomed them. In Matthew 9 we read that Jesus was teaching both His and John's disciples. In the middle of the lesson, a synagogue ruler interrupted Jesus and asked Him to come help his sick daughter. The Scripture records that Jesus got up and went with the man. Jesus didn't ask him to come back later or sigh and reluctantly rise. The text implies Jesus rose immediately and responded to the request.

People must have known Jesus was approachable because this is one of many instances where people interrupted Him. Jesus must have welcomed hurting, scared, and lonely people to come to Him. As Jesus responded with grace to the interruptions in His schedule, God worked miracles, and this time was no exception. But on this day, God worked two miracles.

Before Jesus could get to the sick little girl, a second interruption occurred. As Jesus walked through the crowded street, a woman touched His cloak. This woman, who had bled for 12 years, was instantly healed. Jesus felt power leave Him, and He stopped walking long enough to speak with the woman. After this interaction, Jesus continued to the ruler's house, where He raised the man's daughter from the dead.

Two interruptions, two loving responses by Jesus, and two miracles. Imagine if Jesus had been too busy, or if this man or woman had been afraid to bother Him. Imagine the ministry God might want to work through us when we welcome interruptions.

I'm learning from Jesus to slow down, choose welcoming words, and consciously eliminate rushing from my life. Jesus modeled a life submitted to God's plan—including the interruptions. My prayer is that God will work through me in the ministry of interruptions.

> *Dear Lord, I praise You for Your compassion and patience with me. I know I can always come to You when I'm in need. Help me to be more aware of the needs of those around me. I want to be more like Jesus and allow You to work through me. In Jesus' name. Amen.*

Application Steps

Identify one person who needs more of your time. Commit to changing your words and opening up your schedule to be more available to that person.

10 Do I Want Change?

Melissa Taylor

Search me, O God, and know my heart.
Psalm 139:23 nkjv

Weight has always been a struggle for me. I spent years dieting. Diets work. Each time I followed a plan according to the rules, I lost weight and was happier. The happiness gained through dieting didn't last, though. I never could stick to the rules and would gain the weight back. Then I was sad.

This cycle repeated itself for 20 years. My weight and size went up and down. I don't have to tell you this is not a good thing. Yo-yo dieting is unhealthy for your body and mind. I was in a rut I hope never to revisit.

My journal used to read like this: *8:00 a.m.—My goal today is to eat healthy and stick to the plan. 8:00 p.m.—I ate fruit for breakfast. I exercised. I ate salad for lunch. Then, I don't know what happened. I stressed out. The kids were crazy and the house was a mess. I ate like a pig the rest of the day. What is wrong with me? God, I need You to fix me.*

It saddens me to read those words. I was living in condemnation. In my eyes, I was a failure. If I wanted to change, then why didn't I?

After reading through my old journals, I was amazed at how much time I spent agonizing over weight issues. I would never define my life by my weight, yet it was consuming my thoughts. I consider so many other things more important than food: my husband, my kids, and my friends, to name a few. I love God with all my heart, but I wasn't acting much like it. I was focused on myself instead of Him.

I was finally ready to surrender. Did I want change? Yes, but I wanted real and permanent change, from the inside out. No diet can do that. Only God can.

We can do things our way or God's way. Our way may produce temporary results or pleasure. For instance, diets worked and the results made me happy, but they only fixed me on the outside, and for me, only temporarily. In order for the treasure of true change to occur, I needed God to come to the forefront of the process. So I made Him my focus.

As I spent more time in the Bible, I found eternal treasures that are far better than temporary ones. In Christ I am accepted, loved, and significant! He loves me no matter how much I weigh or how many times I fail. When I turned my focus to God, I dropped ten pounds. Would I like to lose more? Yes, since every weight chart I read says I'm still ten pounds overweight. But that is no longer my main focus.

If you are trying to fight what seems to be a losing battle in your life, I want you to know you are not alone. Join me in searching for your treasure God's way.

> *Dear Lord, Your Word says I am wonderfully made. Please examine my heart and lead me to make choices that honor and please You. In Jesus' name. Amen.*

Application Steps

Make God your primary focus, even above that which you desperately want changed.

11 Victoria's Little Secret

Lysa TerKeurst

*Like an apple tree among the trees of the forest is
my lover among the young men.*

Song of Songs 2:3

Victoria has a little secret and I'm not in on it! This came to me
when I found a gift certificate to Victoria's shop while cleaning out my
office. *Oh, her,* I thought, a little disappointed. Not that I don't like
Victoria. It's just that the thought of wearing something that is scratchy,
over-revealing, and undersized just doesn't give me the motivation I
need to make a special trip to the mall.

Upon closer investigation, I doubled over in laughter as I realized
the certificate was more than ten years old! My husband, Art, found
no humor in the situation and offered to use it to buy me a gift. I
just smiled back at him and requested that he remember two things:
warmth and comfort! Does Victoria make flannel pj's?

Whether it's because of changes in our bodies, sleep deprivation,
time constraints, financial pressures, or a myriad of other things, marriage changes after kids. But it doesn't have to be for the worse. Instead
of hoping things will magically reignite and get better, I've decided to
actively pursue a richer relationship with my husband. It will be a matter
of choice, not chance. Here are some of my newly resolved choices:

Seduce him. Oh, gasp, is that allowed to be said in a Christian book?
Absolutely! I know when my husband has been left wanting for too
many days in a row, he gets cranky. Think for minute if your husband
was your only source for food. But every time you went to him to get
this nourishment you not only wanted but also needed, he said back
to you, "Not now. I'm too tired. I have a headache." Most husbands
would love it if their wives were a little more intentional about initi-
ating intimate connections, so seduce him.

Serve him. I can feel eyes rolling on this one, but when was the last time I really looked for something Art wanted and did it for him? Sometimes the thing we least want to do in our marriage might be the very thing that could help our relationship the most. Instead of becoming offended the next time your spouse asks if you can do something for him, why not see it as an opportunity to invest in your marriage? It just might work wonders.

Simply be sweet to him. Why is it that I can be *so* kind to strangers and then—just seconds later—impatient and *unkind* to those I love most? I don't want short fuses, quick tempers, and rushed conversations to be the legacy I build with my husband. I have to make the choice to swallow my cutting remarks and simply be sweet!

So, my little hidden gift certificate actually has served me well. It was a sign that I need to make some adjustments and investments. I think I'll ask Art if I can accompany him to the mall. And no, I won't be in search of flannel. Maybe I'm starting to clue in to Victoria's little secret after all.

> *Dear Lord, help me to remember that sex within marriage is a blessing for both me and my husband. God, give us a desire for each other that will reignite the romantic spark in our relationship. Thank You, Lord, for the privilege to be a wife. In Jesus' name. Amen.*

Application Steps

You guessed it…seduce him, serve him, be sweet to him!

12 Shattered and Scattered

Van Walton

The LORD appeared…from afar, saying,
"I have loved you with an everlasting love;
Therefore I have drawn you with lovingkindness."
JEREMIAH 31:3 NASB

I walked out on the beach onto hardpacked sand—the perfect consistency for a brisk walk. As I surveyed the ground ahead, I couldn't help but admire the seashells stretched out before me. Scattered as far as I could see were hundreds, no thousands, of pieces of shells. Every once in a while I spotted one that seemed to be flawless. I'd immediately bend down to pick it up, only to realize it was broken and then toss it back. A little later I'd spot another lovely work of nature, beautifully banded and smooth, with unique colors. Once again I'd reach down to collect it, but finding a defect, I'd drop it. When I did manage to find one without blemish, I'd happily tuck it in my pocket.

As I stood on that beach, surrounded by these broken pieces, I thought about the similarity of those shells to my life. I am not perfect and never will be. I would hate to be picked up, studied, and discarded because of my imperfections and defects. At that moment, God reminded me that He doesn't choose His children based on outer appearances. No one is faultless, but God picks us up anyway from the pile of scattered and shattered humanity, and He loves us despite our blemishes and brokenness.

He also uses us, flaws and all, to tell others His message. What is this message? Hope. Hope in something larger than the broken, shattered pieces of our small lives. Often we look around and develop a sense of hopelessness due to our inability to compete with the world's standards. Many of us feel tossed aside or overlooked, but the great news is that God never tosses any of us because of our shattered and scattered lives. He created each one of us and sees us as perfect in Christ. Christ's death on the cross paid the price for our imperfections—our sins. The blood that He shed washes us clean.

After a while I stopped collecting shells. Suddenly the challenge of finding perfect ones lost its appeal. God isn't interested in perfect people. He came to encourage the shattered and gather the scattered.

Dear Lord, I am overwhelmed by Your desire to be a part of my life—to gather my broken pieces and show me Your plans, despite my many imperfections. Pick me up and use me to encourage others in their brokenness. In Jesus' name. Amen.

Application Steps

Are there bits and pieces of your life that are shattered and scattered? In your journal write a letter to God and tell Him about your brokenness. Then, in a prayer, ask Him to show you how much you are valued.

13 Knowing God

Micca Campbell

More than that, I count all things to be loss in view of
the surpassing value of knowing Christ Jesus my Lord.

PHILIPPIANS 3:8 NASB

If someone were surveying my life, they might conclude that my greatest passion is to speak or pen lasting words that will transform lives long after I'm gone. The truth is, my greatest desire is to know God.

Can a person really know God intimately? Of course you can! In fact, this is why you and I were created, to have an ongoing, personal, love relationship with our God.

We meet a tremendous amount of people throughout our lifetime. Some of them are quite special to us, such as a schoolteacher who helped us achieve our goals, an aunt or uncle who always stood by our side, or perhaps a childhood hero we admired. While it's wonderful to know these special people that better our lives, our greatest privilege is to know God.

Sadly, though, most people only take the first step in knowing God at the foot of the cross. It's enough for them that their sins are forgiven and heaven is their future home. If you were to ask them if they know God, most would say they do.

I can't help but wonder. How can you know the Comforter if you've never experienced His comforting? How can you know Him as Provider when you've chosen to live life independent of Him? How can God be your Helper if you've never allowed His hand to lead you through the darkness? There is more to God beyond Savior.

We can have all the intellectual knowledge there is about God and still not know Him. Our Bibles can be color coded, underlined, and frayed at the edges, but it doesn't necessarily mean that we are familiar with God on a personal level. That kind of relationship comes through trusting the Lord's promises in every situation until we are confident that He is faithful and true.

As long as we go through life dependent on our own resources, we will never know how marvelous our God is. We'll never know how He longs to come alongside us and be our provision. Our Lord will not show Himself to the proud and arrogant heart. God will only reveal Himself to those who humbly seek Him with their whole heart. When we acknowledge Him in our helpless state, we discover who the Lord is. Bowing daily before His majesty is where we discover God's holiness, power, love, and true fellowship with Him. Only then we will begin to appreciate His divine nature that makes our God a privilege to know.

Do you hunger to know God? Tell Him! Spend time in His Word and discover His magnificent attributes. Before long you'll come to realize like Paul that all else is rubbish compared to knowing God. He is the prize, the blessing of our lives, and our greatest treasure. He already knows you and me. Isn't it time to get to know Him?

Dear Lord, create in me a hunger for You alone. Open my eyes and reveal Yourself to me. I want to know You, Lord. In Jesus' name. Amen.

Application Steps

Pick a place to meet with God. Ask Him to reveal Himself to you through His Word. Write down any verse that seems to jump off the page at you. Ask God to show you what He wants you to know, and then apply this revelation to your life.

14 Loving Irregular Dads

Sharon Glasgow

Love suffers long and is kind; love does not envy;
love does not parade itself, is not puffed up;
does not behave rudely, does not seek its own,
is not provoked, thinks no evil; does not rejoice in iniquity,
but rejoices in the truth; bears all things,
believes all things, hopes all things, endures all things.
Love never fails.

1 Corinthians 13:4-8 nkjv

Do you have an irregular dad? I did. Most people assume that all dads are normal. Well, some are not normal according to the world's standards.

My dad was always different from other dads. He didn't like crowds, so he didn't come to special events such as award ceremonies, sports competitions, or even graduation. He was a man of few words, never saying "congratulations," "good job," or "I love you." But in my heart I knew he was proud of me and loved me. He just didn't know how to express it.

When I became an adult I would take him out to eat or go fishing with him. I can still remember as if it were yesterday how his pants slid off while he walked, and how he'd click his false teeth in and out in public. I would mention to him that he should keep his teeth in place while we were out, but he couldn't seem to control that habit.

The most challenging thing for me about being with Dad was that he smoked. He couldn't stop, even for the duration of a single visit. I'm allergic to cigarette smoke, so this made visiting with him difficult because I couldn't breathe. But I'd give anything in the world for those times, even if they were hard.

My kids didn't get to know their grandpa. I wish they could have.

He was schizophrenic, and his mind continued to deteriorate when they were young. He is gone now, but I think of him often. I miss him, clicking teeth, smoke, and all, because I loved him no matter how irregular he seemed.

Maybe your dad isn't all this world says he should be either, but he is your dad. It's time to honor him, even if his quirks make him everything you wish he wasn't.

He may never know how to say "I love you" or show that he loves you, but you will be freed when you give him unconditional love. When his profound differences make you squirm, let God give you His wisdom to act and say the appropriate things, and you will reap what you sow—abundant blessing.

Your dad may never give you the approval you think you need, but the truth of the matter is that you only need God's approval. So be filled with the joy of the Lord, and be free to bless your earthly father with love that never fails.

Dear Lord, help me to love my dad in a way that would bring honor to You and him. Help me to see beyond the external and into the eternal. Help me to live out the truth that "love never fails" with my dad. In Jesus' name. Amen.

Application Steps

Honor your father even if he is irregular. God will help you.

15 Ice Princess

Rachel Olsen

People with good sense restrain their anger;
they earn esteem by overlooking wrongs.
PROVERBS 19:11 NLT

I gasped as the ice dancing pair both fell in the final seconds of their routine. They had come out of retirement to skate in the Olympics before their home crowd, and they skated so well in the first round that they were in first place heading into the second round of the three-day competition.

Both partners recovered from the fall in time to hit their final pose as the music ended. They headed to center rink, where they're expected to take bows. It was then that the real drama began. The woman faced her partner with an intense look. Was she hurt? She stood staring at him for the longest time. The camera angle widened, allowing us to see his face also. At first he looked disappointed, then confused, and then he simply matched her stare.

As the staring contest wore on, the crowd grew quiet and uncomfortable. By this point it was clear she was communicating tremendous disapproval with her icy look. I suspect this man wanted nothing more than to take his partner's hand, shrug off their shared disappointment, and take their bows—but his manhood was being challenged, in public no less.

Eventually they bowed and headed over to the "kiss and cry" area to await their scores. She still didn't give it a rest. She was not looking at the scores, crowd, or camera, but mostly glaring at him in anger. As a skating fan, I've seen many drops, mistakes, and falls, but I've never seen a partner behave like this afterward. They dropped from first place to seventh with one round left to skate, and the sun went down on her anger.

The next day the pair entered the arena separately, warmed up separately, and didn't speak a word to each other. This behavior continued until they joined hands on the ice to begin their final routine. Both partners skated beautifully, and the world waited to see what her reaction would be. She was pleased, so she dramatically hugged and kissed him. I've never seen a clearer picture of performance-based love.

Like this ice princess, I am prone to use the icy silent treatment when I'm mad at my spouse. I can say from experience that it's not healthy or productive. The silent treatment communicates: If you do not please me 100 percent, you no longer exist in my world. After reading Matthew 5:21-22, I'm guessing Jesus would consider this method of anger-management murderous.

The Bible advises against performance-based love, and advocates grace-based love instead. Proverbs 19:11 explains we should be slow to anger and quick to forgive. *The Message* puts it this way: "Smart people know how to hold their tongue; their grandeur is to forgive and forget." We're also advised to stop mulling over our grievances. First Corinthians 13 explains that a loving person is not irritable or demanding, and doesn't carry a grudge (verses 4-5). After all, it's hard to be graceful with a grudge in hand.

Have you been loving and full of grace lately, or just plain icy?

Dear Lord, I need help moving from an attitude of performance-based love to a grace-based perspective. Help me to be slower to anger and quicker to overlook offenses. In Jesus' name. Amen.

Application Steps

Pay attention to your nonverbal reactions today and see what they're communicating to those around you. Ask a trusted friend how well you really deal with your disappointment in loved ones.

16 You're Just Like That Little Girl

Zoë Elmore

*Therefore, since we are surrounded by such a
great cloud of witnesses, let us throw off everything
that hinders and the sin that so easily entangles,
and let us run with perseverance the race marked out for us.*

HEBREWS 12:1

As I left the grocery store yesterday, I noticed a small girl holding on to her mother's hand as they entered the store. While I've witnessed a similar scene countless times before, there was something unusual that caught my attention. In her free hand, the tiny girl held on to a large stuffed animal that appeared to be as big as she was. Each time her mom took a step forward, the daughter would step on and trip over her beloved toy. Step-trip, step-trip, step-trip—this awkward rhythm continued as they made their way into the store.

I couldn't help but think about the self-control this mom was exercising with her daughter as she tripped and stumbled along. I thought about how much easier it would have been to leave the dirty and tattered toy behind in order to get on with her day. Wow! This mom deserves a gold star for patience. As we passed one another in the doorway, I noticed the determination of this child and realized that no amount of tripping or stumbling was ever going to persuade her to part with her beloved toy.

Making my way to the car, I thought about what I had just seen, and the Lord whispered into my ear, "Zoë, you are just like that little girl. You cling to Me with one hand, yet your other hand is full of old ragged things, causing you to trip and stumble." As I drove home, I asked the Lord to open my eyes to those things that entangle me, hindering my walk with Him.

One by one, the Lord revealed things I must throw off and leave behind: old insecurities, ragged motives, and worn-out behaviors. These are things that cause me to stumble in my relationship with the Lord. I've held on to these things for many years with the same intensity that that little girl clung to her toy. Now that these have been revealed, I must choose to leave them behind. I must continue to cling to the Lord with one hand while keeping the other hand free to share His goodness with others.

> *Dear Lord, forgive me for clinging to things that impede my walk with You. Enable me, through the power of Your Holy Spirit, to throw off and leave those things behind that cause me to stumble. I want to walk with You unencumbered by the things of this world. In Jesus' name. Amen.*

Application Steps

If you feel entangled, tripping up in your spiritual life, ask the Lord to reveal the things you are holding on to that are holding you back. Then ask the Holy Spirit to empower you to let go and leave them behind.

17 Burned-Out and Calling Out

Wendy Pope

To you, O LORD, I call, for fire has devoured
the open pastures and flames have burned up
all the trees of the field.

JOEL 1:19

I am drawing a blank as I sit to write this devotion. I feel exhausted. I feel burned up. I wonder if you can identify with me. Life is hard and complicated. And frankly, life burns us out. We go and go. We endure. We overcommit ourselves. Sometimes, we sin.

At times we even enjoy the enticing allure of selfishness and sin. Before we know it, however, the enemy has used this allure to destroy the once soft and grassy pasture of our walk with God. The quiet brook where we would go to quench our thirst is dry and hard. The wild-flowers of spontaneous acts of kindness are gone. The trees that gave us shelter and protection from the heat of the enemy's attacks have been destroyed in the fire. So what are we to do now? We stand in the middle of our burned up pasture and call out to a holy God who loves us unconditionally.

I love the picture today's verse paints. In the middle of our destruc-tion, in our burned-out state of mind, we can call to our heavenly Father for help. He reaches out to us with His strong hands and ten-derly lifts us into His arms.

Unfortunately, we can't expect restoration and renewal without repentance. What burned my beautiful pastures was direct disobedi-ence and willful sin in my life. In order for the grass to grow again, the brook to flow, and the wildflowers to bloom, I must be willing to confess the sins in my life and allow God to sow His will in my heart.

In Isaiah 61:3, the prophet tells us God will bring forth beauty from the ashes of our lives. In that same verse Isaiah says that God will exchange our mourning for gladness and give us "a garment of praise instead of a spirit of despair. They will be called oaks of righteousness, a planting of the LORD for the display of his splendor."

Doesn't this verse describe what we want? To have the pain of our mistakes or trials somehow bring forth beauty in our lives? To have the mourning we feel over lost loved ones, broken relationships, or unfulfilled dreams replaced with gladness? What if today we took God up on His Word and put on the garment of praise He has designed especially for us, instead of wearing that tattered garment of despair? Oh, what a display of splendor we'll be!

Dear Lord, take off of me this worn-out garment of despair and help me put on my garment of praise. I want to be a planting for You, a display of Your splendor. Help me to be willing to do what it takes for my heart to be fertile soil for Your planting. In Jesus' name. Amen.

Application Steps

Write out Isaiah 61:3 and memorize it.

18 Do You See Me?

Marybeth Whalen

Our fellowship is with the Father and with his Son,
Jesus Christ. We write this to make our joy complete.

1 John 1:3-4

My seven-month-old daughter loves to be noticed. When her daddy walks into the room, she will lock her eyes on him intently until he sees her and pays her sufficient attention. When we are in a restaurant, she looks around at people at nearby tables until she finds someone who will talk to her and return her blue-eyed gaze. Though she cannot speak, her eyes tell the tale. She is saying, "Notice me! Do you see me?" Even at such a young age, she feels a need to somehow be validated by other human beings. Her need to know that she matters in this world gave me insight into the human psyche.

Unfortunately, we confuse our need to be validated by others with our soul's cry for intimacy with God. For many of us, that means moving from one person to the next, hoping to find the one who will finally validate us and let us know that we matter. We foolishly think that if others notice us, compliment us, and affirm us, we will fill up that emptiness. And yet the emptiness invariably creeps back in as the cycle continues throughout our lives.

However, there is a way to break this cycle. When we draw close to God and discover the soul-affirming joy of fellowship with Him, then we find what we have truly been longing for. We learn that God can fill our empty spaces deep inside. We stop looking to sin-filled people in a fallen, broken world to validate us. While affirmation and validation will always be nice to have, we find we don't *need* them the way we once did. Because Jesus lives in you, people notice something different about you. Your confidence—not in yourself, but in Him—

shines through and draws others to you. In short, people want what you have when you have a relationship—fellowship—with God.

When Adam and Eve walked in the Garden of Eden, they enjoyed sweet companionship with their Creator. Though banished from that paradise, the human soul has never forgotten what that oneness with God feels like. We will continue to search for it in vain as long as we search for it apart from Him. If you are searching for validation in all the wrong places today, I urge you to seek God anew. Ask Him to fill you up. Stop scanning every room you enter for that one person who will finally meet all your needs. That will only happen when you turn your face toward heaven.

Dear Lord, thank You for desiring to have a relationship with me. Help me to look to You when I need to be validated. Help me to not look in the wrong places and to find the peace I am seeking in Your waiting arms. In Jesus' name. Amen.

Application Steps

If you are in a habit of seeking validation and affirmation from others, take steps today to stop and draw closer to God. Remember that people will always let you down, but God never will. He adores you.

19 Plan a Great Date

Renee Swope

*Very early in the morning, while it was still dark,
Jesus got up, left the house and went off to a
solitary place, where he prayed.*

MARK 1:35

I knew my husband was up to something special when he invited me to lunch for the next day. I woke up that morning to find a card with detailed instructions. He'd planned a whole day of anniversary surprises that included a facial, a reserved table for dinner away from the crowds, chocolates and flowers, a walk under the stars, and time to talk—just the two of us.

J.J. had planned the perfect date and every detail spelled L-O-V-E to me! He'd chosen a time and a place. He'd made sure my heart and mind were prepared to enjoy our date, and when it was over, our hearts were closely connected.

So it is in our relationship with God. Each day He wants to spend time with us. As we see in today's verse, Jesus spent time with His Father each day. Just like Jesus, we need to get creative and intentional about planning a date—Determine a Time Everyday—with God. Here are some things we can do to make the most of our time alone with Him.

Choose time alone each day. Set 15 minutes aside each morning to begin your day with God. As your relationship grows, you can increase your time together.

Create a setting for two. Find a comfortable quiet place for your date. I have a favorite chair near a window in my bedroom with a pretty chenille throw over it. Every time I walk by I imagine Jesus waiting there for me.

Prepare your heart. Listen to worship songs to prepare your heart to hear from God. Music that reminds us of who God is drowns out distractions and sets our focus on Him.

Ask God to speak to you. Everything God wants you to know is written in the Bible, His love letter to you. As you read, ask Him to show you what you need that day. You can start by reading a psalm and a chapter from the book of Proverbs each day.

Pray. This is your chance to listen quietly and share openly with God. There's nothing you can tell Him that He doesn't already know. There's nothing too big or small for Him to handle.

Journal. Journaling is like keeping a spiritual scrapbook. Record requests prayed and answered so you can see not only how God can change your circumstances, but how He changes you. Staying connected to His heart through time alone together is the beginning of becoming the satisfied, peace-filled woman you long to be. So set aside some time to spend with the One who knows you best and loves you most.

> *Dear Lord, I want my relationship with You to grow. I want to know You more and be captured by Your love each day. Give me a desire for time with You that cannot be satisfied by anything else. In Jesus' name. Amen.*

Application Steps

Go to bed earlier so you'll have more time in your morning and more energy for your date. Write a time in your calendar to spend with God each day this week. Choose a favorite place and imagine Him waiting for you. Turn off the phone during your date and harness wandering thoughts by writing them down on a sheet of paper. Plan your date today!

20 A Fool's Tongue

Susanne Scheppmann

*Better a poor man whose walk is blameless
than a fool whose lips are perverse.*

Proverbs 19:1

Eccentric people make us laugh. They do funny things. Sometimes they appear foolish in our eyes. Have you ever appeared foolish to someone? I have.

At the beginning of the New Year, I decided I would exercise more. I wanted to walk with my dogs, but they both have arthritis in their hind legs and can't move about much. So I devised an ingenious solution with the help of an old baby stroller. I plopped my dogs in the dilapidated stroller and squinted into the bright morning sun. I decided to grab my sunglasses and off we went.

Two miles into my trek, I saw a woman with a puppy prancing beside her. She appeared startled as I approached. I grinned and said, "I know it's ridiculous to be pushing these dogs in a baby stroller, but they can't walk far." She nodded curtly. Then she snatched her dog up in her arms and strode away without a word.

After my invigorating exercise, I came home pleased with my ingenuity. I lifted the dogs out of the stroller. I took off my sunglasses and placed them on the counter. To my surprise, one of the dark lenses had fallen out. I realized how foolish I must have looked. Strolling with two dogs in a baby stroller and staring out of sunglasses with a missing lens. No wonder the woman grabbed her dog and hightailed it away from me!

I laughed until my sides ached. Although I looked pretty foolish, it didn't harm anything except perhaps my ego.

Unfortunately, some of our behaviors hurt others. A common theme throughout the Bible is the foolish use of our tongue. In the book of

James, we are warned not to use our tongue to bless God and then curse people.

You can read about Balaam in the book of Numbers. King Balak of Moab wanted Balaam to curse the Israelites, but God commanded Balaam to bless them. As the story goes on, Balaam keeps trying to figure out a way to bypass the will of God. It seems he had a penchant for taking out his frustrations on everyone else. Eventually, Balaam's donkey speaks up.

> When the donkey saw the angel of the Lord, she lay down under Balaam, and he was angry and beat her with his staff. Then the Lord opened the donkey's mouth, and she said to Balaam, "What have I done to you to make you beat me these three times?" Balaam answered the donkey, "You have made a fool of me! If I had a sword in my hand, I would kill you right now" (Numbers 22:27-29).

Balaam's foolish decisions made him a fool, not the donkey's behavior. The donkey, although only a beast, held more wisdom than Balaam.

Unfortunately, more times than I care to admit, my tongue makes a fool of me. Words fly out, only to be heard later by the target of my gossip. Or at other times I've insisted my opinion on a subject was correct, and then later I was proved wrong. Yes, I have been a fool with folly falling from my lips.

I might have looked foolish strolling with my dogs while wearing sunglasses with only one lens. However, I pray that my tongue will speak wisdom and blessing to everyone I encounter. I certainly never want to give cause for my dogs to speak to me!

Dear Lord, help me control my foolish tongue. I ask the Holy Spirit to take control of my tongue. In Jesus' name. Amen.

Application Steps

Read James 3:1-12.

21 Going Astray
Luann Prater

You were like sheep going astray.
1 PETER 2:25

My family and I once spent a wonderful week exploring the charming countryside of England. We had chosen to travel by train in order to get a close look at the landscape. We were certainly not disappointed. The striking beauty of the rolling hills and the lush meadows took our breath away.

After arriving at our accommodations, we decided to explore the surrounding grounds. Unprepared for the splendor that stretched before us, the seventeenth-century manor house was right out of a fairy tale. Beyond the scenic garden just outside our patio door was a beautiful green pasture dotted with sheep peacefully grazing on the cool grass. We strolled to the back of the property and came upon a barbed wire fence. It was interesting because there were thick clumps of wool caught on each barb. In fact, little puffs of white were scattered all along the fence as far as I could see in either direction. And then it hit me. I am such a sheep!

When I was a teenager I turned my life over to Jesus Christ, asking Him to come in and take control. But as the years passed, I longed to escape His protection and catch a glimpse of the world and all of its enticements. I did not plan to jump over the hedges of protection placed around my life by the Father. I just wanted to sneak along those boundary lines, getting just close enough to see what it was really like out there, where the grass seemed greener.

One wrong decision—a single deliberate choice to take one tiny step toward that forbidden edge—led to another wrong decision, and then another. Before I knew it, I was swallowed up in the muck and mire of sin, grazing in the wrong pasture on the wrong side of the fence.

Just like the wandering sheep, I found myself caught in sharp barbed wire. I was wounded by the consequences of my choices and longed for the peaceful pastures I had been so quick to escape. I cried out to God, like a lost and broken lamb passionately bleating for its Shepherd. Immediately sensing His presence, my heart was filled with the sweet knowledge that He had been there all along, every step of the way, watching over me and waiting for me to return home. He gently pulled me away from the fence and led me back to the place of obedience where I belonged.

Staring at the barbed wire fence that day, I was reminded of how the Good Shepherd loves us. Not without pain, not without scars or tears, but faithfully and tenderly, I had been released from the hold of sin by the grasp of the Shepherd.

Dear Lord, thank You for being our Good Shepherd. Thank You for snatching us from danger and gently leading us home. Keep me far from the edge as I walk in Your truth today. Lead me and keep me from going astray. In Jesus' name. Amen.

Application Steps

When you make a wrong choice, confess it and let it go, knowing that His grace has already provided the forgiveness you need. Let the Good Shepherd return you to God's pastures of peace.

22 Worth Dying For

Glynnis Whitwer

To me, to live is Christ and to die is gain.

PHILIPPIANS 1:21

One day my 14-year-old son Josh e-mailed me an article he found on a website. It was about a Christian in China who was persecuted to the point of death for his faith. There wasn't any personal note from my son, just the article. I read it and my heart was touched, but then I didn't think much else about it.

Several months later, a magazine arrived in the mail addressed to Josh. It was from the organization Voice of the Martyrs. I remembered the e-mailed article and connected the dots. Obviously, this website interested my son.

When Josh came home from school, I showed him the magazine and asked, "Why are you interested in this?" I thought perhaps he'd discussed it at youth group or Young Life.

Without a pause, and with sincerity shining from his young face, he answered, "I've always wanted to be a martyr."

My heart started to thud and my insides twisted. This was not what I expected to hear. My mind raced frantically, trying to make sense of his answer. *Surely,* I reasoned, *he doesn't know what a martyr is.* Hoping my assumption was true, I asked, "Do you know what a martyr is?"

"Yes," he replied. "Someone who's willing to die for his faith. I want that kind of faith."

After recovering from the shock of his answer, and battling the fear of a mother's heart, God revealed something to me about my son's desire to be a martyr. It's not that my son wants to die, but that he's found something worth dying for.

At 14 Josh looks around him and sees people pursuing things that are meaningless. He's watched friends search for happiness in popularity, music, drinking, and being rebellious and disrespectful. Even his young mind knows that none of these things are worth dying for.

But many years ago, my son met Jesus. And when he did, Josh discovered something that mattered...Someone worth dying for.

I believe God's eyes roam the earth looking for a child of His whose faith burns in her chest...who loves Jesus Christ with such passion that sacrifice for His sake is an honor. The first believers were trained to suffer for Christ's sake, while many today are trained to be happy and comfortable in their faith.

The call is loud and clear—Jesus is worth living and dying for. Jesus is worth living life to the fullest. Jesus is worth dying to self-centered desires. Jesus is worth living as if every day could be our last. Jesus is worth dying to a life that is all about us.

Jesus is worth it all. Josh got this right. Do we?

> *Dear Lord, thank You for bringing meaning and worth to my life. You are worthy of all I can offer. Help me when I focus more on receiving things from You, rather than giving back to You. In Jesus' name. Amen.*

Application Steps

Identify on a scale of one to ten your level of commitment to your faith. In prayer, seek God's direction on how to increase your level of commitment to Him.

23 Who's Got the Whole World?

Melissa Taylor

Be silent, and know that I am God! I will be honored
by every nation. I will be honored throughout the world.
Psalm 46:10 nlt

Recently I attended chapel with my three-year-old daughter's pre-school class. The pastor was playing guitar and the kids were singing along. He was about to begin the next song when he asked the children a question. "Boys and girls, do you know who has the whole world in His hands?" The kids thought about this and one little boy shouted, "I do! I have the whole world in my hands!" Everyone laughed and the pastor explained who really had the whole world in His hands, and then they sang about it.

Sometimes kids say the funniest things. This little boy's declaration of "I do" was indeed humorous, but I also see where he got that impression. I believe that God has everything under control and has the whole world in His hands, yet how many times have I acted as though I do?

I take pride in being a fixer; not of things, but of people. When I see someone hurting, in trouble, or in need, I want to fix everything and make it better. I may take care of a sick friend's children, buy a gift to cheer someone up, write an encouraging note, or take them to lunch trying to find just the right words to help fix their situation. While it brings me joy to serve others in this way, I often find myself feeling discouraged because I can't really fix anything. Sometimes I become burdened or worried. I may be able to bring some temporary comfort, but that's all I can do alone.

Jesus asks and answers a good question. "Can all your worries add a single moment to your life? Of course not" (Matthew 6:27 NLT). Jesus is right. In fact, studies show that worry actually decreases the days of your life. There's just no need for it; worry doesn't fix a thing. Jesus goes on to say that "your heavenly Father already knows all your needs, and he will give you all you need from day to day if you live for him and make the Kingdom of God your primary concern" (Matthew 6:32-33 NLT). Our God knows all our needs and the needs of everyone around us. This same God who created us all can be trusted with every single detail of our lives. We aren't supposed to carry the world upon us. It will crush us if we try. My friends, I encourage you to join me in letting go, giving all our burdens to the Lord, and trusting that He, and He alone, surely has the whole world in His hands.

Dear Lord, help me to trust You to calm the storms of life. I pray that I will not worry, but give all my cares to You. In Jesus' name. Amen.

Application Steps

The next time you find yourself worrying about something that is out of your control, try writing down Psalm 46:10. In your journal, substitute the words "be silent" with "stop worrying" and then with "stop striving."

24 Affluenza

Rachel Olsen

Beware! Don't be greedy for what you don't have.
Real life is not measured by how much we own.
Luke 12:15 NLT

The store-wide clearance sale is going on today at JC Penney's. I'm trying hard to not go in search of a bargain on something I didn't know I needed until I saw it.

My husband laments the fact that every purchase I make seems to lead to more purchases. I buy a mirror for the dining room wall, only to find it throws the room off balance and now I need something for the opposite wall. I purchase a black-and-red sweater, only to discover that my old black pants look faded next to the new sweater, and so I head off to the store for new pants. While at the store I find a fabulous pair of pink shoes on clearance. (Don't ask why I'm in the shoe department to buy black pants.) It seems a crime not to buy a gorgeous pair of shoes at 70 percent off, but now I need a skirt to go with them...

Recreational shopping replaced baseball years ago as our national pastime. We've fallen for the promise of higher self-esteem via retail therapy as we purchase our way to beauty, prestige, and happiness.

In 2002 the term "affluenza" was coined to describe our insatiable pursuit of more, more This relentless drive for affluence ultimately leads to overload, debt, anxiety, and waste. Perhaps you recognize its symptoms: 1) inability to delay gratification, 2) low tolerance for frustration, 3) more stuff than you have space to store, 4) no time for nurturing one's spiritual life, and 5) the expectation that attaining a certain thing will make your life more fulfilling.

We need material things. It's even okay to want or buy some things we don't necessarily need. However, we must keep material possessions in eternal focus or we will fail to bear fruit (Matthew 13:22). Jesus said, "Don't store up treasures here on earth, where they can be eaten by moths and get rusty, and where thieves break in and steal. Store your treasures in heaven, where they will never become moth-eaten or rusty and where they will be safe from thieves" (Matthew 6:19-20 NLT). God wants our focus on living justly, helping others, and loving Him, not keeping up with the Joneses.

"Beware!" Jesus said. "Don't be greedy for what you don't have. Real life is not measured by how much we own" (Luke 12:15 NLT). Christ repeatedly taught that a person's worth is not measured by her talent, money, or clout, but by the fact that she was created in the image of God to have an intimate friendship with Him.

Your life is worthwhile because God created it. You are desirable because you are loved by Him. You are precious because He gave His Son for you. You have purpose because He's ordained the days of your life. Worth, love, value, and fulfillment—these are things money cannot buy. They can only be bestowed and received from a gracious God.

Dear Lord, forgive me for worshipping material things. Help me to focus on following You and developing my character. You've said my heavenly Father knows all my needs and will supply them if I make His kingdom my primary concern. Help me order my priorities. In Jesus' name. Amen.

Application Steps

Grab a trash bag and find at least ten things in your home to donate to others in need. Then put the filled bag into your car to be dropped off this week.

25 Mirror, Mirror on the Wall

Charlene Kidd

So God created man in his own image,
in the image of God created he him;
male and female created he them.

GENESIS 1:27 KJV

For as long as I can remember, a huge mirror hung above my grandmother's couch. All of the grandchildren would jump on the couch and make funny faces in it. When my grandmother died, I inherited the mirror. It was hung in my family room, and I enjoyed seeing my children jump around and make funny faces in it.

We'd recently moved into a new home. I carefully chose the place for the mirror to be placed. I hung it on the wall and reached out to adjust it. It came crashing down the wall and shattered. I checked the screws in the wall, thinking surely I had missed a stud, but they were securely set. Then I noticed a frayed spot in the wire. I cried at the loss of that treasured heirloom. It had hung for ten years in my other home. I never thought to check the wire.

Two weeks later at 2 a.m., my husband's grandmother's mirror that hung in our bedroom came crashing down. I could hardly believe both mirrors broke in a matter of weeks. Turns out, there was a frayed spot in that wire as well! You can bet I checked the wire on every other mirror in my house.

I cried again at the loss. I questioned, "Lord, why did we lose two such treasured memories of our past?" He reminded me that a mirror shows an image, and that we are made in an image as well—the image of God. We reflect His image to the people looking into our lives.

Our wire is our relationship with Jesus Christ. I believe three key things can weaken and fray our wire: disobedience, unforgiveness, and busyness. The opposite of those—obedience, forgiveness, and time with Him—can strengthen us so we don't come crashing down.

Just as we need to check for weak or frayed spots in the wires that hold up our mirrors, we need to also check on our relationship with Jesus, so that our reflected image of God doesn't shatter.

Dear Lord, I pray that each time we look in a mirror today and see ourselves, we will be reminded to take care of the image we reflect of You to the world around us. In Jesus' name. Amen.

Application Steps

In prayer, ask God to reveal any areas of disobedience, unforgiveness, or busyness that inhibit your ability to reflect Him.

26 Beep–Beep
Micca Campbell

Would [she] argue with useless words,
with speeches that have no value?

JOB 15:3

Communication is like dancing the tango. It takes two. However, just because you communicate your thoughts to someone doesn't mean you will be understood. The person I have the hardest time communicating with is my husband. Sometimes it seems that men really do come from Mars and women are from Venus! We simply communicate differently.

My husband and I began learning about good communication skills when we agreed to teach a marriage class. We learned that to communicate clearly you listen, ask questions, and then repeat back what you heard the other person say. Sounds easy enough, right?

Most of the time, couples are not listening to what the other is saying, but rather thinking up their counterpoint or defense and then sharing it—sometimes loudly. In order to teach the class (and ourselves) how to put these principles into practice, we developed a technique called "Beep–Beep." We discovered that practicing good communication skills is as easy as ordering a Big Mac at McDonald's.

Let's review the process of ordering fast food. Before placing your order at any drive-through window, your car rolls over a wire that sounds "Beep–Beep" inside of the restaurant, informing employees they have a customer wishing to communicate an order. Then, a happy person acknowledges you. "May I take your order?"

"Yes, thank you. I would like a Big Mac with fries and a Diet Coke (to balance the calories), please," you state clearly.

The cheerful employee repeats your order. "You wanted a Big Mac with fries and a Diet Coke. Is this correct?"

"Yes, it is," you confirm with mouth-watering excitement.

Likewise, the process is the same when communicating with your partner. To gain your spouse's attention, drive over beside them in your imaginary car and say, "Beep–Beep." This signals to the other person that you need their full attention without interruption. Once you have "placed your order" by making your thoughts known, your partner happily repeats your statements back, nearly word for word just like the employee at McDonald's. Then your spouse asks, "Is this correct?" to make sure he has understood you fully. If so, the payoff is you have successfully made your thoughts known without fuss or fight.

This has become a regular means of communication for my husband and me. Sometimes while I'm reading a book, my honey will sit down beside me and say, "Beep–Beep." Immediately I know there's an issue he needs to discuss. Other times I've stepped in front of the TV and sounded my horn to gain his attention.

Approaching your partner with "Beep–Beep" is a great way to break the ice and let them know you want to talk heart-to-heart. Staying within these guidelines allows each person a turn to speak, the assurance of being heard, and the satisfaction of communicating with success.

With this method, you don't have to wait until Venus is in alignment with Mars to talk to your spouse. You now have the skills to approach your partner, sound your horn, and order up some good conversation. Play by the rules, and you'll always get what you order—clear communication!

> *Dear Lord, thank You for the gift of communication. Teach my spouse and me to talk less, listen more, and meet each other's needs instead of demanding our own way. In Jesus' name. Amen.*

Application Steps

Teach someone how to play "Beep–Beep" and journey together into a world of better communication.

27 My Friend the Atheist

Lysa TerKeurst

God did not send his Son into the world to condemn the world, but to save the world through him.

JOHN 3:17

I have a dear friend who is a wonderful person and terrific mom. We enjoy watching our kids do sports together, and when there is time we work out together. We respect each other and care about one another, but we come from two totally different vantage points. I am a passionate, sold-out Christian. She is a staunch atheist.

Without much discussion on the subject, we basically agree to disagree. But there is something going on behind the scenes that is so very exciting...she is seeing Jesus in me.

Just a few days ago, we were discussing "true beauty" while sweating and straining through sit-ups. She told me her counselor had recently asked her to describe a person who exemplified true feminine beauty, and she'd quickly answered, "Deborah Norville." But after a little more thought, she gave the counselor my name.

I laughed and told her that the only picture that should come to her head when she thought of me was a sweaty woman in workout clothes, a scraggly ponytail hairdo, and no makeup. How could that qualify as beautiful? Her answer stirred my heart. "Lysa, it's what you have on the inside that is so beautiful."

I was amazed. Not because I took the compliment for myself, but rather for my sweet Jesus. I am convinced she sees the reality of Jesus shining through my many cracks and is drawn to Him in me. Even an atheist has God's fingerprints all over her soul. Her innermost being was created by God's hand, and something inside her must recognize Him ever so slightly. So, that is where I start witnessing to her. No lengthy debates. No theological discussions. No hellfire and brimstone.

I simply live and love and make the reality of Jesus known through my interactions with her and others.

She will not care to meet my Jesus until she meets the reality of Jesus lived out through my life. What a challenge for all of us! Many people are turned off by Christians because they hear us say one thing but live out another. I so desperately want to live Jesus out loud. I want to tell the whole world about Him. I am convinced I will have the privilege to one day sit down over a cup of coffee and have my friend the atheist say, "I want what you have. You make me think God could possibly be real. Will you teach me?" And what a day that will be!

> *Dear Lord, thank You for the privilege to know You. Thank You for changing my bitterness into joy, my horrible past into a hope-filled future, and my broken dreams into fulfilled promises. Help me to reflect the reality of You in me. I want to lead many people to the glorious hope that can only be found in You. May it be so, every day of my life. In Jesus' name. Amen.*

Application Steps

Write down the names of a couple people in your sphere of influence who need to meet the reality of Jesus. Make a point to pray for these people. Then look for ways to be Jesus to them. List three things you could do over this next month for each of them.

28 It Is Enough

Wendy Pope

When the centurion, who stood there in front of Jesus,
heard his cry and saw how he died, he said,
"Surely this man was the Son of God!"

MARK 15:39

I love contemporary worship music. God has used it to draw me to Himself in a way I never thought possible. However, I treasure in my heart the memories of the great hymns I learned as a young girl. I remember at my home church, once a month on Sunday nights, we had favorite hymn time. Members would get to shout out the number of their favorite hymn, and the congregation would sing the first verse. The sound of the words from an old familiar hymn by Eliza E. Hewitt, "My Faith Has Found a Resting Place," resonates in my heart: "It is enough that Jesus died, and that He died for me."

Oh, that we would believe the truth in those words. Believe, believe, believe. Not long ago, I discovered I really didn't believe. Even as I write today, this is hard for me to say. I did not believe His death was enough for me. I did not believe I was the apple of His eye. I did not believe I was created in His image. I did not believe He had a plan for me, and the plan was to bring me a future full of hope. I did not believe the sins of my past, present, and future were settled on the cross. I did not believe the gift of grace could possibly be free.

I believed enough to secure my salvation. I believed Jesus came to earth, was born of a virgin, died on the cross, rose again, and will return for me. These were the easy truths to believe. The truths that dealt with my heart and God's affection for me were the difficult ones to believe.

Not believing the simple promises of God's Word and accepting them as truth gave the enemy a foothold in my heart. His weapon of choice for me was shame. Because I did not have a believing heart, I lived in shame: shame of sin, shame of my unworthiness, and shame of not measuring up to others regarding talents, looks, and abilities. Shame first reared its head in the Garden of Eden when Adam and Eve sinned. Their sin made them see themselves for what they were: naked. They tried to hide from God, just like we do. What did God do for Adam and Eve? He made a covering for them so they would not be ashamed. He does the same for us today. The blood Jesus shed on Calvary was enough to cover all our sin and the shame that comes with it. Oh, friend, won't you accept that God's sacrifice of His only Son was enough for you to live in freedom?

Dear Lord, my prayer today is simple: Help me believe and live as though I believe that Your sacrifice was enough for me to live in freedom. In Jesus' name. Amen.

Application Steps

In a journal, write the things you have trouble believing. Search the Bible for verses that speak truth to those doubts. Sing a song of praise after each entry you make. Date each entry, and watch God deliver you into freedom.

29 Ready to Quit
Sharon Glasgow

I will boast all the more gladly about my weaknesses,
so that Christ's power may rest on me. That is why,
for Christ's sake, I delight in weaknesses, in insults,
in hardships, in persecutions, in difficulties. For when
I am weak, then I am strong.

2 Corinthians 12:10

I was exhausted, worn out, and overwhelmed. Between many unfulfilled expectations and too many people wanting too many things from me, I had nothing left to give. I had become so inundated with life that my daily time with God slipped. Soon I felt unworthy and inadequate.

I decided I didn't deserve to teach my sixth grade Sunday school class anymore. After all, how could God use a person like me? All week I rehearsed how I would tell the Sunday school superintendent my decision. Each day passed, and I couldn't muster up the courage to call him. By the time Sunday rolled around, I decided I would just have to find him and resign that very day. I didn't want to teach, and I planned to tell him he'd have to find a quick substitute. I looked everywhere for him, but he was nowhere to be found.

My class was to start in five minutes and I didn't have a lesson planned. I just couldn't teach! These children deserved a teacher who was totally committed to God. Finally, I saw the Sunday school superintendent in the distance, but before I could reach him, I was stopped by a crying little girl, one of my students. "Mrs. Glasgow, I'm so scared. I decided to be baptized today, and I won't be able to be in your class because they are baptizing me in this service. I'm alone, my family is not Christian, and I don't know why, but I'm nervous. Can you stay with me until the second service begins?" By this time the superintendent was out of sight and my class was without a teacher. I told the little girl, "Give me one minute. I'm going to get the other children."

I was back in minutes with the class. We all hugged her and prayed with her before she went into the baptistery. We all ran into the service and sat at the back to watch. Right before the little girl was baptized the minister asked her, "Who helped bring you to the Lord?" Standing on her tiptoes, she looked over the baptistery edge at me in the back and said, "Mrs. Glasgow did." Tears of humility and joy rolled down my cheeks.

I didn't quit teaching. God showed me that His grace is sufficient. His power is made perfect in my weaknesses. I had grown tired and weary, but God gave me His strength when I needed it. He always does when we remember where the power source is and plug in!

Dear Lord, thank You for directing my path. Help me to always follow Your leading and not get ahead of myself. In Jesus' name. Amen.

Application Steps

When God calls you to a mission, He will give you the energy, motivation, and ability to do what He has called you to do. The only way to get the right fuel for service is by spending time with Him. Read God's Word. Listen as He leads you. When you are weak or confused, turn to Him for strength.

30 Crossroads
Susanne Scheppmann

*This is what the LORD says: "Stand at the crossroads
and look; ask for the ancient paths, ask where the good way
is, and walk in it, and you will find rest for your souls."*
JEREMIAH 6:16

I don't remember the bushes on the side of the road looking so green, I thought to myself. Within the next 30 seconds, I drove over a bridge. A sign identified the water below as the Colorado River. On the other side of the bridge, another sign welcomed me to California. I was supposed to be entering Nevada, not California! Somewhere at a crossroads, I had made a wrong turn. Oblivious, I didn't realize my mistake until I'd gone an hour in the wrong direction.

Sheepishly I called my husband to tell him my news. "Hi, it's me."

"Hi, honey. Are you almost home?"

"Not exactly. I'm in California."

"*What?* Are you lost? Didn't you read the map?"

"No, I didn't look at the map. I thought I knew the right direction, but I must have made a wrong turn at the crossroads in Arizona. I am turning around."

My detour added an additional two hours to my long drive home. If only I had read my map or asked for directions, I wouldn't have found myself in the wrong state. I also wouldn't have lost valuable time and energy.

I often make the same mistake in my spiritual life. Big decisions loom ahead. I think I know the right course, so off I go without taking time to pray or read my Bible, and my choices go awry. Eventually I think, *Oops, I should have sought God's advice.*

God promises that when we stand at a crossroads, He will guide us. We need to stop and listen with our spiritual ears for the correct course to take. Proverbs 3:6 advises us to acknowledge Him in all our ways, and He will make our paths straight. I prefer my path straight over crooked, don't you?

The next time life presents a quandary, let's stop at the crossroads of our decision. Let's ask Him which is the better way. Let's reach for our Bible and let God's Word become our road map. "Your word is a lamp to my feet and a light for my path" (Psalm 119:105). God's Word promises to show us the right way to proceed in life.

Dear Lord, help me to remember to ask You for Your direction as I make my decisions today. Guide me so that I do not take a wrong turn. Give me light for my path. In Jesus' name. Amen.

Application Steps

Memorize today's verse, Jeremiah 6:16. Pray this verse when you reach a crossroads in your life.

31 Plate Spinner
Luann Prater

Do not worry about tomorrow, for tomorrow will worry about itself. Each day has enough trouble of its own.
MATTHEW 6:34

Worry: one of Webster's definitions is to disturb something repeatedly. Rick Warren asked the question in his book *The Purpose-Driven Life,* "What is your life metaphor?" For me, it was always the plate spinner at the circus. You've seen him. He starts spinning a plate on top of a stick, and then he moves on to the next one and repeats the process until five or six are whirling. But as soon as the last one is up and going, the first one becomes unbalanced, wobbles, and is in danger of crashing. It demands immediate attention.

Between my husband, kids, job, friends, and service duties, it seemed one plate was always wobbling! And just when I would focus my attention on the current unstable area, out of the corner of my eye I would spot another careening toward the floor. Oops! I forgot to pick that one up from practice. Ugh, I didn't get dinner started in time. Oh, no! The deadline at work is tomorrow!

No matter how hard I tried, someone or something reminded me that my attention was not evenly distributed. I remember dropping to my knees one afternoon in total exhaustion and wailing, "It's never enough!"

Isn't it interesting that it took me collapsing to finally reach the position in which God had been longing to see me—on my knees. In Jeremiah 1:8 (NKJV) God promises, "I am with you to deliver you." And in Matthew 6:33, the key is found to eliminate exhaustion, "But seek first his kingdom and his righteousness, and all these things will be given to you."

Does that mean that plates will never crash if we seek Him first?

No, it means *we* will never crash. The promise is to deliver *you!* Oswald Chambers says, "We put our common sense on the throne and then attach God's name to it." Possessions and people often cause heartache and turmoil. However, when your focus is on the Maker, complaining turns to continuing steadily on.

In Matthew 6:34, Jesus is telling us that if our priority is seeking Him and His righteousness *first,* then there is no reason to worry at all about wobbly situations in our life, for our Deliverer will keep us steady. Therefore, don't worry. Trust Jesus.

> *Dear Lord, thank You for caring about details so we don't have to. Help me to stop worrying today about the unstable things in my life and focus first on my relationship with You. Instead of being repeatedly disturbed, teach me to be repeatedly delivered. In Jesus' name. Amen.*

Application Steps

First, ask Jesus to draw you so near to Him that all other things will dim in the light of His presence. Write down everything that worries you, and then number them in order of priority. Across the top of the page write JESUS in red. Then, place your hand on each item as you pray out loud down the list. When your prayer is complete, write "Jesus" across the entire list, knowing He will faithfully sustain you through it all.

32 God's Arms

Marybeth Whalen

*Surely the arm of the LORD is not too short to save,
nor his ear too dull to hear.*

Isaiah 59:1

I once heard a story about an elderly woman whose husband went to the hospital emergency room complaining of chest pains. After she had waited for hours, a young doctor came out to explain to her that her husband was stable, but he would need to be moved to a larger hospital far away from her to receive the treatment he needed. Though the woman was grateful that her husband would be okay, she was saddened to learn that he would need to be hospitalized so far away. Because of her own health concerns, there was no way she would be able to make the long drive to see him each day. Sadly, she returned home alone.

Later that day, her neighbor and friend came over to check on her. The two women talked about her husband's health, and her grief that he would be so far away from her. Her friend began to pray for her and her husband. "Lord," her friend prayed, "we know that our arms cannot reach to him, but Yours can. Your arms are not too short to reach him, no matter where he is. We will choose to rest in that, and to know that You are comforting him when we cannot." After her friend prayed, the woman felt better. She had the peace of her friend's reminder that God's arms were not affected by human limitations like old age and failing health. She slept well that night, trusting God to care for her husband and to work out the situation.

Is there someone in your life who needs God's arms to reach where you cannot? Perhaps it's a child who needs God's arms to reach the place he has run to. Perhaps it's a loved one who is far away from you but going through a hard time. Perhaps it's your husband, who has withdrawn from everyone—even from you. Whatever your situation,

God's arms are not too short to reach. He can touch that person in a way you cannot. He can take care of that person when you cannot. You need to give the situation to Him and trust Him to resolve it according to His perfect plan.

Sometimes it's hard to give a situation to God. We want to hold on to it and worry over it, as if we can do anything about it by worrying. When you feel yourself tempted to worry, pray instead. Remind yourself that God's arms are not too short, and verbally give the situation to Him to take care of. Tell God you trust Him, and you are placing your loved one in His capable hands. Recommit the situation as often as you need.

> *Dear Lord, thank You that I can trust Your arms to reach where I cannot. I will trust You to take care of my situation and I rest in that. In Jesus' name. Amen.*

Application Steps

God's arms are not too short for any situation, and they are not too short for you, either. Let God wrap His powerful arms around you and comfort you today. Feel the warmth of His embrace and the comfort of His care for you. Rest in that and feel the peace He longs to fill you with.

33 Can-Do Kids

Renee Swope

I can do everything through him who gives me strength.
Philippians 4:13

"I can't!" Andrew shouted. Joshua, his older brother, was trying to help him use an Etch A Sketch. Andrew had barely touched the white knobs when he gave up. It seemed Andrew's response to every obstacle that week was, "I can't!"

"I can't," he cried at the pool when I encouraged him to put his head under water. "I can't," he muttered when I asked him to tell me the first letter in the word "airplane." "I can't! I can't! I can't!"

I can't take it anymore! I thought to myself as I watched him sit in defeat. I knew Andrew was frustrated because he was trying things his big brother could do easily. I could relate. How many times have I resisted doing something I wasn't good at?

I remembered a magazine article I'd read about helping children become can-do kids. In a sudden moment of inspiration I said, "Andrew, Mom has decided to give you a new name. You're my Can-Do Kid, so you can no longer say 'I can't' because there are many things you *can* do. I'll show you how and I'll do them with you."

It was time for dinner, so I handed Andrew the forks and showed him where each one went. I gave him one plate and cup at a time and watched him complete each setting. He was so proud of himself. When he finished, Andrew looked at me and said, "Mommy, I *can* do it!"

How many of us never grow to our fullest potential because we lack confidence and courage? Just like Andrew, we sometimes measure our abilities based on how well we can do something compared to someone else.

That day taught me an important lesson—the power of believing in someone and showing it through words and actions. Here's what I did: I drew Andrew's attention away from something he couldn't do toward something he could. I showed him how to do it by doing it with him until he gained confidence. Then I watched as he completed his assignment with success. Three years later our family still calls Andrew our Can-Do Kid. Recently, Joshua offered to help Andrew feed the dogs and Andrew replied, "Thanks, Josh, but I don't need help 'cause I'm a can-do kid!"

Today's verse reminds us that we're all Can-Do Kids when we look to Christ for strength. Jesus shows us with His words and actions that He believes in us, that He's with us, and that He cheers us when we're willing to become all He created us to be. If you have a child or a friend who needs encouragement, tell them today that you believe in them and God does too.

Dear Lord, show me where my children or friends are comparing themselves to others and need to be encouraged with Your perspective. Help me to see others the way You do and instill in them the confidence to do everything through Your strength. I want to be a woman who helps others become Can-Do Kids for Your kingdom. In Jesus' name. Amen.

Application Steps

Think of someone you know who needs you to believe in her. Show her your confidence by trusting her with something. Communicate encouragement through your words in a letter, phone call, card, or e-mail. If she becomes frustrated, offer to help and encourage her to do all things in the strength that's found in Christ.

34 Dreams Come True
Rachel Olsen

The bride, a princess, waits within her chamber,
dressed in a gown woven with gold. In her beautiful robes,
she is led to the king; accompanied by her bridesmaids.
PSALM 45:13-14 NLT

Once upon a time there was a handsome prince in need of a bride. Far away, in another part of the kingdom, there was a beautiful woman who possessed great potential but was under the oppression of an envious evildoer. So the prince, being a man of justice and mercy, rescued the young woman and set her free.

She in turn couldn't help but fall in love with her noble rescuer. "You are the most handsome of all! You are so gracious! God Himself has blessed you forever!" she exclaimed as she held tightly to his waist to steady herself on the back of his white horse. He took her to the palace, where she was bathed and then covered in beautiful linens and sweet-smelling oils. The prince was captivated by her radiance and called her to his side. It seemed as if they were two pieces of the same whole, destined to come together as one.

She was advised, "Forget your people and your homeland far away. For this royal prince delights in your beauty; stay here and honor him!" In response she declared, "I will bring honor to his name," and she set her heart on a future with him. A wedding date was planned and...you know the rest of the story...they lived happily ever after.

How do you feel about that fairy tale? Do you wish that were the story of your life? Maybe you rail against fairy tales, believing them to be literature used to keep women under men's thumbs. Or maybe your reaction is, "Sweet story but definitely not plausible!"

I am so excited to tell you that this tale does come true for millions of women. If you are a Christian woman—married or single—this is *your* story! Jesus is your rescuer…your handsome prince…your royal husband. He wants nothing more than to rescue you from the evil grip of sin and bring out the best in you. He wants to purify you with His Word and His Spirit and keep you by His side forever. Can you hear Him calling your name today? Listen, He is saying, "How beautiful you are, my darling! Oh, how beautiful!" (Song of Songs 1:15).

Will you respond by leaving your past behind, setting your heart on Him, and bringing honor to His name?

Dear Lord, purify my heart so that it would be worthy of the honor of marrying the Prince of Peace. In Jesus' name. Amen.

Application Steps

Read Psalm 45 today. It is the story of a wedding, paralleling Christ and His bride, the church.

35 The DMV of Life

Van Walton

I have no greater joy than this, to hear of my children walking in the truth.

3 John 1:4 nasb

■ My teenage son and I sat facing each other in the dewy morning air waiting for the doors of the DMV to be unlocked. I studied Ben, realizing the importance of this day. I recalled the first swing of his bat, the first kick to score a goal, and the first run for a touchdown. Today's objective was a bigger milestone: a driver's license. Though it was an exciting day for my son, it was a bittersweet day for me.

Minutes ticked by and God invited me to pray. Ben peeked out from under his hooded sweatshirt to find me staring at him. I mouthed, "I am praying for you." Nodding, he closed his eyes and retreated into the warm folds of his hood. A little later, he popped out, only to find me still staring. This time, with a hint of a smile, he wrinkled his brows.

Ben had prepared diligently for his road tests and gathered all the necessary documents. He felt ready to go before the DMV examiner. When the door finally opened, we were invited in to take a number and a seat. As we waited I wondered, *Is my son as prepared to go before God and be examined?*

Returning from his road test, Ben walked with confidence. "No problem," he declared. "I think he knew when he saw me that I was a good driver. He knew I was responsible." Within moments, Ben was showing off his driver's license.

Riding home with him at the wheel, I congratulated Ben for his newly earned freedom. I shared with him my thoughts from that morning and the comparison I had drawn between his road test and his future appearance at the judgment seat of Christ. I asked him if he had prepared himself as well to go before the Lord.

"Will the only One who can pass you stand at the gates of heaven and invite you in? Will He recognize you as 'good' because you accepted Jesus' work on the cross as your responsible preparation for eternity?" Ben smiled confidently, eyes focused on the road ahead. "I don't have to take that road test. Jesus passed it for me!" My motherly apprehension was replaced with assurance as we continued down the road toward home.

Dear Lord, I praise You for the gift of everlasting life with You in heaven. I thank You that I can teach my children about Your love and the promises You give to those who follow You. In Jesus' name. Amen.

Application Steps

Teach your children about heaven. Show them how to go to the concordance of the Bible, find the word "heaven," and read about God's future plans. Pray that God will reveal Himself to your children and use you to teach them about His goodness.

36 Crucified

Micca Campbell

I have been crucified with Christ; it is no longer
I who live, but Christ lives in me; and the life
which I now live in the flesh I live by faith in the
Son of God, who loved me and gave Himself for me.

GALATIANS 2:20 NKJV

Just the thought of trying to be holy creates despair in my heart. It's not that I don't desire to be holy. I do what I can. I struggle, pretend at times, and even beg God to make me holy—yet little changes.

Often, I find myself studying its definition: "Holiness…one who is perfect in goodness and righteousness." That's a great description of God, who is the essence of holiness, but my life barely reflects the first letter of the word, let alone the whole meaning. Time and again I've been disappointed by my efforts to become holy.

Then one day I realized the reason for my defeat. I was trying to obtain something I can't. God never intended for me or you to be holy by our own efforts. We cannot achieve that high standard by ourselves. That's why we have Jesus. His holiness is imparted to us the moment we receive Him as our Savior. It's not about imitating His life, but receiving His life, and allowing His holiness to be lived through us!

Once Jesus is residing in you and me, we have all that He is. We have His wisdom, faith, power, and holiness. It's almost too wonderful to believe. In order for us to experience His life in ours, we have to make a choice. We can either continue to live our life our way by our own effort, or we can die to self and allow Jesus to live His life through us. It's only by choosing Jesus and abandoning self that we can experience His presence and power in our lives. However, choosing Jesus means we must identify with His cross in order to experience His character.

Most of us are content with Christ's forgiveness and a paid ticket to heaven, never seeking the resurrected life that comes from dying to self. To be crucified with Christ means that I have no more claims on my daily life. Identifying with His death means that I must fully surrender to His will and not mine because I no longer live, but Christ lives...in my thoughts, my plans, and everything I do.

Once we are dead to self, Jesus is then free to invade us with His life and power. Only then will we experience the fullness of His life. He didn't die on the cross so that we can continue to live in defeat. Christ died so that He could impart to you and me His very life and live it through us.

We can try to be holy on our own or even beg God to make us holy, but He won't until we allow Christ to occupy our essence. The choice is ours.

Dear Lord, forgive my sins. Invade me with Your life so that I may exude Christlike character in all that I do. In Jesus' name. Amen.

Application Steps

Crucify your self-centered focus and your attempts to live righteously apart from daily empowerment through Christ.

37 Learning Contentment

Glynnis Whitwer

I know what it is to be in need, and I know what it is to have plenty. I have learned the secret of being content in any and every situation, whether well fed or hungry, whether living in plenty or in want.

PHILIPPIANS 4:12

My middle son Dylan worked for more than a month on his Christmas list. At the top of this 11-year-old's list was an iPod.

Unfortunately, an iPod was out of our budget. My husband and I decided an MP3 player would give our son a similar musical experience. We found one that held 50 songs and reasoned it would be more than enough.

Fifty songs were enough until Dylan learned his friend had 300 songs on his iPod. It wasn't long after that when I discovered my deal-making son had written up a contract, signed by both his brothers, stating they would give him a portion of *their* monthly allowances to help *him* save for an iPod. The trade-off? When Dylan had enough money, little brother would get the "old" MP3 player, and then Dylan would help his older brother save for something big.

When I found out about the plot, I addressed the issue with Dylan. I was hurt that the three-month-old gift was now unacceptable. More than that, I was concerned about his lack of contentment.

In Philippians 4:12 Paul tells the believers in Philippi that he has "learned the secret of being content in any and every situation." How does a man under house arrest learn to be content? How do we learn it?

I believe the secret Paul alludes to is simple. It's not believing your situation will improve, or comparing your situation to others who might be worse off. We learn from Paul that the secret to contentment is making the most of what you have.

- Paul didn't have freedom, but he did have the love of the believers in Philippi.

- He didn't have a lot of money, but he did have the ability to share the gospel of Jesus Christ.

- He didn't have confidence in the health or strength of his body, but he did have confidence in the power of Christ's resurrection.

Paul didn't have a lot in terms of material things, but he focused on what he did have, and that was Jesus. Using that scriptural truth, Dylan and I talked about how he could make the most of what he had. He decided to invest in some Christian CDs and then take the time to switch the songs loaded on his MP3 player.

That was a good start, but we also talked about the heart issue. We discussed how everything we have is a gift from God. I shared that my feelings were hurt at Dylan's discontentment, and that I imagine God's feelings are hurt when any of His children are unhappy with what they have.

It was a lesson I needed to learn as well. The next time discontentment threatens to sneak into my heart, I'll remember the "secret" and focus on what can never be taken away from me—the love of Jesus.

Dear Lord, I praise You for Your faithfulness. Forgive me for the times I've been discontent with a gift You have given. Help me learn contentment in every situation. Thank You for caring for me so generously. In Jesus' name. Amen.

Application Steps

Identify one situation or thing about which you are discontent. Acknowledge that it's a gift from God. Determine how you can make the best of what you have.

38 Before I Fly Off the Handle Again

Lysa TerKeurst

Only be careful, and watch yourselves closely
so that you do not forget the things your eyes have
seen or let them slip from your heart as long as you live.
Teach them to your children and to their children after them.

DEUTERONOMY 4:9

It was a simple request. I had asked my daughters to practice their piano pieces before the teacher arrived for lessons. When they didn't listen to my request, I became angry.

Anger was not the correct response. The way I should have responded was to calmly reprimand their disobedience and give them a consequence for their poor choice. But anger pushed my emotions beyond calm into chaos. My voice went higher in pitch and stronger in volume. Children not practicing their piano lessons should not have caused me to get so angry. What was the real issue here?

The week before the piano teacher had informed me that it was evident my kids had not had enough practice time. When she said this, my mind kicked into overdrive as I defined what she must have meant by this statement. *Good moms make sure their children practice at least 30 minutes a day. Good moms help their kids stay on top of their theory assignments. Good moms ensure each child makes progress that week.*

I held these unspoken but assumed interpretations up against my reality. The reality was I had no idea if my kids had even sat at the piano once that week. When I held my reality up against what I assumed to be her standard, I fell horribly short. I let my kids' poor choices be a defining reflection of what kind of mother I am. Ever been there?

There are three fundamental parenting truths that we would do well to remember in situations like this. First, refuse to dive below the surface of people's comments and blow them out of proportion. We moms can really do a number on ourselves with crazy assumptions, misinterpretations, and dangerous comparisons. The reality was the teacher made a simple statement that my kids could use some more practice. So, tackle that issue plain and simple.

Second, there should be consequences for irresponsibility so that the pressure to remember is on them, not me. My kids are old enough to remember to practice the piano on their own. If they make an irresponsible choice, they should feel embarrassed, not me.

And finally, I must operate in truth when it comes to my identity. Just because someone forgets to practice their piano, or does one of the hundreds of other irresponsible things kids do, does not change my identity. I am not a perfect mom, but I am a good mom. And a good mom's job is to love her kids, correct them, and model godly attitudes, actions, and reactions.

> *Dear Lord, give me Your definition of what a good mom is for my specific children. You have entrusted these precious souls to me, and I don't want to mess up. Help me hold on to Your truths and resist Satan's pull toward comparisons and assumptions. Help me keep my emotions in check and my heart in tune with You.*

Applications Steps

Write these three fundamental parenting truths down on a 3 x 5 card and carry it with you. The next time you start to hear those accusing voices in your head, pull out your card and read them over and over until you can proceed in truth and not anger.

39 My Fab 5

Melissa Taylor

A person standing alone can be attacked and defeated,
but two can stand back-to-back and conquer. Three are even
better, for a triple-braided cord is not easily broken.

Ecclesiastes 4:12 nlt

I am a relational person. I love to be around people. If there's a party, I'm there. If girlfriends are getting together for lunch, I'm there. If there's a good topic on a message board, I'm there. If you call me on the phone, I'll talk to you. My mom says the reason I had four kids was just so I'd always have people around me. She might be right!

There's a particular group of people I get together with weekly. These four women have become fabulous friends of mine. When we gather, my social tank gets filled to its fullest. We talk about our families, jobs, housework, insecurities, fears, trials, and celebrations. We pray for the same things we talk about. We study the Bible together. The difference between these and most of my other relationships is that our friendships are grounded in Christ.

When a relationship is grounded in Christ, a new level of intimacy is achieved. We know what we say to each other is in Christian love, so we can say just about anything without fear of judgment or abandonment. We call ourselves "The Fab 5." We are not just five fabulous friends, but we also have recognized five fabulous qualities that make our friendships solid.

Love. We love each other unfailingly, the way Christ loves us. A true friend loves you even when you are unlovable.

Encouragement. We intentionally try to build each other up. I want these ladies to know I believe in them.

Forgiveness. Forgiveness requires a loving heart and a lot of nerve.

The Lord does not keep a record of our sins, and neither should we. Everyone needs forgiveness at some point.

Accountability. We love each other enough to be real before each other. This is HARD! To give accountability you need to be honest, bold, available, and authentic. To receive it, you need to be humble, open, and approachable. Not everyone wants accountability, but we all need it. In our group, we ask for accountability in certain areas of our lives.

Service. I don't know what I'd do without the service these ladies have provided me with at key times in my life. Meals, housecleaning, taking care of kids, a listening ear, making me a CD (I love music!)… these all come to mind when I think of things they have done for me. Their service is love in action.

Today's key verse reminds me of my Fab 5 group. It says that one can be easily defeated and two can conquer. That's true. When I am alone, I often allow negative and defeating thoughts to take over. Not so when I'm with true friends. They don't put up with that! Now add a third partner to the relationship, Jesus. With just my friends, I am uplifted and encouraged, but when Jesus is a part of the friendship, look out! We are indestructible and we can do anything! That's because "a triple-braided cord is not easily broken."

Dear Lord, thank You for my friends. Help me to be a friend who loves at all times. In Jesus' name. Amen.

Application Steps

Do you have friends like the Fab 5? If not, pray for and pursue such relationships. Join a Bible study or begin a prayer group in your home. Integrate the "Fab 5" qualities of friendship into your relationships.

40 Spouse!

Susanne Scheppmann

May the righteous be glad and rejoice before God;
may they be happy and joyful.

PSALM 68:3

My girlfriend Connie has a hilarious husband. With complete love and tenderness in his voice, he will holler for her, "Spouse!" Now to someone who didn't know the couple, it could be perceived as rude and obnoxious. But for them, it's all in loving fun.

My husband and I have adopted their ritual and started summoning each other with "Hey, Spouse!" It makes us smile. Many times after years of marriage, fun seems to disappear like mousse in wet hair. We know we need it, but where does it go?

After almost 20 years of marriage, I understand that if I want to laugh and have fun, then I need to create some mirth. Other couples can be a great source of ideas. Connie's husband will also grab her in the grocery store and dance her down the aisle. Embarrassing? Maybe. Fun? Absolutely. There is not a woman in the produce section who doesn't envy that woman waltzing by the vine-ripened tomatoes.

God never intended for our relationships to be dour and lackluster. He designed marriage for companionship. Do you recall what He said after He created Adam? "The LORD God said, 'It is not good for the man to be alone. I will make a helper suitable for him'" (Genesis 2:18). I believe He intended for the wife to be a helper in several ways, including to create laughter and fun in the family.

One way to rekindle the fun in your marriage is by remembering what you did when you dated. Perhaps it was going to a park to swing. Maybe you picnicked by the local lake. Could you do similar things now? Of course. Only now, they could be even better because you *are married.* Could you pitch a tent in the backyard, picnic, and then enjoy a warm summer night under the stars? Use your imagination to pick the perfect fun-filled activity for you and your spouse. If you need to, ask your friends what they do to promote laughter and fun in their marriage.

Excuse me. I have to go now. I hear my husband calling. We are going to the local home improvement store. I not only plan to improve my house, but my marriage. Yes, I think I will dance with him down the plumbing aisle or perhaps ride piggyback through the lumber department.

Dear Lord, I ask for renewed joy, fun, and laughter in my marriage. Give me ideas to create times of laughter and enjoyment that both my husband and I will delight in. Father, not only do I ask for the ideas, but give me the desire and energy to implement them into our home daily. In Jesus' name. Amen.

Application Steps

Make a list of things both you and your husband enjoy doing together. List fun activities you did while dating. After looking at both lists, decide to implement one thing this week that will make you both laugh and have fun together.

41 Fill 'er Up
Luann Prater

*Restore to me the joy of your salvation and grant
me a willing spirit, to sustain me.*

PSALM 51:12

Ever go on a trip and forget to gas up?

In my youth, I was the QUEEN of empty fuel tanks. If I had five dollars, rarely would more than one make it into the tank. I drove my dad crazy! Drive down any road in the Midwest, and I've probably been stranded on it. The clincher was when I was 17 and driving down the street while practicing my lines for the school play, oblivious to the gas gauge. I suddenly saw the barricade begin to lower, red lights flashing and the ding-ding-ding announcing I must stop at the railroad tracks. As I impatiently waited on the train, my car spitted, sputtered, and then died. Without hesitation, I jumped out and took off to find the nearest phone to call Dad.

Our next-door neighbor heard the report on the police scanner: Abandoned car near tracks, and then it described my car. Immediately they informed my parents. Dad raced to the scene. When he arrived I was gone; kidnapped, he feared. Then, remembering my bad habit, he checked my gauges and found a neglected gas tank, again! I returned and found Dad waiting at my car with one hand on the car and the other disgustedly propped on his hip. He was not happy.

This week I have drained my tank again. Not my gas tank, my spiritual tank. Racing to be in all the right places at all the right times without checking my gauge left me feeling empty. In the past seven days I've been trying to start the car with no gas. I abandoned His will for mine, and my heavenly Father was not pleased. He wasn't happy when I raced out the door before my devotions. He wasn't thrilled when

I flew through my prayers on the way to work. He was disappointed when I hurried past the hurting friend at church.

After running the wrong race, I am spitting, sputtering, and drained. Why is it so hard to remember that God has given us the answer to an empty spiritual tank—the Holy Spirit? The Magnificent Encourager, Wonderful Counselor, Prince of Peace, who is right there with not just a spare can, but an endless supply of all we need. He is just waiting for us to say, "Fill 'er up."

As my dad always told me, if I start with a full tank, my day will go so much smoother...for everyone! When I start my day with my holy Father, reading His Word and asking Him to fill me with His Holy Spirit, my day goes so much smoother...for everyone in my world.

Dear Lord, fill me with a willing spirit and sustain me this week. Through Christ I can do all things, but left on my own, I am empty. In the hustle and bustle of life, restore to me the joy of Your salvation. In Jesus' name. Amen.

Application Steps

Get up 30 minutes earlier and begin your day with prayer and devotions. Take time to fill your tank before the break of day and the breakdown of your sanity.

42 Pretending
Shari Braendel

How priceless is your unfailing love!
PSALM 36:7

The other day my friend Lindy pulled out a sheet of paper for me to fill out. She had an identical one she wrote on. The paper was a fill-in-the blank with statements such as, "I am happy most when _____" or "I am sad when _____." I took my time responding to the 50 short sentences. Lindy felt this exercise would help us "get real" as we began our mentoring process.

As I pondered each question, I came upon one that, to my surprise, I didn't have to think about at all. I immediately filled in the blank. The statement was, "Sometimes I pretend that _____." My answer was "being a stepparent is easier than it is."

I have been a stepmother to triplet girls for the last ten years. They came with my husband into our marriage when they were just 12 years old, and for some reason I thought it would be easier. Silly me! I praise God that He thought I could handle triplet stepdaughters and that He helped me every step of the way. If left to my own abilities, I would have failed before the first week ended.

They are now 22 and finishing college. Kimmy, Carly, and Jessica each have their own wonderful personalities. Kimmy is bright and caring. Carly is artistic and easygoing. Jessie is free-spirited and easy to talk to. The girls bring such great diversity to our family. I can't imagine life without them, but there were times when I thought it would be easier on everybody if I just gave up.

God calls us as stepmothers to be mentors, discipline providers, and friends. It's gratifying to know I was ultimately able to be that for my girls. And although they aren't home much anymore, I know that my stepparenting role continues.

Many times I pretended stepparenting was a piece of cake. To the outside, I made it look as if things were running smoothly. But when you peeked into the trenches of my life, it was evident things were not as they seemed.

If you are a stepmother of young children, look for a mentor who is further along in her stepparenting journey. Pray a lot, and ask God to fill you with His unfailing love. Love really does conquer all. "How priceless is your unfailing love!" (Psalm 36:7).

Dear Lord, You are a Father to the fatherless, and You have given me the awesome responsibility of being a parent. I pray You will guide and direct my steps today as I try to be a friend and mentor to my children. Help me remember that love covers all things, and fill me with Your love. In Jesus' name. Amen.

Application Steps

As you go about your day, thank God for every person in your family. Thank Him for allowing you to be placed in a family that wouldn't be the same without you, or them.

43 Taste and See

Rachel Olsen

Taste and see that the LORD is good.
PSALM 34:8

Dagoba dark 59 percent is my favorite treat. It's pure, semisweet, organic chocolate I get at my health food store. Just a few bites after dinner gratifies my demanding sweet tooth. It satisfies.

Give me a Hershey's bar, however, and I'm likely to consume the whole thing, lick the wrapper, and ask if there is more where that came from. For me, anything less than rich dark chocolate sets into action a cycle of craving, consuming, and craving more.

I'm so thankful God created chocolate. If anyone should doubt God loves us, they need only to examine the cocoa bean...well, that and the coffee bean. I'm certain that God understands the pleasure chocolate gives a gal. King David also knew such wonderful tastes were a gift from the Lord. He said, "Bless the LORD, O my soul...who satisfies your mouth with good things, so that your youth is renewed like the eagle's" (Psalm 103:2,5 NKJV). I'm thinking King David must have been a chocolate lover. It was also David in Psalm 34:8 who encouraged all to "taste and see that the LORD is good."

God is like the perfect blend of chocolate. He simultaneously satisfies my soul, and yet in this state of fulfilled satisfaction I desire more of Him. I'm content, yet drawn to go further and deeper in our relationship.

The apostle Peter described what should follow our tasting of the Lord's mercy: love and grace. He wrote, "Therefore, rid yourselves of all malice and all deceit, hypocrisy, envy, and slander of every kind. Like newborn babies, crave pure spiritual milk, so that by it you may grow in your salvation, now that you have tasted that the Lord is good" (1 Peter 2:1-3).

Milk—the perfect accompaniment to chocolate! So what is pure spiritual milk? It's the Word of God. The King James Version translates this way, "As newborn babes, desire the sincere milk of the word, that ye may grow thereby" (1 Peter 2:2).

The Bible promises we will be satisfied when we seek God and act according to His commands. Psalm 37:3-4 says, "Trust in the LORD, and do good; dwell in the land, and feed on His faithfulness. Delight yourself also in the LORD, and He shall give you the desires of your heart" (NKJV). Jesus said, "Blessed are those who hunger and thirst for righteousness, for they will be filled" (Matthew 5:6).

Chocolate and milk go hand in hand. So do God's love and God's law. By consuming plenty of both on a regular basis, we grow in our salvation. By laying aside our envious and deceitful ways for the ways of love, we display Christ's character and experience a soul satisfaction like no other. *Bon appétit.*

> *Dear Lord, thank You for life's little pleasures—like chocolate. Thank You even more for the milk of Your Word. May I hunger and thirst to understand Your laws and Your ways. Fill me with Your loving presence today. In Jesus' name. Amen.*

Application Steps

Grab yourself a small bite of chocolate and a glass of milk, and then sit down to study the Word of God today. Choose a verse or passage of Scripture and begin memorizing it.

44 I've Been Scammed

Glynnis Whitwer

For such men are false apostles, deceitful workmen, masquerading as apostles of Christ. And no wonder, for Satan himself masquerades as an angel of light. It is not surprising, then, if his servants masquerade as servants of righteousness.

2 CORINTHIANS 11:13-15

I should have seen it coming, but I didn't. It came wrapped in a flattering official-looking letter, announcing that my son was selected to be in a book titled, *Who's Who of Middle School Students.* It looked wonderful, but it was a scam.

Maybe I was thrown off by the colorful letterhead, the actual street address, the website, and the phone number. Maybe it was the honor of my child being recognized nationally. Maybe it was the fact the letter repeated over and over there was no charge to be *in* the book. I also got confirmation they received the bio. So I was hooked, and I sent my check for $50 to purchase a copy of this wonderful chronicle announcing my son's entrance into the world of officially accomplished children.

When the book didn't arrive after a few months, I called and left a message. No response. I went on the website and sent an e-mail. No response. Finally a year later, I googled: "Who's Who of Middle School Students Scam." Low and behold, I wasn't the only one who'd been ripped off. Ugh!

I thought I was smarter than that. I watched for certain signs scam artists use, and when I didn't see any, I plunged right into deception. In hindsight, I wish I'd seen a copy of an actual book first.

Paul warned about an even greater deception that would come upon Christians. In 2 Corinthians 11, Paul warned believers about false teachers. Verses 13 through 15 read, "For such men are false apostles, deceitful workmen, masquerading as apostles of Christ. And no wonder, for Satan himself masquerades as an angel of light. It is not surprising, then, if his servants masquerade as servants of righteousness."

These false apostles weren't preaching the true gospel of Christ, and they weren't living according to Christ's teaching. Amazingly, the Corinthians still tolerated them in their midst. Paul warned them—don't believe everything you see and hear!

The book of Matthew records the words of Jesus about scam artists. In Matthew 7:15-16, Jesus warns, "Watch out for false prophets. They come to you in sheep's clothing, but inwardly they are ferocious wolves. By their fruit you will recognize them."

These verses warn us that Satan will try to deceive us cloaked as an agent of God, but we can identify deception and deceivers by the fruit they produce. My experience taught me to watch and wait for the evidence of truth. Studying Scripture and learning about the unchanging heart and character of God will prepare us to identify true spiritual fruit when we see it. It will help us recognize the bad, deceptive fruit as well.

> *Dear Lord, You are the source of all truth. I praise You for Your goodness and righteousness. Help me to learn Your truth and ways so I can identify deceptions when I encounter them. In Jesus' name. Amen.*

Application Steps

Identify a time in your life when you were deceived. Consider why you were deceived. What did you miss or overlook that might have saved you from the deception?

45 Confidence in CHAOS
Zoë Elmore

Blessed are those who trust in the LORD...They are like trees planted along a riverbank, with roots that reach deep into the water. Such trees are not bothered by the heat or worried by long months of drought. Their leaves stay green, and they go right on producing delicious fruit.

JEREMIAH 17:7-8 NLT

I'm sure we all have our own definition of chaos. The North American dictionary defines "chaos" as "a state of complete disorder and confusion." Over the last two years my family has experienced my husband's job being eliminated; my mother-in-law falling and our caring for her while her wrist mended; my dad suffering a massive stroke, leaving him partially paralyzed, in diapers, and using feeding tubes; our oldest son having ten tumors that needed to be removed; our youngest son going off to college; having a young man live in our home for six months; and I, myself, spending seven months working for a cosmetic company where I was treated quite rudely.

Maybe your work environment qualifies as chaos, or perhaps entertaining your grandchildren would more accurately define this word for you. Whatever your definition, I'd like to change your perspective on the word "chaos." Replace your definition of chaos with this acronym: **C**hrist's **H**ope **A**midst **O**ur **S**uffering.

When I place my hope in Christ despite my crazy circumstances, I find true rest. What's more, it becomes a wonderful opportunity for others to see Christ in me as I walk through times of chaos.

From my experience, I can tell you that changing my perspective on the word "chaos" gave me the ability like never before to experience the peace, presence, provision, and power of Christ in some very difficult circumstances. God wants to transform our lives into a reflection of Him so that we can impact others for His eternal purposes. Sometimes God chooses suffering to accomplish that goal.

If your life is in a state of complete disorder and confusion, I invite you to look at chaos from God's perspective. You can experience the transforming power of hope in Him as you face the issues and concerns of your life. Christ's hope can empower you to face medical challenges, financial difficulties, and marital or family problems.

Dear Lord, thank You for Your promise to be with me and for Your enabling power that helps me to walk through this life with confidence. May I be one who bears and shares Your hope so that others may experience Your peace, presence, provision, and power. In Jesus' name. Amen.

Application Steps

Change your perspective on chaos. See your chaotic circumstances as opportunities to hope and trust in Christ. Then you'll walk through life with real confidence.

46 Coming Home
Micca Campbell

I say to you that likewise there will be more joy in heaven over one sinner who repents than over ninety-nine just persons who need no repentance.

LUKE 15:7 NKJV

Watching my children enjoy summer takes me back to my childhood. I recall warm summer days when I played in the neighborhood with childhood friends. Each day was a new adventure. We played from dawn to dusk. At sunset, one by one the children would answer the call of their parents to come home. My dad would whistle. No matter how far my journey carried me, my father knew that the sound of his whistle would be heard, recognized, and obeyed.

Responding to his call, I'd jump on my bike and head for home. As my house came into view, I could see Dad standing on the front porch waving. I didn't realize it then, but he didn't have to wait for me. Dad could have continued about his business. Instead, he displayed a father's heart. Dad waited and watched until I was safely home. My arrival seemed to bring him joy. I knew this by the smile on his face and his open arms.

Jesus also revealed the Father's heart toward us, His children, when He told the story about the Shepherd who left his entire flock to find one lost sheep (Luke 15:3-7 NKJV). In the same way, our heavenly Father is troubled over the person who has wandered away from Him.

One summer our six-year-old son went missing. The sun was setting, and like my dad, I stepped onto the porch and called for him. There was no response. Frantically, his dad and I searched door-to-door for him. House after house, all we found was disappointment. With flashlights in hand, our neighbors joined the search. Eventually we phoned the police. I felt my body go numb. We were living out our worst nightmare—our son was lost.

Before the police arrived, some neighbors returning home from the ballpark stopped in front of our house. As the side door of their van slid open, there sat our son. The neighbors had taken him to the ballpark without our permission.

Our son was afraid his dad would be angry at him for going to the ballpark without checking with us first. Instead, he found the comfort of a father's heart. With arms of love, my husband held our son tightly and rejoiced over his homecoming.

Perhaps you have wandered into a distant place and long to come home. You may feel lost for good, but God knows where you are. You have not escaped His attention. The Father knows His children and calls them by name. Those who follow Him will find their way home and be welcomed with open arms. With a Father's heart, God is waiting and watching from the front porch of heaven for your return. If you don't know what to say to Him, use the words from this hymn penned by William J. Kirkpatrick:

> *Coming home, coming home,*
> *Nevermore to roam,*
> *Open wide Thine arms of love,*
> *Lord, I'm coming home.*

Dear Lord, forgive me when I stray from You. I want to come home. Receive me into Your presence. In Jesus' name. Amen.

Application Steps

If God is calling you home, answer yes! Tell Him you are sorry for your sins and turn from your old ways. Recommit your life to Him with regular prayer and Bible reading.

47 He Knows the Plans

Renee Swope

"For I know the plans I have for you," declares the LORD, "plans to prosper you and not to harm you, plans to give you hope and a future."

JEREMIAH 29:11

Have you ever heard the saying, "Failing to plan is like planning to fail"? Isn't that so true? But what about those times when you make plans and your plans fail anyway? Isn't that so frustrating?

I used to avoid planning because I like being spontaneous. I also dislike being upset when my plans are interrupted. However, a busy life without wise planning leads to a life of disarray, so my husband and I try to sit down each week to plan our schedules.

We were going through a season where both of us needed extra time during the week to complete work projects. We met with calendars and plotted each night to make sure our week went smoothly.

We scheduled Monday night as "pizza night" and J.J. would work late at his office. Tuesday night he'd be home by 5:30 for dinner. He would oversee our boys' evening routine while I caught up on work calls and e-mails. I couldn't wait for the peace of mind that would bring!

Monday went just as planned. Tuesday was one of those days that felt like only an hour passed before it was time for me to head home from the office. Hurriedly, I stuffed files in my bag as a wave of anxiety swept over me. Then I remembered *the plan* and sighed with relief knowing I could work from home that evening.

J.J. called at five. He wasn't headed home. He had to work late. I almost burst into tears, but I knew that would make him feel awful, so I said I'd adjust my plans. Although I wasn't angry, I felt anxious. I looked at the files and reminded God of all the people waiting for calls and e-mails. Before I could complete my mental memo, my worries gave way to an unexpected prayer: "Lord, I had plans for tonight; plans that would bring me peace and a sense of completion. But You know the plans You have for me; plans to prosper me, not to harm me; plans to give me hope. Obviously my plans weren't Your plans. Please show me the plans You have for tonight."

I never touched my files. Instead we ate dinner, cleaned the kitchen together, and folded clothes while we watched a family video. Our evening had an unusual sweetness as we sorted socks and snuggled on the couch. God's plan was for me to help my husband, spend time with my kids, and care for our home.

When I surrendered to His plan, a peace that surpassed my understanding came over me. I had planned to find peace in getting things done, but God's peace emerged when my plans came undone, making room for the plans He had for me.

Dear Lord, I want to leave room for Your plans in my life. As I seek to live a life with purpose and peace, teach me how to let You redirect my steps so that my plans align with Yours. In Jesus' name. Amen.

Application Steps

Imagine you are standing before God. Are you willing to place your schedule in His hands? Ask Him if there's anything He wants to replace with something else. Invite Him into every nook and cranny of your day and seek the blessings of a life lived in full surrender to His plans.

48 Satan Yells, God Whispers

Marybeth Whalen

Whether you turn to the right or to the left,
your ears will hear a voice behind you, saying,
"This is the way; walk in it."

Isaiah 30:21

First Kings 19:3-13 is one of my favorite passages in the Bible. In this section of Scripture, Elijah runs to a cave and is hiding from King Ahab, afraid for his life. He is at one of life's low points with which we can sympathize. He wants to know if God is really there. Have you ever asked that question in your heart?

Unfortunately, I don't struggle with knowing whether Satan is in my life. He announces his presence with authority. I see him in my own sinful nature. I sense him lurking, waiting to strike. Like a police officer in a speed trap, he could show up anywhere and catch me off guard. He crawls up on my shoulder, and says horrible, crippling things in my ear. His voice is loud and persistent. I want to silence him forever, but I must wait on God's timing for that. In the meantime, I know I must contend with my enemy.

God, on the other hand, is the great lover of my soul. He does not enter in uninvited; rather, He is always the gentleman. He does not insinuate Himself into my life but waits to be invited. He says, "Here I am! I stand at the door and knock. If anyone hears my voice and opens the door, I will come in and eat with him, and he with me" (Revelation 3:20). In His grace, He asks for entrance to our lives and does not barge in unbidden.

Unlike Satan's evil hiss, God's voice is a gentle whisper. It's something I do not so much hear with my ears as feel in my soul. In the passage in 1 Kings, God does not come in the wind or the earthquake or the fire. He comes in a breeze that soothes and comforts Elijah's troubled heart. He comes to us in the same way. Remember this about His character when you are facing tough times. Just because He is quiet does not mean He isn't there.

He will not yell at you and condemn you. That is the enemy talking. As God's people, we must learn to distinguish between the two voices and not mistake Satan's condemnation for God's loving guidance. There is a difference. Get to know God's character by reading His Word and spending time with Him in prayer each day. Just as you recognize familiar voices on the telephone without having to ask who it is, you can come to know God's voice instantly. When you get to know God's character, you can recognize His sweet voice.

Dear Lord, thank You for caring enough for me to speak to me. Help me to know You so well that I instantly recognize Your voice. Help me to know when it is Satan speaking to me, and to learn not to listen to him. In Jesus' name. Amen.

Application Steps

Get out your Bible and read 1 Kings 19:3-13. Write down any words or phrases that speak to you today. Learn to recognize God's voice just as you would any friend with whom you regularly spend time.

49 A Mother's Trust

Sharon Glasgow

You shall teach [my words] diligently to your children, and shall talk of them when you sit in your house, when you walk by the way, when you lie down, and when you rise up.

DEUTERONOMY 6:7 (NKJV)

I can remember vividly a night years ago that impacted me as a maturing young teenager. My three siblings and I were walking with our mother to our car when a woman approached us, wanting to talk to my mom. She said very proudly, as if she were a child-rearing specialist, "Louise, you've got good kids now, but you just wait (snarling giggle). One day they're going to grow up, and let me tell you, teens bring trouble and you'll be no exception to that rule."

Mom had always been an insecure person because of her childhood. Her father had been abusive, and she constantly struggled with thoughts of failure because of her lack of confidence. She was also a struggling single parent raising us all by herself.

All of a sudden my mom's countenance changed. It seemed as if the wind stopped blowing, the stars grew brighter, and time stopped. Mom looked at me with eyes that penetrated to my soul. Then she locked eyes with Susan, Scott, and Sandy. Her 4' 11" stature seemed to grow to 6 feet tall in a matter of seconds. Confidence and joy swept across her face as she replied to the woman, "My children will be the exception. I have total trust in my kids, through the help of my God."

We didn't say a word on the way home that night. It was after that night that I remember my mom setting aside an hour every night to pray for us. I felt my mom's prayers as temptations came when I was a teenager. Every time I was faced with tough decisions, I would remember how much my mom trusted me, believed in me, and prayed that I would choose the right path.

Today I'm the mother of five daughters. People have made similar comments to me in front of my girls, and I count it a privilege to carry on the legacy of what my mom instilled that night.

Just the other day, I overheard our 23-year-old Heather talking with her sisters about what the worst punishment in the world would be. She said it would be to disappoint Mom and Dad because "they *trust us* so much." I smiled and thanked God for the legacy my mom had given to me. I can't wait to see the legacy lived out in the next generation!

Kids need to know we love them, but just as importantly, they need to know we believe in them, trust them, and are proud of them.

Dear Lord, please give me Your wisdom in raising the children You have entrusted to me. Help me to not lean on my own understanding but to rely totally on You for guidance (Proverbs 3:5). Thank You! In Jesus' name. Amen.

Application Steps

Pray for your children. Care about the details of their lives. Your children should know without a doubt that they are a high priority to you.

50 What's in Your Closet?

Susanne Scheppmann

*If you decide for God, living a life of God-worship,
it follows that you don't fuss about what's on the table
at mealtimes or whether the clothes in your closet are in fashion.
There is far more to your life than the food you put in your
stomach, more to your outer appearance than the clothes
you hang on your body.*

MATTHEW 6:25 MSG

I discovered a lot about myself during a recent cleaning of my clothes closet. Blue stood out as my favorite color. How could I own so many blue tops? I realized that somewhere in the recesses of my mind, I hold the fantasy I am going to fit into those size 10 jeans again. One glance at the floor confirmed my husband's past comment, "You might be a shoe-o-holic."

Spring-cleaning my closet felt like a safari of sorts. I separated, bagged, and hauled out many worn, useless, too small, and even hardly worn items. I sat down exhausted after finishing my mission.

Then I asked myself, *Why do I own so many clothes that a full walk-in closet bursts at the seams?* Two answers settled in my mind—God's blessings and my own self-indulgence.

Starting today, I will attempt to put less value on my clothing and more significance on what I wear on the inside. The apostle Paul said, "Rather, clothe yourselves with the Lord Jesus Christ" (Romans 13:14).

In addition, I will purchase my clothes with more thought. *Do I need it? Will I really wear it? How often?* If I buy a new item, I will remove one old item when I hang the new one in my closet. I also decided that enduring styles, not fads, will populate my wardrobe.

Now, I do love shoes, but I need to be a good steward of my money.

Paul advises us on our footwear, "For shoes, put on the peace that comes from the Good News" (Ephesians 6:15 NLT). Thankfully, Paul is not inferring I shouldn't wear stylish shoes, only that I take into consideration what their true importance is in life. I will determine a shoe budget and stick to it. If it's not in my budget, I will resist the urge to buy...even if they are cheap and adorable.

Next year, my cleaning shouldn't be such a tiring experience. I hope my closet will reveal that I've been a better steward with my money. Moreover, I hope I will look back and see that I better clothed myself with Jesus from the inside out.

> *Dear Lord, remind me of what is truly important in the big scheme of things. Help me to be a wise steward of my money when I shop for clothes. Each morning remind me to clothe myself with humility and love, so that others see You. In Jesus' name. Amen*

Application Steps

Glance through your closet and make notes on what it reveals about your personality and resources. Mark a date on your calendar to give your clothes closet a thorough cleaning. Then when the day arrives, sort into piles: items to keep, to donate, and to be discarded.

51 No More Shame

Lysa TerKeurst

I sought the LORD, and he answered me;
he delivered me from all my fears.
Those who look to him are radiant;
their faces are never covered with shame.

PSALM 34:4-5

■ I still remember the outdated furniture and stale coldness of the room. Women from all walks of life were there. Our paths had crossed at this awful place, a place where life was exchanged for death. We would now share an unmentionable secret.

No one let her eyes meet another's. Though medical fluorescent lights brightly lit the room, the heavy darkness in my soul made true vision nearly impossible. What had brought me to this place? Certainly, I had people to blame. There was the man who sexually abused me in childhood. I could blame my biological father. Maybe if he had given me the love and acceptance I so desperately longed for, I would not have come to this place. I could blame God. Why had a loving God let such terrible things happen to me? Tears filled my eyes and deep sobs poured from my soul in that cold room. I knew I could not blame anyone but myself. I'd walked into this place. I'd signed the papers. I'd allowed my baby to be aborted.

I can just imagine Satan hissing as he writes his name across the victim's heart: Shame. I have felt shame's pain—a deep, constant throbbing of regret from the past mixed with dread of the future.

Let's look at when shame made its debut. Genesis 2:25 says, "The man and his wife were both naked, and they felt no shame." Then Satan slithered onto the scene to deceive Eve. When Eve fell into sin and took Adam with her, their reaction was to hide and cover up their mistake. That's exactly what I did for so many painful years. But keeping my secret in the darkness allowed Satan to use it against me. He is the father of darkness and the author of shame. He would constantly whisper that I was worthless, and that if anyone ever found out about my secret, they would condemn me.

But that was a lie from the pit of hell. When I finally brought my sin out into the light, God met me there with grace, forgiveness, and healing. Then He gave me the courage to let Him take my shame and use it for His good. I can say without hesitation the thing that has brought me the most healing has been to share my story with other women. Now that I have seen God touching and healing others through my testimony, the shame has gone and freedom has come.

Dear Lord, I thank You for seeing me as pure, clean, spotless, and without blemish. You alone have the power to heal those parts of me that I have buried and tried to hide for so long. May Your grace be enough for me today as I trust You to work all things for Your good. In Jesus' name. Amen.

Application Steps

Write down and meditate on these three truths:

1. By His wounds, I am healed.

2. God never forgets His promises. When He says that nothing I have ever done could make Him stop loving me, it is absolute truth. His love for me cannot be shaken.

3. Jesus died of a broken heart so that I don't have to. He thought of me on that cross, and because of His sacrifice I am forgiven and set free.

52 The Duet

Rachel Olsen

A man shall leave his father and mother and
be joined to his wife, and they shall become one flesh.
Genesis 2:24 NKJV

His scarlet red body hopped from branch to branch as he whistled directions to his lady love on the ground below. From my window, I watched the cardinal pair choose a nearby shrub for their new home. Nothing brightens a dull winter landscape like a cardinal's bright red plumage and many-toned songs. Only the male species is brilliantly colored; the females are tan with a hint of muddy red on their wings. The male cardinal is so attractive that seven different states have adopted it as their state bird.

Unlike most bird species, the female cardinal can sing just as well as her male counterpart. She frequently sings to him, whistles when she needs him to bring food to the nest, and often chimes in with him to perform a duet. They remind me of the truth of Proverbs 18:22: "When a man finds a wife, he finds something good" (NCV).

Cardinal couples create and share their own special songs. The female will often sing longer and slightly more complex tunes than the male. (Perhaps all females have the gift of gab.) Take a look at Proverbs 12:18: "Some people make cutting remarks, but the words of the wise bring healing" (NLT).

If you spot a red cardinal this winter, look closely into nearby branches or ground brush for his tan-colored wife, for the two are never far apart. They mate for life. This is God's design for men and women as well. Read Mark 10:8-9: "The two are united into one. Since they are no longer two but one, let no one separate them, for God has joined them together" (NLT).

It seems the female cardinal is content to let her mate garner respect and attention. Though she has skills equally as impressive as his, she's happy to allow him to sing the lead, to wear the bright-red-pants in the family, and to care for both her and their young. "You wives will submit to your husbands as you do to the Lord. For a husband is the head of his wife as Christ is the head of his body, the church...And you husbands must love your wives with the same love Christ showed the church. He gave up his life for her to make her holy and clean" (Ephesians 5:22-25 NLT).

As I watch them at the bird feeder, dining together on sunflower seeds, they take turns offering each other seeds. Their dark beaks touch briefly, as if in a kiss, as they pass nourishment and sustenance to one another. Galatians 5:13-15 reminds us: "You, my brothers, were called to be free. But do not use your freedom to indulge the sinful nature; rather, serve one another in love. The entire law is summed up in a single command: 'Love your neighbor as yourself.' If you keep on biting and devouring each other, watch out or you will be destroyed by each other."

I am thankful for the opportunity to watch this scarlet cardinal and his lady love—and for the visual reminder of what a godly marriage is to look and sound like.

Dear Lord, You are love. Increase my heart's capacity to love the way You do. Give me eyes for my husband only, and help me to honor, respect, and follow him as You guide us both. In Jesus' name. Amen.

Application Steps

Look for ways you can honor your husband today (including your husband Jesus) and focus your attention on blessing him and following him.

53 Meter Reader

Wendy Pope

Check up on yourselves. Are you really Christians?
Do you pass the test? Do you feel Christ's presence
and power more and more within you?

2 CORINTHIANS 13:5 TLB

I have to admit, I have taken pride in knowing the answers to most questions my children ask me, or at least knowing enough to make it sound as though I'm an expert. This was until trucks, bulldozers, and "workermen" came into the picture.

Realizing I could not talk intelligently about such things with my son, I went and got a book on construction equipment. Together we learned. I can proudly say I now know the difference between a skid steer and an excavator, a backhoe and a bulldozer, a baler and a harvester. It thrills me to be able to stop by a construction site and talk "workerman" with my little guy.

As we drove home from preschool one day, he spotted a truck he had never seen before. He was thrilled at seeing the "workerman" and was quick to inquire who he was and what he was doing.

Fortunately, I recognized the vehicle as a meter reader truck. (I don't believe that is the technical name, but it worked for a four-year-old.) I identified the truck and driver for Griffin. His response was, "What does a meter reader do, Mommy?" I answered, "He reads the meter on the house to see how much power the people who live inside the house have used." He was satisfied with my answer and looked around for something else to inquire about. Meanwhile the Holy Spirit became my meter reader, prompting me to question myself: "If I had a meter to measure the amount of Holy Spirit power I've used today, what would it say?"

The question caught me off guard. So much of my time is wasted complaining or whining about situations or circumstances in my life. I forget, until I am the middle of a crisis, that God's Word says that as a child of God I have the power to overcome. In fact, the victory is already mine. As believers, we put ourselves through needless worry and anxiety when we don't use what God has given us, His power. Imagine how effortlessly we could sail through our troubles if only we would use what has been given freely to us.

Dear Lord, You are all-powerful. I know I have power available to me as a believer. Help me to call upon it when I need to and not to try to handle things myself. My efforts have proven futile. I need You every minute of every day. In Jesus' name. Amen.

Application Steps

Using a Bible concordance, look up the word "power." Read several of the verses in context. Learn what it looks like to experience the presence and power of Christ in your daily life.

54 Being Faithful with Little

Glynnis Whitwer

*His master replied, "Well done, good and faithful servant!
You have been faithful with a few things; I will put you in
charge of many things. Come and share your master's happiness!"*
MATTHEW 25:21

I love all five of my children with equal measure, but when I want to get something important delivered to the school office, I know which one will get it there in one piece. I know which one will look for a brother on the playground full of children until he's found, and I know which one will get distracted by the swings and abandon the search.

Of course, children will be children, and most grow out of distractions and a constant preference for play. But I wonder if God doesn't sometimes look at us the same way and decide whom He can trust with something important?

I believe most Christians want more of the *right* things. We want to know more of God. We want more joy in our lives. We want to do more things for Jesus' sake. We would like to have more money to give away. We would like to share more of our talents with others. And we question why we don't have more.

Then we look around and wonder why some people seem to get all the opportunities. Why do some people have money to give? Why are they asked to do important jobs? Why can they work with a good attitude at a boring assignment?

I believe the answer is found in the words of the master in the parable of the talents found in Matthew 25:21: "His master replied, 'Well done, good and faithful servant! You have been faithful with a few things; I will put you in charge of many things. Come and share your master's happiness!'"

The servants in the story were entrusted with "talents" or a unit of coins. Two invested the little they had and offered a profit back to their master when he returned. The story describes the happiness of the master when his servants proved themselves faithful with little. The master was willing to give them more.

God is looking at us to see how faithful we are with what He's given us. He's given each of us an amount of intelligence, personal skills, physical strength, and emotional reserve. For most of us in the world, we've been given shelter, food, and a portion of money. Then God waits to see what we're going to do with what we've been given.

God wants to give us more when we invest what we have for His purposes. I believe God longs to reward His believers with more responsibility, but He needs to be able to trust us. The reward of being faithful with little isn't just getting more, it's also sharing in the happiness of our Lord. An even greater reward is knowing we've played a part in advancing the kingdom of God here on earth. We may never know just how many lives are impacted by our obedience, but God knows, and He already has our next assignment planned.

Dear Lord, I worship and praise You for Your goodness and faithfulness. Forgive me for the times I'm not faithful with what You've entrusted to me. Help me to identify those areas in my life that need changing. In Jesus' name. Amen.

Application Steps

Identify one responsibility in your life that you haven't paid much attention to lately. What can you do this week to be more responsible in that area?

55 Spend Some Time with Me

Melissa Taylor

Let the morning bring me word of your unfailing love,
for I have put my trust in you. Show me the way I should go,
for to you I lift up my soul.

PSALM 143:8

I remember the day well. It was the day in my life I thought everything would change. I expected great things to happen. I expected my circumstances to change. I wanted a magical: "Abracadabra! Life is perfect!"

I invited Christ into my life back in 1979. I was watching a religious program on TV, and I liked what these messengers from God had to say. They said my life would be different, and I would experience a change if Jesus was a part of it. During the previous five years, I had experienced sexual abuse, witnessed my grandfather's stroke, moved several times, and cried over my parents' divorce. I believed Jesus was real, but I had never invited Him into my life. I was quickly learning that this world was a hard place to live.

Maybe you've been where I was. You finally made a decision, and a big one at that, to invite Christ into your life, but what happens next? Where do you go from there? That's exactly what I wanted to know.

My circumstances did not change. In many ways, they became more complicated. If I was a changed person, then why did I still feel this way? Why did I continue over the next ten years to make decisions that were anything but godly? Guilt and shame filled my inner thoughts.

Jesus is all about changing and transforming lives, but He doesn't promise that He will change or fix our circumstances. What He does promise is that He will bring us unfailing love, He will watch over us, and there is no condemnation for those in Christ. I would have known this if I had just spent time with Him.

In every relationship, time needs to be invested in the one you are trying to know. My life began to have much more meaning when I began spending time with God. I was able to find purpose in my circumstances because His Word spoke to my heart. I learned I was a child of the Almighty King; therefore, being a daughter of that King, I am a princess.

When I invite a friend to my home, I don't just leave them at the front door. I bring them to the center of my home. We laugh and we cry. Sometimes we exchange gifts, meal ideas, or family stories. We often share secrets, ask for advice, or even pray together. We listen and we learn. We live life together.

So it is with God. I invited Him in, but I wasn't spending any time with Him. I know now that He was carrying me through certain dark times in life and trying desperately to get me to hear Him say, "You invited Me in. Now spend some time with Me."

Dear Lord, help me to know You better. Thank You for loving me without fail every day of my life. In Jesus' name. Amen.

Application Steps

Have you invited Christ in? If not, I encourage you to pray today, asking Him to forgive your sins and invade your life. Get to know Him, and you'll come to trust Him. Spend time with Him today.

56 A Cheerful Heart

Susanne Scheppmann

A cheerful heart is good medicine,
but a crushed spirit dries up the bones.

PROVERBS 17:22

Pamela's disability keeps her from fitting in with average people. I am not sure what is wrong with her, but she is different—physically and socially. She limps as she busses tables for hustling table servers. She struggles to collect dirty dishes and wipe the tables. Pamela grimaces when she needs to bend over to pick up a napkin lying on the floor. She perseveres until the job is complete. Struggles pervade every area of her life, but she does not give up.

However, that is not the only amazing thing about Pamela. She spreads joy, always keeping a smile on her face. Pam's memory for silly jokes amazes everyone. She provides opportunities for others to smile as she tells them. Sadly, some people laugh at her rather than at her jokes. Once they get to know her, though, they're happily laughing right along with her.

I know a little of Pamela's story. Her life has been difficult from the day she was born with physical handicaps. Children tormented her. They poked fun at the way she walked and talked. Then in early adolescence, Pamela's father abused her two sisters and went to prison. The family fell apart. She was left to fend for herself as a teenager.

However, when you hold a conversation with Pamela, there is no trace of bitterness. She possesses the most positive outlook of anyone I know. Do you remember the old saying, "When life hands you lemons, make lemonade"? No sour lemons exist in Pamela's life. Instead, she pours refreshing laughter into other people's days.

I admire her. Personally, I easily harbor bitter feelings toward people and events. Pamela reminds me that life is too short to be cranky and resentful. I believe God placed her in my life to remind me that terrible things happen to everyone. Even Jesus warned us of this fact in the book of John: "I have told you these things, so that in me you may have peace. In this world you will have trouble. But take heart! I have overcome the world" (John 16:33).

If we carry bitterness in our heart, it can dry up our spirit. Even worse, it can lead others astray. "See to it that no one misses the grace of God and that no bitter root grows up to cause trouble and defile many" (Hebrews 12:15). I don't know about you, but I don't want to turn out a bitter old woman!

So let's take heart. A cheerful heart is good medicine, no matter what the ailment. We can seize cheer, because Jesus has overcome the world. Let's not allow bitterness to crush our spirit and dry up our bones. Instead, let's try to squeeze out some lemonade to sweeten other's lives—just like my friend Pamela.

Dear Lord, help me to keep a cheerful heart regardless of the difficulties in life. Keep me from growing a heart of bitterness. Help me to recall that You have overcome this world. Let me become an example of joy, so that others will come to know You. In Jesus' name. Amen.

Application Steps

Look at Proverbs 17:22 in a few different versions of the Bible. Ponder the different phrasing. Then write your own personalized version of this verse.

57 The Joy of Being a Disciple
Micca Campbell

Jesus said to His disciples, "If anyone desires to come after Me, let him deny himself, and take up his cross, and follow Me."
MATTHEW 16:24 NKJV

Tuesday nights were basketball night. We usually sat among the other proud parents to cheer for our junior high boys as they strived for victory. This Tuesday night was different. The moms were busy organizing a list of foods to bring to Jimmy's house. He was the father of one of the players on our team. Jimmy was dying from diabetes.

When I explained that I would take my dish over myself and visit with Jimmy when I did, I was met with disapproving looks. Suddenly, something that was already going to be hard for me to do just became harder. Hearing their reactions made me not want to go. I struggled with staying home rather than going to comfort Jimmy because I feared their rejection. Still, the Holy Spirit was persistent at nudging me to go. I knew what I had to do, regardless of what the others thought.

I was surprised when the nurse rolled Jimmy out into the living room. Both of his legs had been amputated, and most of his fingers too. Stunned and helpless, I whispered to the Lord under my breath, "Oh, God, how can I minister to this man when I don't know what he's been through?"

Somehow, I knew God would show up to do what I couldn't. And He did.

As Jimmy and I talked, it was apparent that he knew the Father, but I sensed there was more. It wasn't much longer into our conversation when I discovered the real trouble with Jimmy. He was afraid to die.

I told Jimmy Bible stories where God sent an angel to someone in need, much like him, with a special message. "Fear not, for God is with you!" As I shared with Jimmy, I saw peace return to his face as if he received the message for himself.

After I left there that day, my joy was so full it outweighed the cost of those disapproving moms. To my surprise, God did more that day than I realized.

At Jimmy's funeral, his wife shared his last moments with me. Jimmy would often awake from his sleep wide-eyed and call out, "I'm afraid!" She would pat him gently and remind him of God's promise. "Don't be afraid, Jimmy. God is with you." Then he would sleep again.

The last time Jimmy opened his eyes he just stared at the ceiling. His wife asked, "Jimmy, are you afraid?" Jimmy whispered, "No, I'm not afraid. I'm looking at the angels." We embraced.

"If you hadn't come that day," she said, taking my hand, "I wouldn't have known how to comfort Jimmy."

For a little word, "if" carries a lot of meaning. *"If anyone desires to come after Me, let him deny himself."* If I had let the fear of rejection stop me from ministering, I wouldn't have experienced the joy of being God's disciple. It's our choice to follow Christ or not, but we need not fear because the same promise God made to Jimmy, He gives to us, "Fear not, child, for God is with you!"

Dear Lord, thank You for the privilege of serving You. Help me to not fear but to be a bold witness for You in every area of my life. In Jesus' name. Amen.

Application Steps

To grow spiritually and experience true joy, step out in faith and follow Christ wherever He leads.

58 You've Got Charisma
Luann Prater

I long to see you so that I may impart to you some spiritual gift to make you strong.
Romans 1:11

The term "spiritual gift" in the original language is *charisma,* which means "the instantaneous enablement of the Holy Spirit in the life of any believer to exercise a gift for the edification of others."

Our daughter got married last year. The months preceding the wedding were a marathon of planning, spending, and attending showers. Each shower was in a different city and each with its own theme. We had the UK coed shower, the Pampered Chef shower, the "just family" shower, and the "bring anything you want" shower. The giving was generous and the love was flowing.

This madness, coupled with a semester of 18 college hours, drove my daughter to develop a severe stomach ulcer. For weeks she was unable to keep anything down and was shedding pounds like a sheared sheep. Five days before the wedding, as stress levels reached an all-time high, God's still, small voice echoed on my radar screen. "Stop rushing and start praying."

I asked my two daughters to take a break and join me in a circle of prayer. Quietly we came to the Lord asking for His presence, His comfort, His healing touch. As our prayers continued, our high-speed race was disrupted by a tranquil stream of peace that enveloped the room. It was such a delightful time of bonding with our Father and one another. All of the racing, the spending, and the gift giving could not compare to the precious gift that God showered on us at that moment.

We rose from the circle rejoicing. Our lovely bride whispered in my ear, "Mom, I felt my stomach calm down. I don't think I'm going to need any medicine today." And she didn't. Not only for that day, but every day since she has been medicine free.

Now, please don't misunderstand. I'm not saying that things went smoothly from that day on…quite the contrary. The week took many twists and turns. Her stomach, however, did not. Bridesmaid dresses didn't come in until two days before the wedding, and they didn't fit. The caterer got sick right before she was to prepare the rehearsal dinner. The wedding cake was not at all what my daughter had ordered. And yet, peace remained. The most precious gift my daughter received for her wedding? Time spent in prayer with her loving family and her heavenly Father.

God has given each of His family members the ability to share His love with others. Many people are generous with their worldly gifts, but how many take the time to reveal God's eternal gift? His peace that passes all understanding is a gift anyone can afford to give. When it's gift-giving time, whether for a shower, a birthday, or Christmas, take a moment to impart *charisma* to build and strengthen others.

> *Dear Lord, You are such an awesome God. Your goodness is more than we can comprehend. You shower us with Your loving-kindness every day. And You have called each of us to share that love with those who need Your touch. Help me this day to build and strengthen others through my prayers and Your Holy Spirit. In Jesus' name. Amen.*

Application Steps

Find one person today who needs to feel God's love through your loving touch. Listen for God's direction. Pray with them in person, on the phone, or through computer messaging.

59 My Morning Renewal

Susanne Scheppmann

Create in me a pure heart, O God, and renew a
steadfast spirit within me. Do not cast me from your
presence or take your Holy Spirit from me.
Restore to me the joy of your salvation and grant
me a willing spirit, to sustain me.

PSALM 51:10-12

Today my car registration came up for renewal. I also received notification that my magazine subscription will expire if not renewed immediately. Almost everything has a renewal of some sort, including my life.

I struggle out of bed each morning to stumble bleary-eyed to the earthy aroma of coffee. After just a couple of sips, I feel renewed. Caffeine works wonders in my drowsy morning state.

With the ceramic mug in hand, I mosey to my next renewal: a few moments spent with Jesus Christ. The brief morning interlude prepares me for the day ahead. So many times I wake up crabby for any number of reasons—a spat with my spouse, raging hormones, or lack of sleep.

But as I settle into a quiet time with God, I sense His peace. I experience the Holy Spirit renewing my spirit with calmness and serenity. He "renews a steadfast spirit within me." I accept gratefully His reassurance in the day looming ahead.

With my head down, I ask Him to create a purer heart in me. I need Him to wipe the slate clean of my anger with my husband. He calms wild hormones by bestowing self-control upon me. I can manage the monthly moods instead of them managing me. He gives me renewed energy, even though I lack my necessary eight hours of slumber. The words of Isaiah 40:31 spring to life in me: "Those who hope in the

LORD will renew their strength. They will soar on wings like eagles; they will run and not grow weary, they will walk and not be faint."

Suddenly, I feel energized and encouraged. I start the day's chores with an upbeat attitude. Okay, first I'll call my husband and apologize. I will renew the magazine subscription, and then I will head to the DMV to renew my car registration.

Finally, I will come back tomorrow for another replenishing for myself, for without a continuous renewal of my spiritual life, I would surely expire.

Dear Lord, help me to make my quiet time with You a priority every morning. Renew my spirit as I reflect upon You and Your Word. In Jesus' name. Amen.

Application Steps

Make a list of activities that will help you to renew yourself spiritually. Make a promise to yourself to incorporate at least one of these activities in your daily routine.

60 Sanctuary

Van Walton

"Because of the devastation of the afflicted,
because of the groaning of the needy, now I will arise,"
says the LORD, "I will set him in the safety
for which he longs."

PSALM 12:5 NASB

On September 18, 1989, Hurricane Hugo slammed into the eastern coast of Puerto Rico. The violent storm climbed up the anvil-shaped mountain that overlooked the Atlantic Ocean, forging a path of devastation and destruction. Although much of the El Yunke Rain Forest was ruined, its high and strong mountain protected the rest of the island.

The aftermath of the winds and rain revealed major losses in the forest. One loss was that the parrot population had been reduced to an estimated 25 birds. The Puerto Rican parrot, already one of the rarest birds in the world, now faced extinction. Something had to be done to save this uncommon, beautiful bird.

The United States Forest Service collaborated with the Puerto Rican Department of Natural Resources to initiate a recovery program. The plan was to increase the birds' population by breeding them in captivity. So the parrots were captured and placed in protected sanctuaries, high in the mountain landscape, while their numbers increased. As the bird population grew, the birds were systematically returned to the wild. Each bird was tagged and observed so they could be recaptured whenever another major storm threatened their habitat.

God made us in His image, a rare and special creation. He told us to be fruitful and multiply. Throughout history, as the human race populated the earth, storms, diseases, and devastation have constantly threatened mankind in one way or another. Not only do physical trials threaten, but spiritual temptations are common to all. The good news is that God has a plan for our eternal preservation.

Like the U.S. Forest Service, God's plan is to rescue us from the evils that would destroy His unique and precious children. In God's love and mercy, He reached down from heaven and through His Son captured our hearts. Jesus "tagged" us with His love, placed us in His sanctuary, and empowered us with His Spirit so that Christianity would never face extinction. The New Testament gives a detailed account of how Jesus, through His death and resurrection, carried out God's plan of deliverance.

Empowered by the Holy Spirit, we are strengthened to fulfill God's plan. By spreading the Good News throughout the world, all can come under the shelter of God. God is our refuge and our strength. He is our strong mountain. In Him we find power and peace none other can provide.

Conservation efforts are proving productive. Sheltered parrots are prospering and multiplying. Bird preservation taught me a valuable lesson. Because I am frail and faulty, I must live in the Lord's sanctuary. There He will preserve me. It's in Him I find life, both now and eternally.

Dear Lord, I long to live in Your sanctuary. Capture me with Your love. Take all of me. Preserve me for Your service and glory to bring Your Good News to future generations. In Jesus' name. Amen.

Application Steps

Consider those circumstances that threaten to weaken or destroy you, your faith, or your ministry. Be aware that storms will come in various ways. Choose now to rest in the perfect protection and provision of God.

61 Facing a Phobia

Rachel Olsen

Jesus said to the people who believed in him,
"You are truly my disciples if you keep obeying my
teachings. And you will know the truth,
and the truth will set you free."

John 8:31-32 NLT

It hardly weighed anything. If my eyes hadn't confirmed that a large brown tarantula was crawling across my hand, I'm not sure I would have known. It had the ability to bite me. It also had the ability to flick small hairs infused with a highly irritating chemical onto my skin. Given my long-standing fear of arachnids, it definitely had the ability to scare me silly.

Spiders usually cause a shudder to start at the base of my neck, roll across my shoulders, and down my back. This muscular reaction is often accompanied by a high-pitched: "Eww, get it away from me!" Yet this day I willingly let a spider prance across my palm as I held it up for a closer look.

When I planned a family vacation in the mountains, I didn't know this feather-light lesson in facing fears was going to be on the agenda. My young son loves animals of all kinds—the Crocodile Hunter and Jeff Corwin are regulars on our TV. So when I found an attraction called RainForest Adventures, we had to go. After seeing and learning about many creatures, the owner decided to let us handle some of the animals. While my husband held the camcorder, the kids and I interacted with a turtle, an exotic bird, and even a rather tame baby crocodile.

My adrenaline surged when he brought out the tarantula and asked if we were willing to touch it. Everything in my body said, "No way!" In my spirit, however, I felt a prompt. "Face your fear."

I reasoned God was mightier than this spider and able to keep me alive. So I thrust out my hand against all self-protective instincts and welcomed the furry creature aboard. It did not harm me.

I later researched tarantulas. I learned their venomous fangs inject a flesh-dissolving chemical into their prey. Then I read this statement, "No person has ever died of a tarantula bite." I had been deceived all these years, thinking a tarantula could kill me!

When we operate with false information, as I did regarding tarantulas, phobias can develop. A phobia is an irrational fear—a worry that is not consistent with truth or reality.

Where does false information come from? Sometimes we accept the opinions of man as truth. Sometimes we accept the lies of Satan as truth. Other times, in ignorance, we just make up our own notion of truth. The problem is, these are rarely consistent with reality, and when our sense of reality is warped, pain, fears, or tears usually follow.

It matters where we get our truth from. Jesus said if we follow His commands laid out for us in the Bible, we will know the truth and it will set us free (John 8:31-32). This ancient text, provided for us by the Reality Maker Himself, is the best place to check and receive our perceptions of reality. It's the best place to trade in our phobias for freedom.

Dear Lord, I pray Your Word will correct my perceptions and cause me to not operate with a spirit of fear, but of love, freedom, power, and truth. In Jesus' name. Amen.

Application Steps

Find a verse from the Bible that speaks to your fears. Memorize it, and begin to pray it regularly over the situation.

62 The Power of the Word

Marybeth Whalen

So is my word that goes out from my mouth:
it will not return to me empty, but will accomplish
what I desire and achieve the purpose for which I sent it.

Isaiah 55:11

At a craft show recently, I struck up a conversation with an artist I particularly admire. Our conversation led to a discussion on marriage and learning how to "fight fair" with our husbands. Knowing nothing about her background or beliefs, I quoted the verse, "Love does not keep a record of wrongs" (1 Corinthians 13:5 TEV) to her, but I did not identify it as a verse from the Bible. To tell you the truth, I just assumed she would know it was from that famous passage in 1 Corinthians. From my perspective, anyone who has ever been to a wedding would recognize that verse.

I soon discovered how wrong I was to just assume that she would know I was quoting Scripture. Her eyes widened and a surprised look crossed her face. "That's beautiful!" she exclaimed. "Where in the world did you hear that?"

"Well," I stammered, "it's from the Bible. First Corinthians 13 is a beautiful passage on love the way God designed it to work. You should read it sometime."

As I walked away, I thought of how—out of our entire conversation—the Word of God cut straight through to her heart and spoke to her soul. It was not my words that brought about renewal, but His. How blessed I was to have been able to share just that small bit of God's truth with her.

I wonder how many times I have missed opportunities to weave Scripture into an ordinary conversation. I didn't need to philosophize, pontificate, or preach to my new friend. How simple it was to speak

God's truth to her in a natural, unrehearsed way. How hungry she was to hear that truth.

I asked God to make me aware of other opportunities to share His Word. I prayed I'd not make it harder than it has to be. I also prayed that a small seed of truth will sprout up in this woman's life, and that this will be the beginning of many other encounters she has with God's powerful, beautiful Word.

Dear Lord, please help me to remember that Your Word is powerful. Help me to speak it to others in my everyday life. Thank You for placing people around me who need to hear Your Word, and help me to be more aware of opportunities to share it. Please use Your Word in the lives of those I speak to and bring about change and renewal. I don't want to take Your Word for granted. In Jesus' name. Amen.

Application Steps

Make an effort to commit verses to memory, which will enable you to speak the Word as part of your daily conversations.

63 Thank God for Smelly Shoes

Lysa TerKeurst

Do everything without complaining or arguing.
Philippians 2:14

In my motherhood journey, how many shoes will I pick up and put back, only to pick them up and put them back again...and again...and again?

Recently, I counted more than 14 pairs of shoes that were just within eyesight of where I was sitting. I was quite frustrated that these shoes weren't where they were supposed to be. Visions of chore charts and consequences for leaving things out started dancing about in my mind. I even went so far as to think that this was yet more evidence that my kids are not as thankful as they should be. Kids who were truly thankful for their shoes would care enough to tuck them into their closet shoe racks.

But as I mentally chided my children for their ungratefulness, I felt God gently give me a piece of my own reprimand. Was I modeling thankfulness in this moment? Scattered shoes are a normal, everyday thing with a hidden treasure about them. It's all in how I choose to look at these shoes that will determine whether I feel drained and frustrated or filled up and thankful.

I stopped and thanked God for this evidence of life. Some had grass and dirt on them as proof that our kids were healthy and strong enough to run and play. Some had scuff marks from one too many dances on the concrete outside. Some had teeth marks from our beloved dog, Champ, whose favorite pastime is chasing kids, balls, and stray shoes. One had paint on it from a school project. But all were well worn, broken in, and definitely used.

So here I am, walking life's journey in this season with soccer cleats, princess shoes, basketball high-tops, teenager-want-to-be boots, kitten bedroom slippers, and gymnastics flip-flops. Funny how these shoes tell stories of life, if only I make the choice to listen. Games won and lost, girlhood fantasies, dreams of the future, comforts of home, and expressions of style.

Maybe you've felt a little frustrated with the shoes scattered about your home as well. But the next time you pick them up, instead of letting frustration whisk you away, listen carefully to the story they tell. Listen carefully and thank God for each and every precious soul who wears those shoes.

Dear Lord, thank You for the precious people you have entrusted to me who call me Mom. It is a high honor. Please help me keep this perspective through all the ups and downs of raising children. May all of my actions and reactions reflect a gentle patience that I know is only possible in Your strength. Whether it's toys left in the den, homework papers scattered on the table, or smelly shoes by the door, help me have an attitude of thankfulness first and foremost when I see all this evidence of life. Then if You could have the Holy Spirit remind my kids to put their things where they belong every now and then, that would be great too! In Jesus' name. Amen.

Application Steps

Walk through your house today looking for evidence of life. Spend some time thanking God for each member of your family as you come across things that belong to that person. Ask God how you can come up with a system to keep the things that might become an aggravation to you more orderly. Again thank God as you put the things away.

64 Living in the Hear and Now

Renee Swope

I tell you the truth, the Son can do nothing by himself;
he can do only what he sees his Father doing,
because whatever the Father does the Son also does.
JOHN 5:19

I sat on the couch looking out the window, thinking about the months ahead and wondering what that year might hold. A lot had been happening in ministry—book developments, speaking engagements, and great opportunities. My excitement, mixed with the fear of getting overcommitted, ignited rapid-fire thoughts: *Would I be able to do it all? Was God calling me to do it all? Was my ministry about to really take off?*

Instead of worrying, I decided to start praying and wrote my questions in a notebook. "Lord, what should I say yes to? Where do You want me to spend my time? Please show me what You have planned for me this coming year."

I wanted God to give me a sneak peek into His calendar so I could adjust mine. Instead, I sensed Him telling me not to worry about tomorrow but to live in the *hear and now*. I think He may have even spelled it so I would be clear on the point of *hearing*.

I thought I'd been listening, but my prayers reflected that I wanted to know where to invest my efforts. God wanted my ears. He was more concerned about my character than my calendar. Many times I'd sought God for the larger plans in life, convinced that if I figured out what He wanted me to do I could become the person He created me to be. Have you ever thought, *If only God would show me what job to take, what man to marry, what church to attend—then my life would be complete and I could serve Him with my whole heart?*

The problem is, sometimes we get a glimpse of where He wants us to go and then assume we know how to get there. I've made that mistake many times and then wondered why I wasn't getting anywhere.

Jesus depended on His Father for the large and fine print written in His life plan. He listened closely and obeyed quickly. Today's verse reflects His absolute dependence:

> The Son can do nothing by himself; he can do only what he sees his Father doing, because whatever the Father does the Son also does (John 5:19).

Like Jesus, we can't fulfill God's purpose for our lives unless our ears are always listening. We can only discover God's calendar and calling when we live in the *hear* and now—listening for His voice and obeying here and now.

> *Dear Lord, sometimes I have selective hearing. Many days I don't even ask what You think about my plans and choices. When I do, it's often because I am desperate and need to make a big decision. Then I get frustrated because I don't know what You are telling me. Could it be I have a hard time hearing You because I have grown unfamiliar with Your voice? Today, I lean in to listen. In Jesus' name. Amen.*

Application Steps

Quiet your heart and your thoughts. Be still and acknowledge that God is God and you're not. Ask Him to speak to You through His Word and His Spirit today.

65 Pardon Me?

Wendy Pope

Peter came to Jesus and asked, "Lord, how many times shall I forgive my brother when he sins against me? Up to seven times?"

Matthew 18:21

I'd never believed that forgiving others was an issue I had difficulty with. I get upset and angry the way most people do when I am wronged, but then I tend to ignore the problem or the person until I feel better, never really dealing with the offense at hand. God brought me face-to-face with my naïveté. His desire was to work in and through me to surrender parts of myself that were displeasing to Him: self-righteousness and an unforgiving spirit. Oh, the lessons I have learned. Oh, the lessons I am still learning.

A circumstance arose between my family and the neighbors on our cul-de-sac. It's a situation I would like to have forgotten, but the problem and the persons were not likely to go away. The problem and the persons were there, staring me in the face each time I turned down my street. God was teaching me about forgiving others and requiring me to deal with my self-righteousness by having me live right in the middle of offenders.

I have learned that forgiving others is a choice. There are days when the accusations hurled against me make me burn with anger, and the last thing I want to do is bless those who persecute me. The power of the Holy Spirit living in me enables me to live beyond the anger and bitterness to extend forgiveness. When anger and bad attitudes raise their ugly heads, I make the choice to say out loud, "Now, Lord, I have forgiven them already. Help me to live in the forgiveness I have extended." The choice to live in bitterness is mine. The power to make the choice to not live in bitterness comes from God. I am unable to do this apart from Him. The voice of the liar cleverly tries to lure me with memories of the hurt and betrayal I felt. Then I remember his objective for my life is not peace but pandemonium.

Today's verse is taken from the parable of the unmerciful servant. Peter wanted to know how many times forgiveness should be offered. Jesus, in true teacher fashion, gave His answer in story form. He goes on to tell of a master who forgives a debt that a servant owed him. This same servant refuses to forgive a debt owed him. Upon learning this, the master rebukes the servant and turns him over to the jailers to be tortured. Jesus concludes the story by telling Peter, "This is how my heavenly Father will treat each of you unless you forgive your brother from your heart" (Matthew 18:35).

Frightening, isn't it? Are you being tortured by the power of an unforgiving spirit?

Dear Lord, search my heart today. Bring to my attention anyone I need to forgive. Give me the courage and power to pardon them. I can't wait to live in the freedom forgiveness offers. In Jesus' name. Amen.

Application Steps

Continue today's prayer until God brings someone to your heart. Write the person's name on a piece of paper with the offense. Call the person, forgive them, and throw the paper away.

66 Mother of the Year

Micca Campbell

Her children arise and call her blessed;
her husband also, and he praises her.

PROVERBS 31:28

I long to be a godly wife and mother, but my efforts to become this ideal woman can leave me grieved and depressed.

I felt especially defeated the year my youngest son started kindergarten. In Tennessee, kindergartners follow a scattered schedule the first two weeks of school where half of the class attends one day and the rest comes the following day. It helps them adjust. For me it brought confusion.

On Tuesday, I took my son to school, kissed him good-bye, and headed home to work. I was busy at the computer when the telephone interrupted my pace. "Hello?"

"Mrs. Campbell, this is Parker's teacher. I was wondering who would be picking him up from school today."

Stunned that I had forgotten my child, I jumped in the car and raced to the school. He stood on the sidewalk holding his teacher's hand with tears in his eyes and REJECTION stamped across his heart. I took him home, apologized profusely, and made his favorite meal for dinner. I felt like the worst mother ever.

Thursday, we returned to school. All was going well until I was, once again, interrupted by the phone. I had forgotten to pick up my child not once, but twice in the same week!

I sped to school on two wheels. This time he was standing with the room mother, who was obviously a true Proverbs 31 Woman. As she helped him buckle his seat belt, I tried explaining myself.

"You're not going to believe this, but I did the same thing earlier this week."

"Yeah, I know," she replied bluntly.

I had been labeled a "bad mother" and felt like a complete failure. Then, God showered me with encouragement when, later that same year, *ParentLife* magazine named me one of eight Mothers of the Year! Parker's reaction to this surprising news was, "If they lived with us for a while, they'd probably reconsider."

Those were my thoughts exactly. In fact, I asked my husband how I could be given such a great and undeserving honor. With wisdom he shared that maybe it was God's way of saying I'm doing better than I think.

His words helped me put things into perspective. God never said I had to be perfect. That was my expectation. He never said that I wouldn't make mistakes or a wrong decision every now and then. Again, that was my hope. I had assumed that the Proverbs 31 lady did everything right and I was supposed to as well. The problem was, with all her great accomplishments, I never considered her not-so-good side.

Sometimes I let the bad outweigh the good. Perhaps the Mother of the Year award was God's way of saying, "Hang in there. You're doing better than you think, and I'm not the only one who notices."

Despite my many mistakes, perhaps my children will some day rise and call me blessed.

The next time you need encouragement, let God whisper to your heart: "I hear when you pray for your children, and I'm there when you teach them about who I am. I watch you love, care, and sacrifice for them. You're not perfect, but hang in there. You're doing better than you think."

Dear Lord, when I fail, help me to be the mother my children need. In Jesus' name. Amen.

Application Steps

Start a support group for moms in your neighborhood, school, or church.

67 Encouragement in a Bottle

Susanne Scheppmann

Have I not commanded you? Be strong and courageous.
Do not be terrified; do not be discouraged, for the
LORD your God will be with you wherever you go.

JOSHUA 1:9

Do you ever fear where your next path in life might lead? I do. Not long ago I struggled to determine which path God wanted me to take in serving Him. One lazy, late Sunday afternoon, I took some time to sit outside and bask in an orange-pink sunset. Discouragement crept in. I moped about decisions and dilemmas I was facing. Then I began to flip through the pages of my Bible and read the first chapter of Joshua.

As I read, I realized how frightened Joshua must have been when he looked across the dry desert plain and considered the thousands of Israelites he needed to lead to the Promised Land. Joshua's position required him to make the essential decision to lead the Israelites into enemy territory. Suddenly, my own dilemmas didn't seem so big.

God used the same words of encouragement for me as He did with Joshua. God told Joshua three times, "Be strong and courageous." Another time God said, "Be strong and very courageous...Do not be terrified; do not be discouraged, for the LORD your God will be with you wherever you go" (Joshua 1:6-9).

As I stood up and stretched, I felt comforted. I knew that whatever direction my life path took, I could be courageous because the Lord my God would be with me wherever I went.

One week later I went across country to attend the annual She Speaks conference for aspiring writers and speakers at Proverbs 31 Ministries. I had the privilege of attending a preconference session, and as we arrived, we spied a basket of swirled glass bottles with a sheet of parchment inside. We were each instructed to choose one bottle to take back home with us. The conference coordinator said, "Each bottle has a different Bible verse in it. It is our prayer that each of you will be blessed by a meaningful verse that will speak to your individual hearts."

As often happens in a conference atmosphere, more life-questions surfaced in my mind. My head churned with the thoughts, so many ministry needs, so little time, so many directions, and so few resources. Both my head and my feet hurt as I went back to my hotel room with my tortuous high heels in hand. Once inside I gently pulled the paper from the bottle and read the message:

> Be strong and courageous! Do not tremble or be dismayed, for the LORD your God is with you wherever you go (Joshua 1:9 NASB).

Encouragement swept through my soul. I smiled to myself and to the Father. He is aware and in control of everything!

> *Dear Lord, remind me that You are in control. I do not need to be anxious about my path in life. My fretting is futile because You are in complete control. You know the desires and needs of every area of my life. I praise You for going with me wherever I go. In Jesus' name. Amen.*

Application Steps

Read Joshua 1. Underline in red pencil every time you see the words "Be strong and courageous." List things you need to be strong and courageous about in your life. Then ask the Lord to remind you, "The Lord your God will be with you wherever you go."

68 Better Late than Never

Glynnis Whitwer

What do you think? There was a man who had two sons.
He went to the first and said, "Son, go and work
today in the vineyard." "I will not," he answered,
but later he changed his mind and went.

MATTHEW 21:28-29

My husband and I didn't pick the smartest time to get married. We were juniors in college and got married two weeks before classes started. Although we prepared all summer for the wedding, we had little time for a honeymoon before school and jobs started again.

Between moving into our apartment, working part-time, and taking full-time classes, writing thank-you notes for our wedding gifts fell to the bottom of my to-do list. Months passed, and it was Christmas break before I seriously thought about them again. By that time, I was too embarrassed to send out notes.

That breach of etiquette has always bothered me. In hindsight, I should have sent out the notes at Christmas. Truly, "better late than never" should have been my guiding principle.

Jesus spoke about a similar principle in the parable of two sons (Matthew 21:28-32). Both were asked to work in the vineyard by their father. One said no, but later he changed his mind and went. The other said yes, but he didn't go. Jesus asked the poignant question, "Which of the two did what his father wanted?" The answer was the first.

Jesus used this parable to show the religious leaders that tax collectors and prostitutes were entering the kingdom of God ahead of them. The religious leaders professed to obey God, but they didn't in their hearts. I think this is a principle we can apply to our everyday life.

Many times we know God is calling us to do something. It could be to share our faith with a coworker or family member. Perhaps God has been tugging on our heart to increase our financial giving. Maybe we need to take a leap of faith and change our career, go back to school, or do mission work. We say yes when God first prompts us, but then we do nothing. Time goes by and we think, *It's too late now.*

Unfortunately, that type of thinking leads to disobedience. This parable shows us that it's never too late to obey God. It doesn't matter how old you are or what you've done since God first asked you to do something. It doesn't even matter if you've stomped your foot, crossed your arms, and told God no. Today you can make your heavenly Father happy by doing His will.

We serve a gracious God who doesn't hold our disobedience against us. We may need to confess it as sin, but when we do, it's as good as gone. If God has asked you to work in the vineyard and you've said no, or delayed obedience, make today the day you get to work. *Hmm, I wonder if I still have that wedding gift list...*

> *Dear Lord, I praise You for Your compassion and kindness. You are worthy of my praise and all I have to offer. I confess the times I have disobeyed You by saying yes and then not following through. I pray for strength through Your Holy Spirit to walk in obedience. In Jesus' name. Amen.*

Application Steps

Identify one thing the Lord has asked you to do that you haven't done yet. Commit to following through. Write down specific action steps to accomplish the task.

69 Money Lessons

Sharon Glasgow

Honor the Lord *with your wealth, with the firstfruits
of all your crops; then your barns will be filled to
overflowing, and your vats will brim over with new wine.*
Proverbs 3:9-10

Did you know that, according to the *2004 Field Guide to Estate Planning*, it costs an average of $250,000 to raise a child from birth to the age of 18 in a household with an income of at least $65,000? Gulp—I have five children! That makes my costs more than a million dollars, and these figures don't include college tuition or weddings. That's mind-boggling!

I think one of life's greatest tests of our obedience to Christ is how we spend our money. God is not the only one watching how we spend it. Our children are witnessing our spending habits too. It's imperative we teach our children good money skills by example.

Spending money wisely is challenging, but the benefits are priceless. Make your children aware of the value of saving and budgeting everywhere you go. When they are young, don't yield to the constant begging for candy and toys. As they grow, use every spending venture as a teaching tool.

At the restaurant, show them how much you save if everyone drinks water instead of soft drinks. At retail stores wait until clothes are on sale and then show how waiting saved a large percentage. Bring a calculator and show how percentages work. When grocery shopping, show your children the budget and let them calculate products as you put them in the basket. If they see that you consistently watch your money, they will begin to understand how to spend money wisely.

In our family our kids know everything about our finances. We talk about paying taxes, retirement, savings, our monthly bills, our monthly income, tithing, and every other money issue. This helps them understand how carefully money has to be managed. We set budgets for special events such as vacations, and oftentimes they go on the Internet looking for better deals.

I have a list on the refrigerator of chores for which the children will be paid. These chores are separate from what is normally expected. The expected jobs without pay are: clean your room, make your bed, take your clothes to the washroom, and pick up your messes. Paid jobs are more time intensive and the payment amounts are based on the extensiveness of the job. The kids have to work hard to make money, and a lot is expected without pay because that's how families function.

If we truly spend nearly $250,000 on each child, a lot of money will be exchanged in front of them in 18 years. That's a lot of teaching opportunities! Let them watch, for instance, as you research the most cost-efficient health, car, and life insurances. Also, teach them why credit card use can be dangerous.

God blesses us when we honor Him in the way we spend our money. Our children are blessed when we spend our money wisely, and the cycle continues on to the next generation. Blessings follow obedience!

> *Dear Lord, thank You for everything You have given and are giving me. Give me the wisdom to not only survive, but also to thrive in the financial trials that face me every day. In Jesus' name. Amen.*

Application Steps

Seek godly counsel on financial matters. Make a family budget you can live with. Avoid borrowing against credit cards. Don't forget to give a portion of your earnings to the Lord and people in need as the Bible instructs.

70 Finding Sure Footing in a Slippery World

Rachel Olsen

He lifted me out of the pit of despair, out of the mud and the mire. He set my feet on solid ground and steadied me as I walked along.

PSALM 40:2 NLT

CRACK! I heard bone break, followed by sharp pain racing through my foot. I had rearranged the living room, forgotten where I'd put things, and walked smack into our sofa. My right foot swelled and bruised within seconds of making contact. A cast was not necessary, but I was now sentenced to wearing flip-flops until my toes healed.

The next week some friends planned a gathering to celebrate my birthday, so I climbed into my husband's car and headed out for lunch with the girls. The entrance to our subdivision sits on a small hill. At the stop sign, with my car leaning forward downhill, I waited for a break in traffic. Suddenly my flip-flop-clad foot slipped off the brake, rolling me into the line of traffic. Looking out the window, I saw cars headed for me in both directions. With the sandal hanging half off my foot and my broken toe now throbbing, I stomped in a panic, searching for a pedal that would deliver me from death.

My husband's car is manual transmission, so my impulse to hit the gas only sent me into a near stall. I thought, *Oh, God, help me!* Then I managed to find the gas *and* the clutch and started moving forward again. Watching out the window as the car slowly picked up speed, I held my breath waiting to see if I was going to make it to the other side before the oncoming traffic made it to me. Thankfully, I did. I praised God for His protection, took off my flip-flops, and drove barefoot to the restaurant.

Before I placed my life in the hands of Jesus Christ, I experienced a series of crashes and near misses. I thought I was capable of driving my life, but my foot kept slipping off the brake when I should have been staying put. I kept stalling out when trying to do good. To tell you the truth, I wasn't even sure where I was going. I just wanted to go someplace fun. I didn't know just how near I was to death. Then, Jesus lifted me out of the mud and mire I kept involving myself in and gave me sure footing on solid ground (Psalm 40:2).

Today, I am no longer in the driver's seat of my life. I've handed over the keys to Christ, and together we're cruising a narrow path with light traffic and great scenery (Matthew 7:13). The ride can get bumpy at times, but I know I can fully trust my Navigator. After all, He has driven this road before. And I'm thrilled to know my final destination will be nothing short of paradise.

Are you in need of a similar rescue from the slippery slopes of this world?

Dear Lord, there are many troubles, trials, and temptations in this life. Please set me on the solid rock of Christ. Take the keys to my heart and determine my direction with Your perfect wisdom and will. In Jesus' name. Amen.

Application Steps

Take a few minutes to search Scriptures for guidance regarding a problem you are facing today. Release that problem, and your day, into Christ's capable hands.

71 I'm Not...I Am

Melissa Taylor

God replied, "I AM THE ONE WHO ALWAYS IS."
Just tell them, "I AM has sent me to you."
EXODUS 3:14 NLT

It was one of those days. I wasn't feeling like my usual happy, chipper self. I was feeling just plain sulky.

I've found that when I'm down, a door opens to my mind and I begin thinking down too. It's the perfect opportunity for Satan to take a step through that doorway and do some damage. For me, he begins with the "I'm nots." Here are some of my "I'm nots" with which I battle...

I'm not as good of a mother as Lisa. I'm not very dependable. I'm not on time. I'm not as good of a cook as my family deserves. I'm not a good friend. I'm not as good at speaking or writing as Kim. I'm not a good homemaker. I'm not doing enough at church. I'm not as thin as I should be. I'm not organized. I'm not disciplined.

Sometimes I even bring others into my depressing thoughts.

My kids are not turning out the way I imagined. My husband is not in tune with my feelings. My friends are not interested in me. My church is not meeting my needs.

Thankfully, I am not defined by what I'm not. The "I'm nots" of life aren't true. They are lies that the enemy wants me to believe.

Satan may gain some temporary ground in my thoughts, but I've learned how to fight him off. For every "I'm not" Satan plants in my head, God says, "I Am." What I'm not, He is.

I Am the unconditional love you are able to give your kids. I Am your Redeemer. I forgive you; forgive yourself. I Am your provider. I Am there for your friends. You aren't supposed to fix everyone. I Am living in you; therefore, you have great things to say and write. I Am your audience, not

the world. I Am your husband, kids, and friends. The hole they can't fill
in your heart, I can. I Am your Creator. Love the body you were given
and take care of it.

"Away from me, Satan!" Those are the words Jesus spoke when He
had an encounter with the devil. "Away from me, Satan!" These are
the words I speak today.

James 4:7 says to "resist the devil, and he will flee from you." How
can we resist the devil when his words are knocking so loudly on the
door to our heart? Keep reading. James 4:8 has the answer. It says,
"Come near to God and he will come near to you."

Satan's attacks may be strong, but God is stronger. His Word offers
assurance that He is always there and is always accessible. You can
believe that.

> *Dear Lord, help me to find my identity and truth in You. In*
> *Jesus' name. Amen.*

Application Steps

The next time you find yourself thinking of all you are not, remember
all that God is. He is the great I Am. He loves you dearly. Defeat
thoughts of "I'm not" with the truth of "I am" in Him.

72 He's Still God

Micca Campbell

We are hard pressed on every side, but not crushed;
perplexed, but not in despair.

2 Corinthians 4:8

I was away when the tornado struck the mid-South where my family and I live. My children were in lockdown at their school for hours.

My husband felt helpless as our daughter begged from her cell phone, "Come get me, Daddy. Please, hurry!" He was desperately trying to retrieve both of our children, but debris from the raging winds blocked his every path. Two hours later, he finally reached the school and found it, along with our children, untouched by the tornado. Our house had been passed over as well. Others were not as fortunate.

As I drew nearer our home, I looked on in disbelief as I weaved my way through the devastation. It felt as if my town had been ransacked by intruders. I felt cold and naked as I viewed the homes of friends and businesses that had been stripped bare.

Then, I saw the church. It once was a magnificent church standing tall and proud in our community. It was a symbol of all that was good and right. Now it was wounded and exposed; stripped of its beauty and glory. "Not the church, Lord," I prayed. As destruction surrounded me, I looked to the heavens and questioned, "How will we survive this awful tragedy?"

Jesus promised that we would encounter trials and tribulation in this fallen world, but we need not despair. Why? Because our hope is in God. Hope helps us see the God of restoration instead of becoming paralyzed by the mess of destruction.

Volunteers, workmen, friends, and neighbors all worked together to rebuild our city. It was a precious sight. It was the evidence of hope and the reflection of love.

Right now you may be surrounded by trouble too, but you are not alone. You cannot be hedged in because you are not without help. You have great support. God is your helper. You don't have to be perplexed, uncertain, or concerned about your future. God has promised to deliver you. Even if you are being persecuted by enemies or rejected by loved ones, God says, "I will never leave you." You can trust Him despite the disaster.

Months later this truth became apparent as I drove by the church. The yard had been cleaned up and the walls patched. It looked as if she had been lovingly dressed up. Still recovering from near destruction, her message had not changed. Draped in a large sign that covered the front of her structure, she declared to all, "HE'S STILL GOD!"

In this life we will be pressed—yes, even crushed sometimes—and perhaps perplexed, but we need not despair. No matter what storm we face, no matter what kind of trouble presses in, no matter who is out to get us, the truth remains the same: "He's still God!"

Dear Lord, may I not despair when trouble comes my way, but trust in the fact that You are still God. In Jesus' name. Amen.

Application Steps

Make a list of all your doubts and fears. Then, confess them to God and ask Him to replace them with trust in what only He can do.

73 Don't Look Down
Marybeth Whalen

Make it your ambition to lead a quiet life,
to mind your own business and to work with your hands,
just as we told you, so that your daily life may win the respect of
outsiders and so that you will not be dependent on anybody.

1 Thessalonians 4:11-12

When I was a little girl, I took dancing lessons. I was never an especially terrific dancer, but I enjoyed learning the routines and gearing up for the big recital at the end of the year. Yet it always seemed that no matter how much I practiced and concentrated, I could never remember all the steps to the dances.

I learned that it helped if I focused on the dance teacher, who was usually standing where we could see her, dancing right along with us. I also learned that the worst thing I could do was pay too much attention to my own feet shuffling through the steps. Inevitably, by looking down at my feet, I would lose my concentration and fall sadly out of step.

I have learned the following lessons about staying in step with God:

Stay focused on your own routine and don't try to follow the dance others are doing. Sure, they might be performing a ballet that takes your breath away, but don't let that distract you from performing the tap dance of a lifetime.

Don't let the critics stop you from dancing with all your heart. Invariably, others will make negative comments that have the potential to convince you to trade in your tap shoes. Keep dancing to your own beat and embrace the uniqueness of your dance.

Don't let the sin of vanity or pride keep you from thinking you don't need to practice your routine. Daily time with the Teacher will further your skill. Don't grow complacent about the honor of dancing for the King—give God your best performance every day.

If you are tempted to look down at your feet and take your focus off Him, pray that He would convict you and redirect your steps. Ask God to be the "lifter of your head" so that you can refocus on Him.

Dance for an audience of One, and don't use your dance in an attempt to bring glory to yourself. If you find yourself seeking significance, identity, purpose, or validation from the rest of the world, go back to spending time with the Teacher. Dance solely for the joy that He will certainly bring you.

> *Dear Lord, You are the Lord of the dance. Thank You for crafting a routine that only I can perform. Help me to focus on You as I try to stay in step. I trust You will make my dance a thing of beauty. In Jesus' name. Amen.*

Application Steps

Don't spend time looking down at your feet. Look up! Spend time in God's Word and in prayer. Ask Him to help you stay in step with the routine He has designed for you.

74 Letting Go
Luann Prater

"Come to Me..."
Matthew 11:28 nasb

Toddlers invaded our house last week. We love it when the grand-kids come to visit! They teach us so many things about God and faith.

One afternoon I called my grandson up from the basement play-room for a snack. His little hands were loaded with toys: a truck and action figure in one hand, a ball in the other and a book tucked under his arm. His tiny fingers reached for the railing, but his arms were gripping his toys so tightly that he couldn't grab it. He was ready to join Grandma in the kitchen, but he couldn't bear to leave his toys behind.

I watched him struggle as he took that first step. He wobbled to and fro, so I reached out my hand to help. "I do it!" he proclaimed. I kept my hand outstretched, offering but not forcing help. Finally one foot triumphantly reached the next step, he glanced up as if to say, *"See, I can do it."* As his weight shifted to pull the other leg up, the book at his side began to slip. He paused to readjust, and the ball popped from his hand and bounced back down.

His lip quivered, but he was not giving up the battle. Looking at me now would just be too humiliating, so he pretended not to see me or my hand. With each step came the same scenario: wobbling, slip-ping, readjusting, frustration. Those eyelashes that bat my face with kisses eventually lost the battle with his tears, and moments later his small cheeks were wet. Only then did the fingers that once gripped his treasures purposely loosen and reach for my hand.

Aren't we so like that with our Father? He stands with outstretched arms saying, "Come to Me," but we won't make eye contact because we want to do it our way. Often it just seems too humiliating to admit we're refusing to let go. It may not be a doll or a ball, but we compulsively hold on to other things: jobs, relationships, grudges, money, security, possessions, and pleasures.

We would rather muddle through life than give up control or admit defeat. We would rather slip and stumble than let go of our pride. We would rather readjust our grip than reach out for help.

When my grandson was safe and secure at the top of the stairs, I picked up all of his treasures and brought them to him. Then we shared some quality time and a yummy treat. Hmm...I wonder what Christ would give us back if we surrendered it all today?

Isn't it time we totally trusted the outstretched, nail-scarred hands that beckon us "Come to Me"?

> *Dear Lord, today I drop my treasures at Your feet and ask You to forgive me for hanging on so tightly to the things of this world. Break the strongholds in my life that keep me from drawing close to You. Teach me to trust You as I reach out and grab Your hand. In Jesus' name. Amen.*

Application Steps

Examine your life. List the things that occupy too much of your time and attention. Now pray over them and ask God to give you the ability to let go of each treasure that made it onto your list. In permanent red marker write Jesus across the entire list. Today make Him the most important priority of your day.

75 I Don't Love My Husband Anymore

Lysa TerKeurst

Marriage should be honored by all,
and the marriage bed kept pure.

HEBREWS 13:4

I was saddened by what my friend was sharing. She was tired of her husband, and because she had found the man she dreamed of being with, she was leaving her spouse. I was shocked by her decision.

I had been in their wedding and heard the lifetime promises made from their hearts. I had been with them to celebrate their first anniversary. I had been with them just after the births of their first and second child. I had shared their laughter, encouraged them through their tears, and enjoyed doing life with them.

While their relationship had not been perfect, they did love one another. But something was broken in their relationship, and neither of them knew how to fix it. This brokenness led to a stale quietness that seeped into their home and made each feel lonelier and more isolated than they ever knew was possible for a couple. He had grown distant. She had grown frustrated. Life was busy and finances were stressful, and they stopped making time for the romantic conversations they used to enjoy. They used to be a team and felt they could beat anything life sent their way. Now they just fought against each other. Then she met an attentive, financially secure man who seemed to be the answer to all of her unmet longings.

She traded her life for the thrill of something new, the lure of something she perceived would be so much better.

But just two years later I ran into this friend and was stunned by her confession. With tears in her eyes she admitted that she'd discovered that fairy tales don't exist. Every relationship feels exhilarating at the beginning, but then real life happens and marriage is hard work no matter whom you are married to. When I asked her to tell me about her new husband, she smiled shyly and said, "Well, he's hairy."

What?

What did she just say? My mind was spinning. Of all the words, all the descriptions, all the romantic terms I expected her to use, "hairy" was nowhere on the list. How telling that the man who was once so irresistible that she traded everything for, had now been reduced to one word…hairy!

I'm convinced that in marriage the grass isn't greener on the other side. The grass is greener where you water and fertilize it.

Dear Lord, please help my husband and me to see our marriage for the sacred gift that it is. May I always understand that being married was not meant to make me happy but rather holy. Being married is less about having the right partner and more about being the right partner. Shape me into the wife my husband not only needs but deserves. Help me to pause before I speak or react out of anger, frustration, or selfishness. Show me how to respect, love, and give to this man in a way that honors You and brings joy to our home. In Jesus' name. Amen.

Application Steps

Write a list of all the things you love and admire about your husband. Find some time today to share the list with him. Spend some time in prayer for your marriage and for your husband.

76 Don't Waste It

Micca Campbell

This world is fading away, along with everything it craves.
But if you do the will of God, you will live forever.

1 JOHN 2:17 NLT

The other day when I was driving with my youngest son in the car, he reached over and took hold of my hand. I looked at him lovingly and thought to myself, *What a sweet child.* Then he spoke. "Oh my gosh, Mom! Look at the wrinkles in your hand. Don't you think my hand looks much younger than yours?" *Well, duh.*

The years have a way of sneaking up on us, just as a lion sneaks up on his prey. A naive little antelope is minding her own business while cooling her hot, tired hoofs in the water when POUNCE comes the lion. Suddenly, it's all over. What was the meaning of her life? What did she leave behind that made the world a better place for her furry friends? If she knew her life would end so quickly, would she have lived any differently?

In a similar way, the years pounce on us, sapping our youth, energy, and passion. Sobered by this truth, I ask myself, *What have I done with my life? How will my family and friends remember me? Has my life been a reflection of God's glory, or have I wasted it?*

No matter how old or tired we are, it's never too late to start living life with meaning.

Remember Esther, the Jewish girl with a book of the Bible named after her? She was adopted by her cousin Mordecai after the death of her parents. He instructed her to keep her nationality and family background a secret when she found favor in the eyes of King Xerxes. The king loved Esther and made her his queen. It's unlikely for a Persian king to make a Jewish girl his queen—unless God planned it.

Just when all seemed to be going well, Mordecai overheard a plot to kill the Jews. That's when he realized that Esther was queen for a special reason. In this position she could influence the king and save her people. However, this was risky business. Because Esther was a Jew, her life was also in danger. Despite the risk, she chose to live her life beyond herself. As a result, she saved herself and the Jews.

Why has God placed you where you are? Are you in an ungodly place of work? Perhaps you're in a bad relationship. Maybe you're living beside unbelieving neighbors. God has placed you there to make a difference.

Like Esther, you have a decision to make. Risks may be involved, but think of the difference you could make in someone's life—or even a whole community!

When my life is over, I want others to remember how I loved and served the King no matter how tired, busy, or old I got. A life is a terrible thing to waste. Live yours to the fullest. Whether your hand is beginning to wrinkle or not, use it to make a difference today.

Dear Lord, help me to see and fulfill Your plans and purpose for my life. In Jesus' name. Amen.

Application Steps

Read the book of Esther. Then ask yourself how you can make a difference where you're at. Journal your thoughts, act in obedience, and celebrate the results!

77 Empty Nesting
Susanne Scheppmann

If they obey and serve him, they will spend the rest of their days in prosperity and their years in contentment.

Job 36:11

My chicks have flown the coop, and I'm enjoying life now as an empty nester. However, that wasn't always the case. I mourned for my first son when he left home. His empty seat haunted me from across the dinner table. I dreaded it when my daughter graduated and moved to California. I bawled when my younger son joined his older brother in Minnesota, 1700 miles away from me.

But now? Although I love my children dearly, I am glad they are competent and independent adults. I will always be their mother, but now I can be their friend too. I realize that when certain seasons of life pass, such as raising children, God provides pathways to new adventures. Because He promises to prosper us and give us a hope-filled future (Jeremiah 29:11), life is not over when our children leave home. It's just a new beginning.

An exciting and unknown journey begins each time we enter a new phase in our life. We should look back upon milestone events and consider what we learned through the years. Then we should ready ourselves for the next step in a new direction. What's in your past that you can use to fulfill your future? What dusty dreams do you still hope to achieve?

For example, I recently spoke at a Mothers of Preschoolers event. I met a woman who was on a brand-new adventure. Her children were grown up and long gone from her home. Yet she held a darling foster daughter in her arms. My new friend told me she had always wanted to nurture abused and neglected children. However, she did not have enough room in her home until her own children went to college. This motivated woman had now transitioned her home into foster care and loved every minute of it. Then, with a smile and chuckle, she introduced me to her married daughter. She sat beside her mother bouncing her own cooing baby on her lap. Yes—grandmother, foster daughter, grown daughter, and granddaughter all attended the same MOPS group.

Have your kids flown the nest? If yes, it's your time to fulfill the next plan God has in store for you. Let your imagination and dreams soar. Write your book. Finish your nursing degree. Volunteer at church. It's your turn to fly!

Dear Lord, thank You for this new opportunity to soar as I fulfill Your eternal purposes for my life. Help me to discover my new purpose. Give me the courage to step out into the new adventure that awaits me beyond my empty nest. In Jesus' name. Amen.

Application Steps

Spend some time reviewing your life. Jot down a few dreams you would like to accomplish. Then determine to step out in faith to achieve what God's purpose is for you in the future.

78 Fear and Love
Rachel Olsen

God has not given us a spirit of fear,
but of power and of love and of a sound mind.
2 TIMOTHY 1:7 NKJV

Shortly after being tucked into bed, Alaina came downstairs announcing "scary noises" were in her room. My husband identified the humidifier as the culprit and tucked her back in. Once we headed to bed, we stopped by Alaina's room to deliver the last kiss of the day. Her bed was empty.

We searched her room and closet. We headed across the hall to her brother's room. He was sleeping peacefully, but she was not there. We looked in corners, closets, even bathtubs and shower stalls. My heart quickened as each place proved empty. We searched downstairs in every conceivable spot, loudly calling her name. We reluctantly deducted that she was not in the house.

I ran out into the cold, barefoot and coatless, calling her name as I fought back tears. I saw a black SUV with the engine running parked nearby. Fearing someone might drive off with my daughter, I charged towards the vehicle. I flung open the driver's side door and reached inside for the car keys. The car was packed with five startled teenagers—Alaina was not with them. I apologized, explained, and headed home to dial 9-1-1.

Inside, I walked to my office while praying earnestly. Suddenly I caught sight of little toes underneath my desk. I pulled out the chair and knelt down to discover Alaina sitting with her knees pulled to her chest, wedged behind the file cabinet that juts out slightly from under my desk. She was hiding in a 32" x 42" space, sound asleep. The next morning she offered this explanation: "I was scared and I thought if I told you, you'd be upset and take me back to bed, so I snuck downstairs and hid."

The missing child incident provided me a few more grey hairs and a compelling visual of a spiritual principal: Fear is a powerful force that will back us into the tightest of corners and isolate us from the help we need if we let it. Alaina did not feel secure in her room that night or sure that her parents would understand her fears. She did not trust us to never leave her alone in a place that was unsafe. If only she understood how much we love her, she would not harbor such doubts.

In Ephesians 3:17-18 (NKJV), Paul desires "that Christ may dwell in your hearts through faith; that you, being rooted and grounded in love, may be able to comprehend with all the saints what is the width and length and depth and height" of Christ's love for you. Our Father's love is something we can never be separated from once we lay hold of it through faith.

In reality, Alaina was safe in her room with parents downstairs who greatly love her and protect her. Reality is you and I are also safe in God's hands. He understands our fears and will protect us. If we'll trust in and focus on the great extent of His love, we'll discover true security and not need to hide from the scary noises of life.

Dear Lord, make Your love real to me today. Fill me with the fullness of love so that I won't fear my circumstances. In Jesus' name. Amen.

Application Steps

Meditate today on the greatness of God's love for you. Make a list of ten ways God has shown His love for you.

79 Choosing Forgiveness

Zoë Elmore

Get rid of all bitterness, rage and anger,
brawling and slander, along with every form of malice.
Be kind and compassionate to one another,
forgiving each other, just as in Christ God forgave you.

EPHESIANS 4:31-32

We've all experienced the unpleasantness of hurtful words or actions wrought against us by others. I know from personal experience how easy it can be to allow a root of bitterness to take hold in our lives.

Think of bitterness as a dangerous and powerful poison. Bitterness will eat though our joy, our confidence, and our testimony. When we allow bitterness to grow as a reaction to someone's wrongdoing, we poison our own hearts and minds as well as the testimony of God's grace in our lives. Bitterness is never a legitimate response for a child of God.

Joseph's brothers were so jealous of their younger brother that bitterness began to poison their hearts, minds, and even their behavior toward him. Their bitterness became so intense it caused them to consider doing harm to Joseph, even to the point of murder.

Although the details of our lives differ from Joseph's brothers, the steps to bitterness and ruin are the same. Their jealousy and anger led them to hateful thoughts toward their brother. They rejected him, and deceitful and dangerous behavior consumed them. They quickly fell into the downward spiral of bitterness and suffered the pain and poison it brings.

Joseph could have allowed bitterness to take hold in his life, thus destroying his opportunity to be used by God to save a nation as well as his own family. In Genesis 50:20-21, Joseph declares his forgiveness toward his brothers: "'You intended to harm me, but God intended it for good to accomplish what is now being done, the saving of many lives. So then, don't be afraid. I will provide for you and your children.' And he reassured them and spoke kindly to them."

Because Joseph chose to forgive, he experienced the presence and pleasure of God instead of the pain and poison of bitterness.

What unresolved anger are you holding on to? Whom do you avoid because of ill will? If you're willing to confess your sin, turn to God, and forgive your wrongdoer, you too can be set free from the pain and poison of bitterness. Remember that a bitter root will always produce bitter fruit. If you desire to live a life that produces rich and royal fruit, dig up any bitterness that may have taken hold in your heart and throw it out.

Dear Lord, please help me choose forgiveness over bitterness. I don't want to experience the pain and poison bitterness brings. Thank You for providing the perfect model of forgiveness, Your beloved Son, Christ. In Jesus' name. Amen.

Application Steps

Pray for help and then extend forgiveness to those who have hurt you.

80 And They Were Amazed

Glynnis Whitwer

*Coming to his hometown, he began teaching the people
in their synagogue, and they were amazed.
"Where did this man get this wisdom and these
miraculous powers?" they asked.*

MATTHEW 13:54

When was the last time something truly amazed you? I've been amazed lately at the price of gas, at the size of my clothes, and at a teenager's driving as he cut me off in traffic. Perhaps it's more appropriate to say I've been shocked and disgusted rather than amazed.

True amazement, the kind that's mixed with surprise and awe, is a rare emotion. It's that emotion first-time parents experience upon the birth of their baby. Few things have that capacity to wow us.

Maybe advances in technology have dulled our capacity for amazement. A television screen the size of a whale, or the size of our palm, barely elicits a "wow." A thousand songs in a matchbox-sized container aren't enough. More! More! We want more!

Celebrities or powerful leaders sometimes impress us, but it's rarely long lasting. It's not long before we read unflattering news of their actions or character.

Nature still has the power to amaze, but lines of tourists and scattered trash can sour the experience. People, places, things…is there anything left to incite our amazement?

Flash back two thousand years. A humble man teaches a gathered crowd and they were amazed. He drives out a demon and a mute man speaks, and everyone was amazed (Matthew 9:33). He heals the crippled, a lame man walks, and a blind man sees (Matthew 15:31). He tells the people to pay their taxes and they are amazed (Matthew

22:21). He calms the storm and completely amazes His friends (Mark 6:51). Basically, Jesus was amazing.

Today, Jesus is still amazing and miracles are still being done in His name. Jesus Himself made it clear that He hoped His disciples would continue what He started. In John 14:12 Jesus said, "I tell you the truth, anyone who has faith in me will do what I have been doing. He will do even greater things than these, because I am going to the Father."

Scripture tells us in light of the amazing things Jesus said and did, people praised God (Luke 5:25-26). Yet, in spite of the potential for people to be drawn to God by the amazing things they hear and see today, we allow religion to become routine and we keep Jesus tucked away in a history book.

As believers, we are called to portray to the world a God who is truly amazing. May our mouths speak God's truth in a gracious and compelling way. May our lives model the excitement of walking daily with God. And may miracles still be performed in the name of Jesus.

Let's amaze the world by telling them about a God who still has the power to amaze!

Dear Lord, You are amazing in all Your ways. You are clothed in majesty and worthy of all our praise. Thank You for the record of Jesus' life and for His promise that we can do greater things. Help my unbelief. In Jesus' name. Amen.

Application Steps

Think of one amazing thing God has done in your life. Commit to telling at least one person about it.

81 Growing Friendships

Van Walton

Be alert. If you see your friend doing wrong, correct him.
If he responds, forgive him.

LUKE 17:3 MSG

Recently my gardening girlfriends gathered to refurbish a friend's yard that had been neglected due to a season of family illness. Each one of us took on a task. Some trimmed vines and bushes. Others gathered misplaced limbs or raked up piles of leaves. The most enjoyable chore was mixing fresh dirt with nutrients and fertilizer and planting lilies and daisies. The job that made the greatest statement in the yard, however, was creating the borders. A lot of raking, digging, and trimming clearly defined the flower beds and pointed out the clean-cut walkways. The borders set apart the highlights of the landscape.

The work was hard, but as I bent over vines gone wild with sweat pouring from my brow, I gleaned important lessons about real friendship.

While pulling, snipping, digging, and planting I observed other women on their knees performing similar tasks. Real friends get on their knees together—in prayer and in doing the sometimes dirty work of life together.

Friendships are a lot like gardening. We need to dig deep to understand one another. Sometimes it's important to weed out seemingly unimportant habits that, when they take control, might destroy or distort a relationship. Gossip and grumbling must be removed immediately or they can consume entire communities.

Perhaps the toughest responsibility in healthy relationships is that of creating and maintaining borders. If we neglect these boundaries, we destroy respect for one another. If we ignore the fine lines, it becomes easier and easier to take advantage of good nature and generosity. A strong personality, like a hearty vine, can creep into the life of a friend and wind up manipulating and eventually choking her. When this happens, we need to gently correct her.

A yard must be tended or it becomes unmanageable. It's the same with friendships. There have been many times that I comfortably allowed weeds to take root in conversations. I have allowed gossip and grumbling to become the theme of my conversation. I know there is a constructive way to dig up that which would bring death, but I just stand by, preferring to stay clean instead of addressing the messy problem. As believers, we need to encourage and sometimes correct each other to prevent weeds that can destroy our relationships and disrupt our walk with Christ.

Before leaving we swept away the dirt and carried away the debris. Suddenly, inviting walkways, vibrant ground cover, and a hospitable landscape appeared. Content with my labor, I was confident in having learned a lifelong lesson. Friendships, like gardens, must be tended.

Dear Lord, I want to mature in Your garden, growing in godliness and establishing healthy relationships. Remind me to tend my friendships. In Jesus' name. Amen.

Application Steps

Evaluate your time spent with friends. Is it constructive or destructive?

82 On Guard
Micca Campbell

Be strong in the Lord and in the strength of His might.
Put on the full armor of God, so that you will be able
to stand firm against the schemes of the devil.
EPHESIANS 6:10-11 NASB

When spring arrives, my husband and I love to walk on the nature trail at the park. One day, we were on our last lap when, suddenly, I noticed a long black snake poised on my side of the trail as if he were simply a stick. I stopped dead in my tracks and let out a piercing scream. The snake kept his position, while my husband turned and ran the other way. I knew then it was everybody for themselves!

My husband remembers the event differently than I do. He recalls protecting me from the snake by fearlessly attacking it with his bare hands, whirling the snake around, and slinging it back into the woods. Then, I supposedly rushed him with rewards of hugs and kisses while exclaiming, "Oh, my hero, you saved me from that evil snake!" What puzzles me is how two people at the same incident can walk away with two such different stories.

After I returned home, I wondered how many times we had passed that snake while unaware of his presence. Now during our walks, I'm on guard, looking for the snake behind every bush and tree. As we walk through the Christian life, there is another snake we should be aware of. He is described as the serpent of old who is called the devil and Satan, who deceives the whole world (Revelation 12:9).

As you and I serve the kingdom of God, the enemy is going to be found in our path from time to time. He knows we are a threat to his kingdom, and he intends to try stopping us. During our journey, he may show up in all kinds of forms, such as trials, broken relationships, and temptations. Yet our Lord has provided a way for us to stand guard against the devil's tactics.

First, we can guard ourselves against the devil by remembering that Christ conquered him on the cross. He no longer holds us in bondage to sin, nor can he hold death over our heads.

Secondly, we can guard against the devil by resisting him. While he still has the power to tempt us, we can experience victory. As we submit to God, the devil will flee.

Finally, be on guard by dressing daily in the full armor of God. When we dress ourselves each day in the armor of God, it acts as a hedge of protection that keeps the enemy from showing up on our path and bestowing hardships on us.

During my walk with Christ, the "snake" has crossed my path many times, as I'm sure he has yours. If we are wise, we will stand firm in the Lord and discover that our God is able to defeat the serpent of old. Then, with praise due Him, we will proclaim the victory of our Defender.

Dear Lord, thank You for being my Defender and providing me with ways to stand against the enemy's schemes. May You grant me victory from every trap and snare so that I might glorify Your name. In Jesus' name. Amen.

Application Steps

When you put on your clothes each day, also dress yourself for spiritual battle. Through prayer, dress yourself with each protective piece of armor found in Ephesians 6:14-17. Then, stand firm.

83 Look, I Made God Smile

Wendy Pope

When you give alms, do not let your left hand know
what your right hand is doing, so that your alms may be in secret;
and your Father who sees in secret will reward you.

MATTHEW 6:3-4 RSV

At one time we had a problem in our home: Our children would not talk kindly to one another or treat each other with respect. In order to teach them that good manners and kindness pleases God, we invented the game Make God Smile. The object of the game was to get caught speaking kindly or treating the other person with respect. When someone in our home did something or said something kind or respectful we said, "That makes God smile." The game worked, but it created another problem: wanting recognition for good deeds. Now when my five-year-old says or does something that would make God smile, he wants credit for it.

His desire to be recognized for good deeds reminds me of today's verse. So often we do kind things or say encouraging words with the wrong motive. There may be times when our motives start out pure but become tainted with pride along the way. We begin to feel justified in desiring recognition and even crave it. It's our nature to want to be thanked or recognized. However, we are to take on the nature of Christ and bear the fruit of His Spirit—love, joy peace, patience, kindness, goodness, faithfulness, gentleness, and self-control (Galatians 5:22-23)—no matter who is watching.

We only take on His nature and bear His fruit if we are willing to lay down our rights and motives. Paul reminds us of what Jesus did: "Taking the very nature of a servant" he "became obedient to death" (Philippians 2:7-8). God wants us to be willing to die to ourselves and the things we desire. We have to lay down our right to be recognized in return for the reward He will give us in secret. I don't know about you, but I love secrets!

> *Dear Lord, create in me a clean heart. Give me a desire to take on Your nature today and to lay down my own. Forgive me for being prideful and wanting recognition for any good I have done. Thank You for the promise of a secret reward. In Jesus' name. Amen.*

Application Steps

Spend some time in prayer asking God to reveal your motives for serving Him. Confess with your mouth anything He brings to your mind. Write in a journal the things God is asking you to do, and then do them without seeking credit from others.

84 You're the One I Want

Renee Swope

You are a chosen people, a royal priesthood, a holy nation, a people belonging to God, that you may declare the praises of him who called you out of darkness into his wonderful light.
1 PETER 2:9

Christmas was only days away and we didn't have a tree. Living on a college student's budget with a baby on the way made it hard to spend $25 to $50 on something we didn't need. It seemed kind of trivial, but I told God how sad I was that we couldn't afford a tree. Then I felt guilty knowing there were many people who needed much more than us.

God didn't think it was selfish. Instead He provided. Two days later we discovered that a nearby tree lot had marked all trees down to $10.

For this pregnant woman, choosing a tree was almost like choosing a child. I walked down each row to find just the right spruce to fit in the corner of our one-bedroom apartment. Unfortunately, the sun went down quickly, the employees turned the spotlights off and the tree lot turned pitch-dark.

My creative and very patient husband pulled our car *into* the rows of trees and flashed on his high beams. The bright lights dispelled the darkness, and standing in front of me was the most precious little tree I'd ever seen. Although it had some droopy branches and a gap on one side, I pointed and said, "That's the one I want!"

Later I sat on our couch looking at my cute little spruce. I'd felt sad earlier when the darkness made it impossible to see the trees, but when the beams of light illuminated the lot, my heart filled with hope. Etched in my mind was a picture I wouldn't forget, a picture that drew me back to another time marked by darkness—a time when I wasn't choosing but needed to be chosen.

Just when it felt as though all my dreams had died and my hope was gone, God's light punctured the clouds of depression surrounding my mind as His love poured into my heart. It happened on another winter's eve when Jesus looked at me and said, "That's the one I want!"

At some point in our lives, I think most of us can identify with that little tree. Scarred by disappointments, we wonder if anyone would ever choose us. With gaps that make us feel like candidates for rejection, we hope no one will see the holes in our hearts. Like the fate of my little spruce, it seems the only way we'll get chosen is if all the good ones are already taken.

First Peter 2:9 reminds us that through Christ we are chosen. God sent His Son to light our darkness and fill the gaps in our hearts. Hold on to the truth that God sees you today and in His heart He's saying, "You're the one I want!"

Dear Lord, that spruce tree and I have a lot in common. Yet even with my gaps and broken branches, You chose me and made me part of Your family through Jesus. Thank You for sending Your Son to illuminate the dark corners of my life and bring hope to my heart. In Jesus' name. Amen.

Application Steps

Are there times when you feel rejected or forgotten? Ask God to heal the broken places that leave you feeling unwanted. Ask Him to show you how He sees you—holy and dearly loved—chosen and belonging to Him.

85 Expressions of Joy

Micca Campbell

The redeemed of the LORD shall return,
and come with singing unto Zion;
and everlasting joy shall be upon their head;
they shall obtain gladness and joy;
and sorrow and mourning shall flee away.

Isaiah 51:11 KJV

Have you ever wondered what good could come out of a bad situation? My neighbor asked herself that question when she was bitten on the leg by a brown recluse spider. As a diabetic, the poison attacked the weakest part of her body—her eyes. Through many surgeries, doctors were able to prevent further deterioration of Kathy's eye loss so she doesn't have to live completely in the dark. Though she can no longer drive, she can still see shapes and figures.

At first, Kathy experienced all sorts of emotions. She questioned God's love and protection. She wondered, *Why me?* and felt sorry for herself much of the time. Her husband, on the other hand, was very supportive and full of faith. "We'll get through this. You'll see," he said daily in response to her depression.

His confidence in God surprised Kathy. For more than 15 years, she had been going to church alone while praying for Don to find his faith. Now, in the face of suffering, it appeared that Don had more faith than she did. Kathy decided to hang up her woes and trust God. While she didn't understand why He had allowed her pain, Kathy chose to believe in the promise of Romans 8:28, "We know that God causes all things to work together for good to those who love God, to those who are called according to His purpose" (NASB).

Because Kathy couldn't drive, Don dropped her off for church every Sunday. On the ride home, Kathy would share about how nice the service was and how loving the people were. Then, one Sunday morning, Kathy noticed that Don was all dressed up.

"Where are you going?" she asked.

"Well, you're always talking about how great church is, so I thought I would go with you today," Don replied.

Don not only went to church that day, but he returned to the Lord, was baptized, and became a member of God's forever family.

Suddenly, it all became clear for Kathy. "My suffering was nothing like what Christ suffered for my salvation, but I would go through all my pain again knowing now that God was using it to bring my sweet husband to Him," Kathy testifies with great joy.

Sometimes it's hard to see the love of God at work in our lives, especially in suffering. Nevertheless, God is always at work on our behalf.

The Lord never promised that our journey would be easy. In fact, He told us that we would encounter much suffering on earth. What He promised was to be faithful to use every bad situation for good. Not just any good, but the kind of good that puts joy in our hearts and praise on our lips. In the end, we will look back like Kathy and be able to say, "Ah, it was all worth it. Look at what the Lord has done!"

Dear Lord, when my circumstances are blurred and I can't see what's ahead, help me to trust in the dark. Thank You for always having my best interest at heart. In Jesus' name. Amen.

Application Steps

Look for evidence that God is at work in the midst of your trial. Let your faith grow.

86 Conversation Hearts

Susanne Scheppmann

Listen and hear my voice; pay attention and hear what I say.
ISAIAH 28:23

Conversation Hearts top my list of favorite things. I remember elementary through high school attempting to converse with my friends by passing the tiny sugary messages underneath our desks. Short, sweet, fun. But you must pay attention to the words or you might miss the implication of the sender.

For example, a friend of mine woke up one Valentine's Day to a trail of Conversation Hearts left by her husband. A couple placed near the coffee pot. One or two left by the bathroom sink. A few cute sayings greeted her as she sat in her favorite chair.

Later that evening her husband asked, "Well, what do you have to say to the message of love I left for you this morning?"

My dear friend realized she had missed something important. She responded, "I didn't read them, I just ate them as I found them." Oops!

I think we miss many messages God sends us from His heart. We rush from one task to the next. We attempt to squeeze in a few moments of devotional time. We read our Bible and pray a quick list of our needs. We check Quiet Time off our to-do list and head out for an hour-long conversation with our girlfriend over a latte.

What if today we decided to discover little conversations placed strategically by God throughout our day? Maybe while reading our Bible, a phrase might jump out at us. Or perhaps, as we pray, a thought will pop into our minds from the Holy Spirit. Possibly a meaningful daily devotional could speak God's heart to us. Conceivably, we could discover God's conversation to read something like the following:

My Bride (Songs of Songs 4:8)
Now Listen (Isaiah 44:1)
Be Still (Psalm 46:10)
Hear Me (Luke 6:27)
I AM (Exodus 3:14)
Everlasting Love (Jeremiah 31:3)
My Love (John 15:9)
Endures Forever (Psalm 117:2)

As you meander throughout your day, keep your eyes and heart open for a sweet message from the Lord, a love declaration given for your heart only.

Dear Lord, help me to hear You today. Remind me to slow down my hectic pace of life so that I don't miss any special messages from You. In Jesus' name. Amen.

Application Steps

Buy some Conversation Hearts. Write a meaningful reply from your heart to God by placing the tiny candies on a plate. Have fun with this and let your imagination flow freely. Then write your message on a piece of paper and place it in your Bible as a reminder to listen for whispers from the Lord.

87 Bridezilla

Rachel Olsen

The king is enthralled by your beauty;
honor him, for he is your lord.

PSALM 45:11

Having been a flower girl, a bridesmaid, and a bride, I know weddings can be stressful. No other day in a gal's life is more romanticized in her mind than her wedding day. That is, until her wedding day arrives and the cake looks lopsided, a ring gets lost, a family member steps on the hem of her gown, and the soloist hits a sour note. For my wedding reception we rented a grand piano and hired an accomplished Christian pianist. The piano arrived but the musician never did. How would I have a father–daughter dance without music? I'd have to skip the tradition of the bride-and-groom's first dance too. Though some disappointment lingered, we piped in hotel music over the ballroom speakers and made the best of things. Imagine my horror when I later learned the pianist had died the week before my wedding.

You may have seen the television show *Bridezillas.* This reality series takes viewers inside the wedding preparations of brides-to-be who are determined to have the perfect wedding—no matter how many tantrums they must throw with their families, friends, and future husband to achieve that dream. I've watched a little of the show, gawking at how self-centered, rude, and controlling these brides behave. They take the notion "a wedding is the bride's special day" and run marathon distances with it!

A bridezilla can wear a gorgeous gown in a grand cathedral, receive a large, sparkly diamond ring, toss an exquisite bouquet of flowers, and still be an unbecoming bride because her attitude is demanding and self-focused. The Gospel of John says the church is to be the bride of Christ collectively, and that we are each His bride individually. I wonder, does Christ look at my life and see a bridezilla? Am I self-centered? Am I rude or demanding of my family or friends? Am I trying to control every aspect of my life to make it flatter me or conform to my view of perfect? Yes, at times, I act just like a bridezilla.

If anyone deserves to garner everyone's attention, it is Christ. If anyone is in a position to demand perfection, it is Christ. But He doesn't demand; instead, He serves. Every battle Christ has fought, every pain He has endured, every enemy He has laid low, every obstacle He has overcome, and every ounce of mercy He has offered has been in service of you—His bride.

He rides in majesty on behalf of truth, humility, and righteousness (Psalm 45:4). He's defeated Satan and death, and He is blessed by God forever. Who really cares about wilted flowers, a wrinkled veil, or a missing-in-action musician when they're marrying someone like that? *He* should be our focus, and our desire should be to honor Him.

Realize that today is a gift—a wedding gift from our amazing Bridegroom who is enthralled with us. Let's see how far we can run with that notion and honor Him today.

Dear Lord, I am grateful You have chosen me to be Your bride! You are so praiseworthy—I want to honor You today. Please show me how. In Jesus' name. Amen.

Application Steps

Read Psalm 45. It tells an allegorical story of King Jesus and us, His bride.

88 The Pineapple Principle

Lysa TerKeurst

With man this is impossible, but not with God;
all things are possible with God.

MARK 10:27

Let's face it. A pineapple is only sweet to eat if you know how to get inside it! For years I didn't have a clue about how to cut up a pineapple. I would walk by the produce aisle looking at fresh pineapples with such longing. I wanted what was inside it; I just didn't know how to get beneath its tough outer skin. I had visions of me slicing and dicing, dripping with sticky juice and so completely mangling the fruit that not even the dog would be tempted to partake.

But one day I watched a friend accomplish what I thought was impossible. She didn't miss a beat as she sliced and diced a pineapple with ease. First she cut off the top and then the bottom. Next, she sliced the cylinder into four equal pieces. She then slid the knife along the back edge to cut off the skin and along the pointed center to cut off the hard core. Laying the long wedges down on the cutting board, she chopped them into bite size pieces and viola! Fresh-cut pineapple was served. Watching her gave me the courage to try it on my own. And, finally, I was able to help myself to the yummy fruit.

This might sound strange, but learning to cut a pineapple became a real life lesson for me. I learned I had bought into the notion that there were just some things I couldn't do. I was challenged by the thought that I might be missing out on a lot in life simply because I had talked myself into thinking it was impossible.

Mark 10:27 reminds us that with God all things are possible. When we ask for God's help, we dedicate our endeavor to Him. We admit that in our strength this would not be possible, but we proclaim that God can accomplish anything through someone who is willing. We put God's courage into our heart with His truth. We retrain our mind by taking the words "I can't" out of our vocabulary.

What is blocking your path to a victorious life with God? Do you sometimes struggle with being a good steward of the time and money God has entrusted to you? Do you struggle making healthy choices with diet and exercise? Maybe your struggle is your temper. Whatever it is, the first major lesson can be found inside this pineapple principle...no more "I can't"! Everything about our lives should proclaim, "With God all things are possible!"

Oh, and the next time you see a fresh pineapple, buy it. Cut it open and let its fruit inspire you that there is sweet victory on the other side of every conquered challenge.

Dear Lord, to say "I can't" about something is to deny Your power that surely resides in me. I am a child of God, which means I am a conqueror. Help me to walk in that truth. Show me where, how, and from whom I am to get educated on this challenge in my life. Give me the courage to face it honestly and bravely. I want to taste sweet victory. In Jesus' name. Amen.

Application Steps

Write down one of the "I can'ts" in your life. Beside it write: "With God all things are possible." Now pray and ask God to show you what your first step toward victory should be.

89 God's Promptings

Marybeth Whalen

With this in mind, we constantly pray for you,
that our God may count you worthy of his calling,
and that by his power he may fulfill every good purpose
of yours and every act prompted by your faith.

2 THESSALONIANS 1:11

When God prompts you to do something, do you do it? Or do you, like me, tend to argue with Him? I am guilty of feeling God's urging in my heart and either 1) quietly ignoring it and going on with my day, 2) listing out a few reasons why I should not obey, as if God needs to be reminded of my limitations, or 3) arguing outright with Him like a rebellious child.

I was recently the recipient of an unexpected blessing because someone obeyed God's prompting. I was preparing to leave for a women's event in Houston, Texas, where I was to speak. I was excited to go and meet with the ladies there, but I was also dreading the trip, as it meant leaving my eight-month-old daughter overnight for the first time. As the time of my departure neared, I felt heaviness in my heart.

About an hour before I was leaving, my phone rang. The caller ID revealed that the caller was our former neighbor who had moved to Houston many years ago. Though we kept in touch through Christmas cards, it was not normal for us to speak by phone. Therefore, I was surprised to see her number and expected her to tell me she had heard about my trip to Houston somehow.

Imagine my surprise when she revealed that she had not known about my visit! She went on to explain that she had awakened that morning with thoughts of me weighing on her heart. The thoughts stayed with her all day until she finally looked up our number and called—knowing that God must have put me on her heart for a reason. She was as shocked as I was at how God had orchestrated the timing of her call. In just a few hours, I would be landing just a short drive from her home.

I made a few quick changes to my plans, and we were able to meet for dinner that very night. What a sweet reunion and time of fellowship we were able to have. Because of her obedience, instead of dreading the trip, I found myself looking forward to it. God never ceases to amaze me at the way He cares about the details of our lives—if we will only live them aware of His activity.

Obeying God's prompting can impact someone's life forever if you will simply do whatever He is laying on your heart, even if it sounds silly. Even if you question it or feel foolish—do it any way. Being a part of His blessings in someone else's life is a blessing in itself. Don't miss out on it by not responding to His prompting. You will be so glad you did—and so will they!

> *Dear Lord, help me to listen to what You want me to do and to do the things You ask of me. I want to bless others in Your name and be part of Your activity here on earth. Thank You for allowing me to be part of Your kingdom. In Jesus' name. Amen.*

Application Steps

Keep a journal and write about the things you are hearing from God. Write down the names of any people God places on your mind or heart—He will guide your next steps.

90 Dylan's First Day

Melissa Taylor

You both precede and follow me.
You place your hand of blessing on my head.
PSALM 139:5

Today was Dylan's first day of kindergarten. He has been so excited to go to school with his two brothers. He has been wearing his backpack around the house for a week and making pictures to give to his teacher. I remembered when his brothers went to school for the first time. They were so nervous and afraid. It seemed as if it was going to be different for Dylan, and I was thankful. Our family had been praying for this day. Over the summer, we began praying for our children's teachers, their friends, and their school. Each of my boys had their own personal prayer requests for the school year as well. One prayed for less homework than last year, and the other prayed that he would go the entire year without going to the principal's office. As for Dylan, he asked that we pray for him to learn a lot and make new friends. They were covered in prayer and prepared for this day.

During breakfast, I noticed that Dylan was not saying much. He is usually quite a talker, so this sent up a red flag for me. I asked him why he was so quiet. Looking up at me with his big blue eyes, fighting back tears, he said in a loud shaky voice, "I am scared to go to school! I am not smart enough to go to big school. Can I please stay home with you and Hayley Grace (his little sister)?"

If you have ever had a child hurting, you know what it does to your heart as a mother. I wanted to scoop him up and say, "Dylan, you just stay with me today. You can grow up and go to school another day." It was all I could do not to cry right along with him.

As I thought about what I should really say, I was reminded of who made Dylan and who loves him even more than me. I decided to turn to God's Word. I read Psalm 139:1-6 aloud. In those six verses, we were all reminded of how God knows everything about us. He knows everything we are doing. He makes the path ahead of us, and every moment He knows where we are.

The key verse that helped Dylan the most was Psalm 139:5: "You both precede and follow me," and it reassured my frightened child that God would be all around him. "You place your hand of blessing on my head," told him that God would continue to bless him even when he is away from home. I then placed a hand on the heads of my children and told them to imagine that it was God's hand, and I prayed for them.

Then I cracked some jokes, got Dylan laughing, and they headed off to school. As they went down the road in their father's car, Hayley Grace and I waved and shouted, "We love you very much! Have a great day!" Then it was my turn to cry...and go to my Father, who knows everything about me, precedes me and follows me, and has His hand of blessing on my head.

Dear Lord, thank You for placing Your hand of blessing on my head—today and always. In Jesus' name. Amen.

Application Steps

Release your cares to Christ today. Let Him comfort and bless you.

91 A Promise Kept

Glynnis Whitwer

For no matter how many promises God has made,
they are "Yes" in Christ. And so through him the "Amen"
is spoken by us to the glory of God.

2 Corinthians 1:20

A broken promise can be devastating. Someone promised to be faithful to you—but they weren't. Someone promised to pay you back—but they didn't. Someone promised to stop a sinful habit—but it continued.

Unfortunately, instead of being an unbreakable covenant from one person to another, a promise is more often a temporary commitment. It lasts until something easier or more attractive comes along—or until our willpower eases and selfish desires assume control.

It would be easy, and somewhat satisfying, to list everyone who has broken a promise to me. But to be honest, I've broken my share too. There's only One whose word is faultless, whose character is faithful, and who keeps every promise, and that's God.

Each Christmas, we celebrate the wonderful fulfillment of God's promise to His beloved people: the birth of Jesus. The Israelites had been waiting many years for the promised Messiah. Although it wasn't in the Israelite's timing, God faithfully kept His promise. Today, God still keeps His promises.

A common definition of faith is: choosing to believe what God says is true. Another common definition is: believing that God will do what He says He'll do. Here are a few promises we can believe:

- God will never change. (Malachi 3:6)
- We are not alone. Jesus promised to send the Holy Spirit

(John 14:15-17), who will be our Comforter and teach us truth.

- Jesus loves us and comes to live within us. (John 14:18-21)
- Jesus is preparing a place for us to live with Him forever. (John 14:1-4)
- We are safe in the care of Jesus. (John 10:27-29)
- God will provide financial blessings when we tithe. (Malachi 3:10)
- Nothing can stop Jesus from loving us. (Romans 8:38-39)

In difficult times it's easy to doubt that God's promises are true. We may think God has forgotten us or that His promises apply only to "good" Christians. But the truth about God is that His promises stand firm for all who love Him.

In 2 Corinthians 1:20 we read that God loves to keep His promises and has given us Jesus as proof. That Scripture says, "No matter how many promises God has made, they are 'Yes' in Christ. And so through him the 'Amen' is spoken by us to the glory of God."

When life seems filled with deception and abandoned commitments, remember the promises of God and His unchanging character. Let a resounding "Amen" sound across our lips as we bring glory to God through our lives and faith.

Dear Lord, I praise You for Your unchanging nature. I praise You for Your faithfulness in keeping Your promises throughout the generations. Please forgive me for the times that I doubt You and give up waiting for You to keep Your promise. Thank You for keeping Your promises in spite of my unfaithfulness. In Jesus' name. Amen.

Application Steps

Think about God's promises. Identify those you have doubted in the past or doubt today. Choose to believe God's promises.

92 The Pumpkin Patch

Sharon Glasgow

He said to them, "The harvest truly is great, but the laborers are few; therefore pray the Lord of the harvest to send out laborers into His harvest."

LUKE 10:2 NKJV

I love pumpkins, gourds, Indian corn, and corn stalks tied together in the fall. Last spring I planned ahead, buying packages of pumpkin seeds. I proudly planted my pumpkin patch and, using the dates on the seed package, estimated I should be overflowing with pumpkins by fall. In the following months I watched my pumpkin patch, but nothing happened. I never saw the first pumpkin vine or leaf. My pumpkin patch was empty. After all the planning I was disappointed. I knew I had planted them at the proper time, the rains were good, and the ground was fertilized. I gave up on the idea of growing pumpkins this year. Why try when I was such a failure at growing them last year?

Two weeks ago I was taking a walk around the barn and saw a huge orange thing peeking out from among the wildflowers. I walked over to it and, to my amazement, found a big pumpkin. In fact, it was so big I couldn't budge it or even put my arms around it! It was one of those state fair-sized pumpkins! Instantly I knew this was a pumpkin grown from my planting the previous year.

I was so excited! I sat down in my pumpkin patch with my big pumpkin and said, "What happened to you last year? Didn't I give you everything you needed to grow?" As the beautiful wildflowers brushed against me, I felt overwhelmingly blessed by this unexpected harvest. I could sense God speaking to my heart. "Sharon, you don't always see the harvest of your labor in *your* expected time frame. Don't stop planting when you don't see growth. Plant! And in due time you will harvest what you have sown."

After visiting with the pumpkin and God, I came back to the house to find an e-mail sent from a young man I had taught in Sunday school ten years earlier. He was writing to me from Africa.

Dear Mrs. Glasgow, thank you for introducing me to the Lord of my life, Jesus Christ. I am helping lead the lost to Him in Africa. Please pray for me.

I was so touched. I'd planted a seed so long ago, and now I got to see the harvest! I quickly jotted some notes to remember what God had just taught me and stuffed the paper in my purse. Last night, as I waited to pick up my children from choir, a young girl ran to my car. She said, "Mrs. Glasgow, pray for my mom. She doesn't know the Lord." I quickly reached for a piece of paper in my purse on which to write her phone number. The girl left. I flipped the paper over to find the words I had written earlier, "Plant seeds, Sharon. God will do the rest." Planting seeds can be done by calling a lost woman in need of a Savior, teaching a Sunday school class, inviting a coworker to church, helping a needy family, or giving a Bible to your next-door neighbor. Don't worry about the harvest. It will come in due time. Just keep planting!

Dear Lord, help me to minister to those You put in my path. Then please help me to follow through with the planting. I leave the harvest to You. In Jesus' name. Amen.

Application Steps

Just plant! Planting seeds can include inviting your neighbors to church, helping a needy family, or letting others see Christ through your generosity.

93 Are You a Salt Lick?

Susanne Scheppmann

You are the salt of the earth. But if the salt loses its saltiness, how can it be made salty again? It is no longer good for anything, except to be thrown out and trampled by men.

MATTHEW 5:13

Traveling along the highway, I gazed at cattle huddling around scattered salt licks. I noticed how contented the cattle seemed as their long tongues stretched to lick the milky-white blocks of salt.

A Bible verse rose to the surface of my thoughts: "You are the salt of the earth." It dawned on me that God desires me to become a salt lick. Of course, not a hard block of minerals resting in a grassy field, but to be a solid witness to His power in my life. A place my friends might come for a little spiritual nutrition.

Ranchers place salt licks amid green-grassy fields for their animals. Why? Because without salt health deteriorates. Cattle, sheep, horses, and wildlife will seek out salt licks. Occasionally, a natural salt lick appears in the wild. Harsh weather can expose a salty mineral deposit that will draw animals from miles away for a taste of needed nutrients. Animals crave salt. They must have it.

Christ stated, "You are the salt of the earth." What did He mean by that statement?

Jesus desires for us to be spiritual salt in a tempestuous world. He calls us to be a place where hurting people can come for a taste of God's goodness. Just as weather exposes a salt lick in nature, storms in our lives that we weather with faith reveal something that is attractive to others.

People aching with problems study us who handle our difficulties with joy and contentment. They will approach us, as spiritual salt licks, with their need for hope. They yearn for an explanation of how we withstand squalls of perpetual problems with serenity. As they come eager to discover our secret, we can share how Jesus Christ is sufficient for anything life throws in our path.

However, Christ added another interesting dimension to the concept of us being the salt of the earth. We can lose our saltiness and our worth in God's kingdom. If we allow life's circumstances to make us bitter, we lose our saltiness. If we become a mental martyr, our saltiness vanishes into self-pity. If we lose our saltiness, those who crave the salt of God's kingdom will look to others, or even worse, taste what temptations the world offers in consolation.

We must guard against anything that siphons our ability to witness Jesus' peace, love, and joy from our spirits. As we maintain our saltiness, hurting people will come and taste the goodness of God. Do you consider yourself a spiritual salt lick?

Dear Lord, help me to become a spiritual salt lick. I want to be a witness of Your goodness to others. When life gets hard, let my life be a testimony for those who are in need of a bit of spiritual nutrition. In Jesus' name. Amen.

Application Steps

Write a prayer asking God to nudge you each time He brings opportunities for you to be a spiritual salt lick for someone else. Place a saltshaker by your telephone as a reminder to tell others of God's goodness in your life.

94 Fluffy Deception
Luann Prater

I am afraid that just as Eve was deceived by the serpent's cunning, your minds may somehow be led astray from your sincere and pure devotion.

2 Corinthians 11:3

Flying over the clouds on our way to Europe, I was fascinated with their appearance. It was the most serene view. Fluffy balls of cotton and translucent puffs of down—they looked so inviting. My eyes glazed over as I daydreamed of plopping into the middle of that billowy blanket. It seemed so peaceful, but I was so incredibly wrong.

As the pilot began the final descent we penetrated the edge of that seemingly soft pillow. The seat belt light came on and the plane began to bump and rock as we fought our way through the darkness. The wings were shaking and so were my hands.

Webster describes "deceit" as "misrepresenting the truth" or "purposely misleading."

Satan wants to make the world look soft and cozy and compelling. He wants temptation to appear as the best choice. "Look at what I'm offering you here! It's beautiful, it's easy, it's peaceful," he whispers. If he threw up a sign that said DANGER, no one would ever dive into temptation. But he is crafty and cunning, and he longs to trip us up with lovely things.

What tempts you?

When we are feeling low, Satan doesn't send spinach, he sends donuts and candy and things we "deserve." When things are rocky at home, he doesn't send a dirty, smelly ogre, he sends another man with a soothing voice and gentle touch. When you don't have a good answer, he doesn't send a whopping tale no one would believe, but rather a small, seemingly insignificant stretch of the truth.

Think about it. Satan hasn't come up with anything new since the beginning of time. In the Garden of Eden he didn't tempt Eve with rotten, wormy, nasty smelling fruit. He pointed out fruit that looked good and then discussed the benefits of eating it. He made it seem so natural, so right. He is trying to do the same thing to you and me. Let's recognize him for what he is...a liar!

That cloud he wants you dreaming about is a lie. It's not soft, it's not comfortable, and it's not safe. It's deadly.

After bumping along on that endless flight, we finally broke through the stormy cloud and to find solid ground below. Rather than basing our choices today on how tempting something seems, let's place our feet on the solid Rock of Ages and stand firm in our devotion to Him. There, we know we are safe from deception.

Dear Lord, give me clear vision into the lies Satan is putting before me today. Help me to see my life through Your eyes. Where there is temptation, make it ugly and noticeable. Reveal his lies with Your truth. In Jesus' name. Amen.

Application Steps

Examine your life. Write down any deception Satan is using on you. Dig into Scripture and find a corresponding verse that will combat each lie. Remember, Jesus fought Satan with Scripture when He was tempted. Let's follow His example.

95 Hallelujah

Rachel Olsen

I heard what sounded like the roar of a great multitude in heaven shouting: "Hallelujah! Salvation and glory and power belong to our God."

REVELATION 19:1

At the dinner table one evening my four-year-old son sang a praise song with the word "hallelujah" in the verse. I asked him if he knew what "hallelujah" meant. My little darling replied with a serious face, "Yes. It means to go to bed." While I tried to figure how he arrived at this conclusion—had I sung him lullabies containing that word?—my husband quipped, "That's because Mommy shouts 'hallelujah' every night once you kids are in bed!" We all had a hearty laugh.

According to *Nave's Topical Bible,* "hallelujah" is "an exclamatory expression of praise or adoration." It's kind of like shouting to God: "All Right—Yippee—Way to Go—Hoo Ha—You're the Best!" You'll often hear it spoken in the midst of favorable circumstances, like when something desperately hoped for finally comes to pass.

God is just as deserving of our hallelujahs, however, in our difficult circumstances—while we are still hoping and waiting on the breakthrough.

A certain musician discovered this truth during his despairing times. Facing bankruptcy and struggling to afford a shabby apartment in London, he often went without food. One evening in 1741, he wandered the city streets all night long, depressed. When he returned to his room he found an envelope on the table from fellow composer Charles Jennens. Examining the pages, he found them covered with words from Scripture.

He crawled into bed to sleep, but dreams would not come. The words on the pages kept returning to his mind:

Comfort ye, comfort ye, my people, saith your God...The people that walked in darkness have seen a great light...For unto us a Child is born...Glory to God in the highest... Hallelujah!

He got up and went to his piano, where music began to flow out of his fingers. For three weeks straight, he composed feverishly. On the day the work was finished, a friend came to visit. There sat the composer at the piano, sheets of music strewn around him, with tears streaking down his face. "I think I did see all of Heaven before me, and the great God Himself," he exclaimed. The composer was George Frederic Handel, and the composition was *Messiah,* featuring the world-famous "Hallelujah Chorus."

No one is more deserving of a hallelujah chorus than our Messiah. The Pharisees told Jesus to rebuke His disciples for exclaiming, "Blessed is the king who comes in the name of the Lord! Peace in heaven and glory in the highest!" Jesus replied, "I tell you, if they keep quiet, the stones will cry out" (Luke 19:38-40). Friends, I pray that the rocks around us never have cause to cry out because we are failing to praise the Lord. In good times and bad, join in with the heavenly hosts shouting "Hallelujah!" to the One to whom salvation, glory, and power belong.

Dear Lord, You are truly worthy of all my honor and praise. I praise You for who You are—You are majestic, loving, and true! I praise You for what You've done—salvation, healing, and blessing come from You alone! I praise You for what You will do in the future—the enemy will be eternally destroyed and a New Jerusalem will be established for Your people! Hallelujah!

Application Steps

Simply praise Him today.

96 Grandpa
Micca Campbell

Though you have not seen him, you love him…
and are filled with an inexpressible and glorious joy.
1 PETER 1:8

My dad's father died before I was born. Although I've never met him, I still adore him. I've come to love, respect, and accept my grandpa's ways of life from the stories shared with me over the years by my father and family.

From their stories I've learned how much family meant to my grandpa and how he was a softy when it came to his children. I've discovered that Grandpa was a fun person who loved to laugh, enjoyed good food, and participated in the sport of boxing.

I have seen my grandpa in our family customs, in our beliefs, and through the specialized fabric that makes up our unique family. One day I'll meet him face-to-face, but for now, I know and love him by faith.

In a similar way, I've come to know and love God by faith. I've never seen the Lord with my eyes or touched His physical body with my hands. It's only by faith, as I've listened to the stories written by my brothers and sisters in Christ long ago, that I have come to understand and accept who God is.

Because I've seen God by faith, I've chosen His ways—to take on His character, live by His laws, and love with His heart. In doing so I've seen His goodness, tasted His compassion, been held by His comfort, surrounded by His love, and sheltered by His grace.

Why is it easy for some to believe in the unseen God while others find it difficult?

Thomas had a hard time believing without first seeing:

One of the disciples, Thomas, was not with the others when Jesus came. They told him, "We have seen the Lord!" But he replied, "I won't believe it unless I see the nail wounds in his hands, put my fingers into them, and place my hand into the wound in his side" (John 20:24-25 NLT).

The Lord is always willing to help our doubt. John 20:27 (NLT) tells us that Jesus came to Thomas and said, "Put your finger here and see my hands. Put your hand into the wound in my side. Don't be faithless any longer. Believe!"

Once Thomas saw, he believed. Then Jesus told him, "You believe because you have seen me. Blessed are those who haven't seen me and believe anyway" (verse 29).

What about you? Do you believe in God, even though you haven't seen Him? Does the hearing of His attributes compel you to love Him? God loves you, and one day we will all see Him face-to-face. For now, the stories of faith that tell of His greatness can compel us to believe.

Dear Lord, like Thomas I need to see to believe. Help my doubt. Make Yourself real to me. Open my eyes so that I may see Your truths, and open my heart so that I may receive Your life. In Jesus' name. Amen.

Application Steps

Ask God to show you His wonders. Plan a day to watch the sun rise or set. Visit a zoo or an aquarium and be an eyewitness to God's handiwork. Don't doubt any longer—believe!

97 Confessions of a Recovering Shopaholic

Wendy Pope

She sees that her trading is profitable.

PROVERBS 31:18

To be honest with you, there was a time when I wished Proverbs 31 Ministries' Principle Five, "The Proverbs 31 Woman contributes to the financial well-being of her household, being a faithful steward of the time and money God has entrusted to her" did not exist. Being a faithful steward of the time and money God and my husband entrust to me has not always been an easy task.

I suppose it started years ago when I rode in the Country Squire station wagon with my mother from destination to destination searching for the "bargain of the century." My mother taught me to be an expert bargain shopper. So much an expert that even now, many years later, friends call me for shopping tips and questions about where to get the best deal on what they're looking for.

What I believe my mother meant for good, the enemy used for evil. Somewhere along the way, through disappointing times in my life and low self-esteem, I began to see shopping as an escape. It became the way I brought myself happiness. I use the word "happiness" because happiness describes a temporary emotion based on circumstances. Joy is something within yourself that remains regardless of your circumstances.

I entered my marriage in debt and managed to keep us in debt during most of our early years together. The debt I accrued became my secret. I hid credit card bills from my husband, as well as new things I bought. Each month, I would scrape enough money together from my household budget to make the minimum payments. The lie kept me from having an honest and open relationship with my husband. It also kept me from experiencing the real joy that comes with an intimate relationship with Jesus. It was a true sickness.

The first step I took to rid myself of this sickness was commit to meet each morning with the greatest financial advisor who ever lived, Jesus. This was before my shower, juice, and kisses from my family. In my quiet times, I asked God to change me. I begged Him to give me a heart to know Him. I invited him to teach me, refine me, and make me pleasing and acceptable in His sight.

I also made the choice not to go to the mall or other stores unnecessarily. Something else that was helpful to cure the sickness was to see where I was spending money by recording the amount for *every* purchase in a small notebook. The final step I took to financial freedom was to cut up my credit cards and confess my lifestyle to my husband.

I now know where real joy comes from. This joy can't be stolen.

Dear Lord, You are Jehovah-Jireh, the God who provides. Help me to trust You to provide my physical needs as well as my emotional needs. Forgive me for making foolish choices when it comes to spending the money You entrust to me. Reveal to me changes I need to make in my spending habits. In Jesus' name. Amen.

Application Steps

Write down all "frivolous" debt you have, such as credit cards and department store cards. Begin praying over it. Ask God for the discipline and courage to cut up the cards and come clean. If you don't have any such debt, praise the Lord for your freedom from it.

98 A Surprising Answer
Susanne Scheppmann

"My thoughts are not your thoughts,
neither are your ways my ways," declares the LORD.
"As the heavens are higher than the earth,
so are my ways higher than your ways and my
thoughts than your thoughts."

ISAIAH 55:8-9

"I hate you!" she said as the door slammed behind her. I recalled, with a sigh, the ten long years I had been praying for the Lord to bring my stepdaughter a Christian friend. Since she was living in another state, we held little sway of influence as Christian parents. My husband and I longed to raise her in our Christian home.

Now, however, she was 16 and attending high school. I doubted we would ever have the opportunity for her to live with us. So what could I do? I prayed for a Christian friend to enter her life.

I wrote this prayer in my notebook. I saw few positive results. In fact, just the opposite appeared to happen. We discovered she was getting involved in some questionable relationships. She started down a path of self-destruction. I began to question if God even heard my prayers.

Suddenly, through some unexpected circumstances, my stepdaughter came to live with us. It was just before Christmas. She arrived angry and full of rebellion. Turmoil decorated our home, not pleasant Christmas memories. Little did I know I had just begun one of the most difficult seasons of my adult life. As a blended family adjusting to a new member, we felt we were being pureed in a family-dysfunction blender. We fought, we cried, and we prayed. I did not think we would survive. My faith ran low in believing any change could occur. Although my faith faltered, my prayers prevailed.

The night she yelled, "I hate you!" I sought refuge in bed, discouraged and exhausted. Again, the question surfaced, "Lord, do You hear me at all?" I picked up my prayer journal from the nightstand, and thumbed through the pages of the past year. The written record of my prayers pleaded, "Lord, bring her a Christian friend!" Suddenly, I saw the answer to my prayer. God could use *me* as the friend who would point her to God.

From that moment on, I worked diligently to win her confidence and trust. She stayed with us until she graduated from high school two years later. As our friendship grew, I had the honor of seeing her accept Christ at a youth conference and then be baptized shortly afterward.

Was it easy? No. Does she still struggle with life issues and rebellion? Yes. Do I still pray for her? Absolutely. I know God hears and answers my prayers.

God affirms this verse in my life time and again, "'My thoughts are not your thoughts, neither are your ways my ways,' declares the LORD. 'As the heavens are higher than the earth, so are my ways higher than your ways and my thoughts than your thoughts'" (Isaiah 55:8-9). He often surprises—and challenges—me with His answers.

What surprise-answers lie within your prayers?

Dear Lord, remind me how You always hear my prayers. Open my eyes to the answers You give in response to my requests. Help me to understand when You answer my prayers in completely different ways than what I may expect. Let me accept that Your thoughts and ways are better than mine. In Jesus' name. Amen.

Application Steps

Record your prayers in a journal. Begin to ask yourself, "Has God answered any of these prayers? Have I overlooked His answer?"

99 Overcoming Our Enemies of Doubt and Fear

Renee Swope

Go in the strength you have...I will be with you,
and you will strike down all the Midianites together.

Judges 6:14,16

I woke up dreading my day before it started. All I could think about were deadlines, laundry, and a gazillion things I had to do before we left town. My husband and kids had been sick, and my hormones were robbing me of much needed sleep.

Clouds of doubt and fear loomed over me. *What if I can't get it all done?* Faces of those I'd disappoint at work appeared before me. *What if we don't leave on time for our trip?* Frustrated family members paraded through my mind. I wanted to shut the curtains and hide under my pillow for the day.

Just as I was about to pull the blankets over my head, I remembered Gideon, a man in the Bible who tried to hide from his enemies too. Although his enemies weren't deadlines, doubts, and hormones—they had as much power to defeat him.

One day while Gideon was hiding from the Midianites, God's angel came to him and announced that Gideon was going to defeat them. Gideon responded with doubt-filled questions—the same ones we ask: *Who me? How can I? Why is this so hard?* Gideon was overwhelmed by uncertainty and fear. He doubted his strength and ability to overcome his enemies, even with God's help.

"The Lord is with you, mighty warrior," the angel promised Gideon. Then God spoke, "Go in the strength you have and save Israel out of Midian's hand. Am I not sending you?…I will be with you, and you will strike down all the Midianites together" (Judges 6:12,14,16).

My fear of not being able to do it all led me to doubt as well. *Had I heard God wrong when I made these commitments? If God is with me, why has He allowed my circumstances to be so difficult?*

Eventually Gideon believed God and with His help he defeated his enemies and his fears. His story reminded me that whatever I had to face, God would be there to help me too. I chose to believe God that morning. Through Gideon's story, I was challenged to stop focusing on what I couldn't do and get up and go in the strength I had—God's strength.

We may not be able to do all we want to do when we want to do it, but we can do what God is sending us to do today. Let's choose to focus on the strength we have—God's strength—so we can overcome our doubts and fears with confident trust because He promises to be with us.

> *Dear Lord, I confess that many days I focus on my circumstances instead of focusing on You. That's when I become discouraged and overwhelmed. Help me see myself and my life through Your perspective. Remind me that You are with me and that I can do all things through Christ who gives me strength. In Jesus' name. Amen.*

Application Steps

When doubt or fear threatens you, stop and remember God is with you. Then make a list of strengths you have and things you can do with His help. If you feel tempted to hide behind television, food, busyness, sleep, or anything other than God, confess your fear and find Scriptures to remind you of His provision, presence, and promise to be your hiding place.

100 Born to Be

Marybeth Whalen

Whatever you have learned or received or heard from me,
or seen in me—put it into practice.
And the God of peace will be with you.

PHILIPPIANS 4:9

At the annual Proverbs 31 She Speaks conference, I had the privilege of leading a critique group for beginning speakers. I enjoyed getting to know these ladies and hearing their courageous stories. At the end of the weekend, as we said our goodbyes, one of the ladies in my group gave me a sweet compliment. "You are a born encourager," she told me emphatically.

I have been mulling over her comment ever since. Me? A born encourager? I wish! If anything, I am a born critic who has had to practice being an encourager. I have learned that people respond to encouragement much better than criticism. "You catch more flies with honey than with vinegar," as the old saying goes. If I want to grow closer to, feel emotionally connected to, or be trusted by the people I love, I have to let go of my fleshly bad attitudes and negativity. Instead, I must learn to speak words of life, hope, and affirmation.

I have intentionally set out to build up instead of tear down—even if it means actually biting my tongue sometimes to make that happen.

God has taught me through the Bible and some godly people the value of practicing the things in life that don't come naturally. I may not have been born to be an encourager, but I can make efforts to change that. Likewise, I may not have been born with a servant's heart, but I can certainly practice the attitudes and actions of a servant while letting God work on my heart. Additionally, I may not feel like being obedient, but I can practice obeying God and trust Him to take care of filling me with joy in the process.

What is God asking you to do that doesn't come naturally? Submit to your husband? Practice good stewardship? Exemplify the fruit of the Spirit? Conquer a bad habit? Surrender control? Display unconditional love?

While you may not have been born to do those things, you can decide today to practice them in your life. As you practice, you will find that they get easier and easier. And in your diligence and willingness, God will show up and take care of the rest. As we practice obedience, it becomes an exercise in faith. We don't see how God is going to accomplish a change in us, yet we say to Him through our obedience, "I trust that You will, Lord."

God is asking us to simply submit to Him with the knowledge that only He, as our Creator, can determine what we were really born to be.

Dear Lord, thank You for working in my life to make me all that I can be. Help me to practice in faith the things I know You are requiring of me. In Jesus' name. Amen.

Application Steps

Determine what God is asking you to step out and practice doing. Don't go by ability or emotions. Go by truth and God's leading in your life. Set a goal to practice whatever that is, and watch God work on the rest!

101 Daddy, Do You Love Me?

Lysa TerKeurst

I am always with you; you hold me by my right hand.
You guide me with your counsel, and afterward you
will take me into glory. Whom have I in heaven but you?
And earth has nothing I desire besides you.
My flesh and my heart may fail, but God is the strength
of my heart and my portion forever.

Psalm 73:23-26

When I was eight years old, I remember wanting one thing more than anything else...my daddy's love. I remember standing beside his chair twirling around while my heart cried out for his attention. *Daddy, do you notice me? Daddy, am I beautiful? Daddy, am I your special little girl? Daddy, do you love me?* But my daddy never gave me those words of affirmation.

While my earthly daddy didn't notice me, my heavenly Daddy did. God promises to be a father to the fatherless and fill in the emotional gaps left behind from those who have abandoned us. Throughout my whole life, He has brought experiences my way that reveal the depth of His love for me.

Last summer I had the privilege to attend the Billy Graham crusade in New York City with Billy's daughter, Ruth. Ruth and I have been friends and prayer partners for several years. We met and instantly bonded at a women's conference. To me, she is just Ruth. My friend with whom I laugh, cry, pray, and experience life. I often forget about the celebrity status of her family.

But at the crusade there was no forgetting. Famous people were all around us as we made our way through the crowd to our reserved seats. My 11-year-old daughter, Hope, who was with me, kept exclaiming,

"Mom, there is Amy Grant and Vince Gill! Mom, there are the Clintons, who used to live in the White House!"

I kept wondering, *Who am I? I don't belong here with all these famous people.* But just as the questions and doubt started to creep in, Ruth handed us badges to wear. All the famous people had them on. However, our badges had a gold star on the bottom. I quickly realized the meaning of this gold star as we walked past the famous people and sat with the Graham family. The gold star meant we were part of the family.

I sat down and wiped the tear that started to make its way down my cheek. I looked up to heaven and winked at my heavenly Daddy. His voice was so tender as He once again whispered to my heart, "Lysa, you are not the child of a broken parent who couldn't give you love. You are a child of God. Yes, Lysa, I notice you. Yes, Lysa, you are beautiful. Yes, Lysa, you are my special little girl. And yes, Lysa, I love you."

Dear Lord, help me to know, believe, and walk in that truth every day. As I think back on my childhood and the gaps my biological parents left in my heart, help me to forgive and release those into Your loving hands. As Psalm 73:26 states, be my strength and my portion today and always. In Jesus' name. Amen.

Application Steps

Picture yourself as a little girl standing on the edge of your parents' bed. You see God standing a few feet away with outstretched arms, telling you to jump. Feeling full of confidence, you leap from your past into a glorious truth-filled future. Hear God's whispers of love as He wraps you in His embrace.

102 Finding Balance in a Tilted World

Glynnis Whitwer

You, LORD, give perfect peace to those who keep their purpose firm and put their trust in you.
ISAIAH 26:3 GNT

Balancing the needs of our families, jobs, homes, and sometimes ministry seems a never-ending task. There's always someone who needs our help, an assignment that needs to be finished, and laundry that piles up. And there are never enough hours in the day to do it all. We're stretched thin.

One of the most effective ways to live a balanced life is to live according to your priorities—those that are in line with God's priorities. A challenge every woman faces is identifying her priorities and then making regular choices that reflect them.

A balanced life starts with being clear on the things that should take top priority in your life. If you aren't sure about your priorities, ask yourself the following questions. I've offered you some of my answers in parentheses.

- What can only I do? (I can develop my faith, take care of my health, be my husband's wife, and be my children's mother.)

- What has God entrusted to me? (God has entrusted me with the care of a home, the care of children, the care of my body.)

- Am I a good steward of what I already have? (I try to manage money well. Every day my goal is to love my husband and children the way I should.)

- What passion has God put in my heart? (I have a passion for helping women draw closer to God.)
- What has God asked me to do that I haven't done yet? (For years I knew God was calling me to write, but I did nothing about it.)

Once you've identified your priorities, list them in order of importance to you. Then, allocate the number of hours each week you devote to each one. If you're like most of us, you'll find your priorities and time are out of balance. The things you value most receive the least amount of your time, and often the lowest amount of energy and enthusiasm.

Only you can make the tough decisions necessary to live a balanced life. It often means sacrificing something you enjoy doing. Rick Warren said, "If you want your life to have impact, focus it! Stop dabbling. Stop trying to do it all. Do less. Prune away even good activities and do only that which matters most."

Finding balance in your life might take time. Some things you can prune immediately, while others may take time to fulfill a commitment before stepping away. Once you've identified your priorities, ordered them, and cut some activities out of your life, you'll enjoy your new-found sense of balance in this tilted world.

Dear Lord, You are holy, righteous, and true. Forgive me when I neglect to live according to the priorities You have in mind. Help me discover Your purpose for my life, and give me the courage to prune activities that keep me from that purpose. In Jesus' name. Amen.

Application Steps

List the top five to ten priorities in your life. Identify how many hours a week/month you dedicate to those priorities. Pray about whether these priorities are in-line with God's priorities for you. Make one or two changes to live according to your priorities.

103 Don't Give Up
Rachel Olsen

What is faith? It is the confident assurance that what we hope for is going to happen. It is the evidence of things we cannot yet see.
Hebrews 11:1 NLT

Being a former gymnast, I am a huge gymnastics fan. I spent countless childhood hours perched atop a four-inch beam, swinging between uneven bars, tumbling across a spring-filled floor, and hurling myself over a horse, hoping I'd stick my landing. One summer I tried training away from home at one of the nation's elite-level gyms. Visions of the 1988 Olympics in Seoul, Korea, danced in my head.

As it turns out, I didn't have the mental toughness to compete at that level. The coaches were unrelenting in attitude and expectation. Sympathy was unheard of. I had never felt so much pressure daily. An encourager by nature, I didn't exactly flourish in an environment where praise was rarely offered.

My biggest problem, however, was not with the coaches but within myself. When I made a mistake in a routine, I had trouble not letting it negatively affect the rest of my performance. I accepted defeat too easily in my mind—often before my body or circumstances even produced it. Really great athletes never accept defeat before the competition is over.

Watching the men's all-around gymnastics competition in the 2004 Olympics, I witnessed a great illustration on overcoming defeat. American favorite Paul Hamm performed a quality vault but fell drastically on his landing—off the mat and onto the judges' table! Before this Hamm was in first place; afterward he dropped to twelfth. This is not a mistake one generally recovers from when competing against the best in the world. It seemed his shot at an Olympic all-around medal was dashed. I empathized with his feelings of defeated dreams.

However, if we could have looked forward in time at that moment as God can, we would have seen that Hamm had not been defeated. With two events left, the other top gymnasts each made a few mistakes. Hamm stayed focused and turned in two stunning performances. He did something I always struggled with after a fall like that. He refused to accept defeat. He went on to capture the Olympic gold medal.

Let Hamm's triumph be an example for us. It's always too early to give up! Faith is the substance of things hoped for, the evidence of things not seen" (Hebrews 11:1 NKJV). Hamm's gold medal was definitely unlikely, even illogical after his disaster on the vault; nonetheless, it was a reality in his future. Faith often defies logic, as does God.

Accepting defeat in our mind can prompt us to live it out in our life. By the same token, praying and acting with hope allows God to move mountains on our behalf. Let's not look at our circumstances, our mistakes, or the world's scoreboard and conclude that we are defeated. We serve a mighty God! He uses our faith—no matter how small—to activate His power in our lives (Matthew 15:28). For this God we serve, nothing is impossible.

Dear Lord, I want to persevere in the faith, especially when I make mistakes. Help me to trust Your hand is at work in my life, even when I can't see it. In Jesus' name. Amen.

Application Steps

In a journal, list two or three areas of your life where you need God's active power and victory. Then pray specifically, with hope and expectation, for God's hand to move. Persevere in faith.

104 The Haircut

Melissa Taylor

Therefore, if anyone is in Christ, he is a new creation; the old has gone, the new has come!

2 CORINTHIANS 5:17

My daughter was in need of a haircut. She has beautiful long brown hair. There's only one problem with that. We can't brush it without major tears in the morning! While I knew her hair needed to be cut, the thought of those sweet locks being trimmed just broke my heart. She didn't want it cut, either. The reality of someone cutting her hair terrified her. We decided to visit an expert on the matter, a hairstylist at a local salon.

As soon as we walked in, the stylist said, "Oh, I see we have a swimmer here. I'd know dry split chlorine hair anywhere!" At first I was offended that she would talk to us that way, but then I realized that she was speaking the truth. Hayley Grace's hair was dry and split. I was pretty amazed that she also knew why. How could she tell? She could tell because that's what she does. She's in the business of hair. She's an expert! She went on to explain how with a simple wash and trim, Hayley Grace's hair would be a new creation. The cut would take off the old and a healthy vibrant head of hair would be revealed. My daughter was fascinated by this. She said, "Let's do it, Mommy. I want pretty new hair."

Where are you right now? What kind of condition is your life in? Is it cracked? Are you suffering? Do you feel defeated or unworthy? That's not the way it's supposed to be. Just as I took Hayley Grace to an expert to repair her hair, we have an Expert who can repair our lives. I'm talking about Jesus Christ, the true life makeover artist.

The Bible says if anyone is in Christ, he is a new creation. That means that you can become brand new, transformed, and repaired. It requires one thing though: You must allow Christ to do the work for you. He is there for us; we just have to believe in Him. Then we need to trust Him to do His work in us. Change can be difficult and painful, but the end result is worth it. When we give our lives to Christ, the old is gone. We are new creations in Him. The makeover Jesus gives is not temporary. It lasts forever.

I wish you could see my daughter's new haircut. She looks like a little princess. Her hair is healthy. No split ends or dryness remain. The old is gone. Unfortunately, her new hairstyle is just temporary. We'll have to continue to take care of it to keep it looking this way. Only the changes Jesus makes are eternal, which reminds me that Hayley Grace really is a princess. She is a daughter of the King. Are you?

Dear Lord, I know changes need to be made in my life. I need Your help to make them. In Jesus' name. Amen.

Application Steps

Do you have old habits you need to shed? Write them down and ask God how you can make lasting changes. If you have not asked Jesus Christ to be your Lord and Savior, why not do it now? There's no better time to make permanent changes in your life. You can be a new creation today.

105 Behold the Body of Christ

Micca Campbell

*Jesus said to him, "'You shall love the L*ORD *your God
with all your heart, with all your soul, and with all your mind.'
This is the first and great commandment. And the second is
like it: 'You shall love your neighbor as yourself.'"*

MATTHEW 22:37-39 NKJV

Someone said that the Bible can be summarized in two statements: "Love God" and "Love others." Jesus is teaching us that people, and caring for them, is what's truly important in life. In fact, showing kindness and caring for others is an act of worship.

Have you ever considered loving your neighbor an act of worship? Perhaps you pick up your neighbor's mail, water their flowers, feed their pet, or mow their yard while they're away. That's all good, but how well do you love the neighbor on the outskirts of town, the person you meet in the grocery store, or the beggar on the side of the street? We don't often think of these people as our neighbors, which conveniently frees us from responsibility...or does it?

I heard a story about a man who was a great admirer of Mother Teresa. While visiting in her area, the man had high hopes of meeting her. Time and again he would visit the places where she often ministered to people, but he never saw her.

One day, while worshipping in the local church, the man found himself in the presence of Mother Teresa, who was attending services as well. He could hardly believe it! He excitedly began pointing and whispering about Mother Teresa to those around him. Quietly, she stepped out of her pew and escorted the man outside into the poverty-stricken streets.

Without saying a word, she led the man to an alley where the walls were lined with old boxes, junk, and smelly trash. She told the man to push aside the rubble. Obeying her command, he began to remove the fragments of garbage one piece at a time. To his surprise, he found a naked, frail old man lying under the rubbish. He stood speechless as Mother Teresa proclaimed five of the most powerful words he had ever heard...

"Behold the body of Christ."

In one short sentence, Mother Teresa echoed the words of Christ spoken long ago, and yet still relevant today.

> "For I was hungry and you gave Me food; I was thirsty and you gave Me drink; I was a stranger and you took Me in; I was naked and you clothed Me; I was sick and you visited Me; I was in prison and you came to Me." Then the righteous will answer Him, saying, "Lord, when did we see You hungry and feed You, or thirsty and give You drink? When did we see You a stranger and take You in, or naked and clothe You? Or when did we see You sick, or in prison, and come to You?" And the King will answer and say to them, "Assuredly, I say to you, inasmuch as you did it to one of the least of these My brethren, you did it to Me" (Matthew 25:35-40 NKJV).

Loving others is how we love and worship our God, who is the author, creator, and meaning of true worship. The next time you see a person in need, don't shrug it off. Instead, behold the body of Christ.

Dear Lord, help me to be a blessing to someone today. In Jesus' name. Amen.

Application Steps

Ask God to show you a neighbor in need. Then, meet their need.

106 Specks
Susanne Scheppmann

One thing I do know. I was blind but now I see!
John 9:25

Recently, I decided to wear a contact lens for my left eye. Just one. I needed it to enhance my close-up vision. I grew tired of scrambling to find my reading glasses, so I decided that a mono-vision contact was the answer to my problem.

Although now I can read without glasses, I have developed a new set of problems. For example, if my eye becomes too dry, the plastic lens glues itself to my cornea. A couple of months ago this occurred when I was staying at a hotel. After sitting through several conference meetings, the air-conditioned rooms seemed to zap the moisture from my eye. By the time evening came, my contact lens had affixed itself to my eyeball. No amount of wetting solution seemed to be able to release me from my predicament. Finally, after prayer and panic, it loosened enough for me to peel it off.

Undeterred, I persevered with my new vision adventure. Next, a fleck of lint flew past my lashes to crash land on the runway of plastic in my eye. Blinding pain flashed in my head. I felt like screaming, "Once I could see. Now I am blind!" I poured an entire bottle of eye drops into my eye attempting to wash away the speck.

This episode of momentary blindness gave me an appreciation, not only for the physical sense of sight, but spiritual sight as well. Many times spiritual blindness plagues us and we are not even aware of it.

Jesus specialized in healing the blind, both kinds—spiritual and physical. In John 9, Jesus gives sight to a man born blind. When questioned about the physical healing the man replied, "One thing I do know. I was blind but now I see!"

Isn't that amazing? But it gets better. Let's look at his new *spiritual* eyesight. Verses 35-38 reveal the rest of the story. "Jesus heard that they had thrown him out, and when he found him, he said, 'Do you believe in the Son of Man?' 'Who is he, sir?' the man asked. 'Tell me so that I may believe in him.' Jesus said, 'You have now seen him; in fact, he is the one speaking with you.' Then the man said, 'Lord, I believe,' and he worshiped him." This man saw Jesus and chose to believe in Him.

Jesus came to relieve us all from spiritual darkness. He said, "I am the light of the world. Whoever follows me will never walk in darkness, but will have the light of life," and "I have come into the world as a light, so that no one who believes in me should stay in darkness" (John 8:12; 12:46).

Although my physical vision needs assistance, I possess spiritual vision because of Jesus.

I'm going to continue to wear my contact lens because the benefits outweigh the hazards. Specks that blow into my eye do give me temporary physical darkness, but I am grateful nothing can remove the light of Jesus from my soul. Because I know Him as my God, I shout, "Once I was blind, but now I see!"

Dear Lord, thank You for spiritual light. I am grateful for Your forgiveness. In Jesus' name. Amen.

Application Steps

Read John 9. Underline the word "blind." Circle the words "sin" or "sinner." Rewrite this into a short story. If you know a youngster, tell them your simplified version of Jesus giving sight to the blind.

107 Toppled by the Pressure

Zoë Elmore

I pray that out of his glorious riches he may strengthen
you with power through his Spirit in your inner being,
so that Christ may dwell in your hearts through faith.
And I pray that you, being rooted and established in love,
may have power, together with all the saints, to grasp how
wide and long and high and deep is the love of Christ.

Ephesians 3:16-18

Several years ago our two sons encouraged me to give their new Rollerblades a spin. Now, I'm not the most coordinated person, so I try to avoid situations that would showcase my lack of athletic ability, especially in front of all the neighborhood children. Reluctantly I strapped on the Rollerblades and headed down the street. I successfully navigated my way for a short distance, bobbled a turn, and headed for home. I slowed myself down and reached for the mailbox to complete my stop; however, things went from bad to worse in an instant. I remember my feet going out from under me and the Rollerblades flying over my head. The next thing I knew, I was on the ground and the mailbox with its wooden post was lying on the ground beside me. As I looked up, my husband, sons, and all those neighborhood children were standing there with opened mouths wondering how I could possibly uproot the entire mailbox and its post.

I know you're thinking that I must be the new "Wonder Woman," so let me put your mind and imagination to rest. There is a simple explanation to the toppling incident. The base of the wooden post buried in the ground was completely rotten. Until this incident, there was never any indication that anything was wrong with the wooden post. The mailbox worked perfectly every day without even a wobble, and the flowers planted at the base of the post were as beautiful as ever. Yet the base of the post hidden from sight was so compromised by neglect that only a little pressure was needed to uproot the entire thing.

As you and I continue to feed and nurture our spirit by reading the Bible and spending time in prayer each day, we keep our spirit strong and steady, ready to withstand the pressures of life. Perhaps you're like me and experiencing many different pressures at the same time—one right after the other, they press in on every side.

I daily seek to keep my spiritual life strong and steady; now is not the time to become neglectful and allow it to become weak and wobbly. Neglect would only ensure that sooner or later, I'll be toppled by the pressure. I've been there before, just like my mailbox. So let me encourage you to keep the foundation of your spiritual life strong, especially when the pressure is on.

Dear Lord, I'm so thankful You are always strong and steady. When the pressures of this life bear down on me, You are there to offer me comfort and stability. Help me to rely on Your strength as I move forward in faith. In Jesus' name. Amen.

Application Steps

What are the obstacles keeping you from a strong and steady spiritual life? What can you do to make certain you're not toppled by everyday pressures?

108 You Deplete Me
Luann Prater

A quarrelsome wife is like a constant dripping on a rainy day; restraining her is like restraining the wind or grasping oil with the hand.

PROVERBS 27:15

A quarrelsome spouse can quickly turn the familiar words "You complete me" to "You deplete me."

Water torture…it's when you are restrained, lying face up, with water hitting you on the forehead between the eyes one drip at a time. Its been known to drive people crazy. The craving for it to stop is maddening.

For 30 years I've been observing, operating, and owning businesses. For seven years in the '80s I owned a salon where six styling chairs were occupied with cackling women. The clatter would roll like a wave, first the low rumble of chitchat, building with the latest gossip, and finally the uproar of laughter filled the room. Often the familiar refrain centered on the grumblings and shortcomings of their spouses. It was not uncommon to hear, "He came home from his business trip and I just let him have it." Quickly the other women would chime in with similar stories until the shop noise escalated to a crescendo of negative emotion.

In the past two decades my business ventures have taken me into industries that are predominantly male. It has been interesting to hear "the rest of the story" from the men's point of view. They are often required to be at the beck and call of not only the boss, but the customer as well. The mental and emotional drain of being "on" all week has wiped them out. Bombarded with compliments, complaints, and temptations at every turn, their emotional, mental, and spiritual tanks may be empty.

They look forward to coming home. At one point in their life they courted you, they longed for you, and they married you. Now they work for you. They go out, kill the buffalo, and drag it home for the family to eat…or at least that is the way they feel after a grueling week at work. However, they still envision their princess waiting for them with a warm smile, a gentle hug, and an affectionate kiss.

The homecoming greeting for the weary warrior is more often a snippy remark, a screaming child, and a frozen bed. Immediately he wants to turn and run back to the wilderness where at least he felt he had a fighting chance.

Are you practicing water torture on your spouse? Are you killing your marriage one nagging drop at a time? Marriages don't fail overnight; it takes months, sometimes years, of maddening quarrels to snap the final thread of sanity.

It's a choice. Choose today to be the towel that wipes the sweat from your weary warrior's brow, not the drip that drives him mad.

Dear Lord, I praise You for giving us Your words of wisdom. Teach me how to be a wife who encourages and not discourages, who hugs and not harms, who lifts and not drips quarrels onto my husband's heart. In Jesus' name. Amen.

Application Steps

Pray today and ask God to make you aware each time you are dripping on your loved ones. Read 1 Peter 4:7-11. Refrain today from saying anything that could cause a quarrel.

109 Right or Left Thinking

Marybeth Whalen

Be careful to do what the LORD your God has commanded you; do not turn aside to the right or to the left. Walk in all the way that the LORD your God has commanded you, so that you may live and prosper and prolong your days in the land that you will possess.

DEUTERONOMY 5:32-33

God has recently shown me the importance of walking in the way He has commanded me without looking around to see what others are doing or seeking their approval. How easy it is to get sidetracked when we take our eyes off what He has asked of us. Like a horse with blinders on, we should be focusing straight ahead and not looking to the right or to the left. This is easier said than done.

I know I can get sidetracked very easily. I look at my friend's unique calling and think, *Maybe I should be doing what she is doing.* Or I look at a family in church that seems to have it all together and think, *God, I could handle their life so much better than my own.* I call this "right or left thinking." I look to my right and think—maybe I should be serving more in the church like her. Or I look to my left and think—how nice it would be to have the financial resources to give the way they do. The problem with looking to the right or to the left is that, when I do, I am taking my focus off the "one thing [that] is needed" (Luke 10:42). I am not centering my gaze on Him.

God has called me according to His unique design for me. I have learned to not feel obligated to fulfill a calling that is not my own or feel inferior for having a calling I might see as less important. God has designed the body to work together, incorporating each individual calling for His glory. Because I cannot see His master plan, I must trust that my calling is part of His greater purpose and walk in that trust.

May I challenge you today to embrace your calling wherever God has you? Thank Him today for His plan for you and His calling on your life for such a time as this. Most importantly, I urge you to seek God's will—His good, pleasing, and perfect will (Romans 12:2)—for your life and then keep your focus on Him as you walk in that will, looking neither to the right nor to the left in the days to come.

Dear Lord, help me to focus on You as I carry out Your tasks for me—whatever they may be—each and every day. Help me not to become distracted by what others are doing and to not look to the right or to the left. Lord, please keep my gaze fixed on You. In Jesus' name. Amen.

Application Steps

What is your calling in life? If you do not know what your calling is, spend time praying, reading Scripture, and asking God to reveal it to you. Try taking a spiritual gifts questionnaire. If God has you in a season of a certain calling (for example, mothering small children), also journal about any callings you feel He might be preparing you for in the future.

110 For Those Who Love Him
Glynnis Whitwer

We know that in all things God works for the good of those who love him, who have been called according to his purpose.
Romans 8:28

When we moved to Charlotte, we purchased our house the first weekend it was on the market. I wrongly assumed it would sell just as quickly.

With its dark green-and-gold entrance, cranberry-colored family room, and dark blue master bedroom, I was sure it would appeal to someone else who loved vibrant colors. In spite of our Realtor's advice to paint everything white, we put it on the market in its colorful glory.

Weeks turned into months. My husband moved to start his new job, while I tried to keep the house ready to show with three small boys running around.

I focused a lot on prayer and praise during that time. Although I trusted God had a plan, my prayers turned to pleading for a buyer. Finally, God brought a young Christian family into our lives. They had just moved to the area and wanted to purchase a home, but they couldn't qualify for a loan yet. Plus, they loved the house just as it was. We arranged for a lease with a purchase option and praised God for answering our prayers.

Little did we know that within six months our renters would experience a devastating miscarriage with no health insurance. Their finances were in ruins, and they returned to their family in Florida, leaving us again with a rainbow-painted house to sell. Only this time we were 2000 miles away.

Even though I could see God's care, I still wondered why He allowed us to go through that cumbersome experience. So I searched for the "good" mentioned in Romans 8:28. Besides helping us to trust God more and developing our character, I learned something new.

When you tell God He can use you, prepare to be inconvenienced for someone else's good! Not only was God working out the situation for our good, but I believe He was working it out for our renters' good as well. That little family of believers needed a home for that time. And when they lost the baby and needed to move near family, they benefited from a landlord who wouldn't sue them for the broken contract.

Perhaps God wants to help one of His children and writes a willing, yet unknowing, servant into the story to do it. When we consider the model of Jesus, sacrificing His own life for our good, I believe we see God's character revealed. While God could accomplish His purpose without us, He chooses to use us. That includes a sacrifice on our part to bring good into another's life.

The next time you can't see the obvious good in a situation, or God's purpose, consider if He's using you to bring good into someone else's life. Always trust that He will bring good to you as well in due time. When considered in this eternal light, it makes our light and momentary troubles worth it all.

By the way, we had the house painted white, and it sold within two weeks.

Dear Lord, You are perfect in all ways. Your plans and timing are perfect. Help me to trust in Your goodness to those who love You, even when I don't understand why I'm experiencing a trial. In Jesus' name. Amen.

Application Steps

Identify a recent personal challenge. List the good that God brought out of it for you. If another person benefited, thank Him for how that person was blessed.

111 I Don't Want to Tell You

Rachel Olsen

If we confess our sins to him, he is faithful and just to forgive us and cleanse us from every wrong.

1 JOHN 1:9 NLT

I walked into the kitchen to find my almost-three-year-old covered in peanut butter and jelly. The two sides of his lunch sandwich had been pulled apart without as much as one bite eaten. On one piece of bread a smiley face had been finger-painted into the peanut butter. Jelly had been thoroughly licked off the other slice. Looking at the telltale mess on the table and his face, I asked him calmly, "Caleb, what are you doing?" Knowing our house rule against playing with food, he answered, "I don't want to tell you." I am hearing this line a lot from him lately. Though he is caught red-handed, when confronted with his crimes my young son will respond with, "I don't want to tell you!" More often than not he is crying as he blurts this out.

Just a few months back I marveled at his willingness to confess to me anything and everything he did wrong. Oftentimes he volunteered the information before I even knew a transgression had been committed. A few times he bypassed me altogether, putting himself in time-out. When I found him there he would say, "Forgive me, Mommy." I assumed I was doing a fabulous job of instilling morals. However, as he approached the ripe old age of three, he suddenly found it hard to admit his wrongs and ask forgiveness.

He knows I always find the broken pieces of his latest mishap stashed behind the fridge. He knows his big sister eagerly gives me a full account of his wayward actions. He will also tell you that his mommy loves him even when he does something wrong. Still, he will not willingly confess his sins. He does not plead innocent of the crime. He does not plead ignorant of the crime. He simply does not want to talk about it. I can relate to that.

Many Christians, including yours truly, struggle with admitting sins. We know our heavenly Parent sees all, yet we act as if we can hide our sins from Him. We know He loves us with an everlasting love, yet we choose to believe He could never forgive us. We simply don't want to talk about it, preferring to ignore our sins. In Psalm 32 King David indicates that ignoring our sins is detrimental to our health and vitality and attests to the liberating power of confession:

> When I refused to confess my sin, I was weak and miserable, and I groaned all day long. Day and night your hand of discipline was heavy on me. My strength evaporated like water in the summer heat. Finally, I confessed all my sins to you and stopped trying to hide them. I said to myself, "I will confess my rebellion to the LORD." And you forgave me! All my guilt is gone. Yes, what joy for those whose record the LORD has cleared of sin, whose lives are lived in complete honesty! (Psalm 32:2-5 NLT).

I wanted to forgive Caleb for playing with his food and get on with the process of cleaning the peanut butter from his face so he could get down and play. My only requirement was that he confess and apologize first. God too wants to forgive our sins, so much so that he gave His only begotten Son, Jesus, to do it. No sin is too big or too small to confess to Him. Confession can be a joyous experience that restores intimacy with God and others. Regular confession releases us to spiritual vitality. So let's declare with David: "I will confess my rebellion to the Lord!" Our God is faithful and just to forgive us our sins and cleanse us from every wrong.

Dear Lord, thank You for dying for every single sin I commit. Purify me from my sin and release me from my guilt. Hear my confession and restore to me health and spiritual vitality. In Jesus' name. Amen.

Application Steps

In prayer ask God to reveal to you any unconfessed sin. Wait patiently for His full response. Accept responsibility for these sins, big or small, and then release them under the cleansing blood of the cross.

112 Summer Vacations

Sharon Glasgow

He answered and said "'You shall love the LORD your God with all your heart, with all your soul, with all your strength, and with all your mind,' and 'your neighbor as yourself.'"

LUKE 10:27 NKJV

My favorite childhood vacations were trips to our relatives, the Caleys. They lived in Indiana. We lived in Virginia, so the trip was long, but well worth every second of traveling. The legacy I gleaned from this family has made an eternal difference in my life.

We didn't have enough money to travel, so my uncle would always send money for the gas, food, and a motel. He was a farmer and schoolteacher, so he didn't have a lot of money, but he sacrificed his needs for ours for the sake of our families spending time together.

Before we could even get out of the station wagon, everybody was in the car hugging and crying. Uncle Bob was the first to start the sobbing, and then we all followed his lead. He squeezed us all as if he'd never seen us before, and then he would pull out his handkerchief, wipe his face, and tell us to shape up and get in the house for dinner!

It was a modest farmhouse with three small bedrooms, a bathroom, and no air-conditioning. The kitchen was small, but despite its size, Aunt Gaye-Lynn knew how to turn out a feast that could have served an army. The smells and sight of food overflowing in bountiful portions was not only a feast for the stomach but also our tender hearts.

Who could sleep on those first nights? In the hot attic bedroom, all of us cousins squished together like sardines, giggling and talking for hours. Daybreak brought bean picking and stringing. While we were stringing those beans, I remember overhearing Aunt Gaye and my mom talking about us kids with pride and thinking, *One day I want to be just like them.*

What made Uncle Bob remarkable was that he was a former in-law. He'd married my mother's sister, but she died after their four children were born. He then married Gaye. He wanted his children to keep their ties to our family, so he did everything in his power to keep relations and traditions with us flourishing.

He taught me unconditional love. We had nothing to offer him, but he treated us as if we were royalty. He used what little money he had to give us summer vacations while forfeiting his own needs. He taught me about family priorities and how important traditions are within the family. Today he still lives out his love for Christ. You can see by the way he lives that he loves God with all of his heart, with all of his soul, with all of his strength, with all of his mind, and he faithfully and passionately loves others as himself.

Summer vacations in Indiana were not only memorable, they also created indelible legacies. What kind of family legacy are you creating by the way you live?

Dear Lord, help me to live out the greatest commandment, to love You with all my heart, soul, strength, and mind, and love others as myself. Help me to see through Your eyes the needs of my family and to follow through on what You reveal to me. In Jesus' name. Amen.

Application Steps

Love God with all your heart, soul, strength, and mind. When you do this His attributes become yours. He will give you His ability to love people despite their flaws or frailties.

113 His Banner over Me

Lysa TerKeurst

*When the Holy Spirit controls our lives, he will produce
this kind of fruit in us: love, joy, peace, patience, kindness,
goodness, faithfulness, gentleness, and self-control.*
GALATIANS 5:22-23 NLT

I had just settled into my seat when I noticed a nice-looking young
woman boarding the plane. She was tall and slender with a pleasant
smile. Wearing jeans and a casual top, nothing particularly made this
girl stand out until she got close enough for me to notice the pageant
banner draped across her shoulder. "Miss USA" it read in sparkly
letters.

My first thought was, "How cool...a real Miss USA." Visions of
me and my sisters as little girls glued to the television danced through
my mind. We would all pick a favorite, root for her the whole pageant
through, and giggle and prance about as if we were being crowned.

As others noticed Miss USA's banner they started asking her questions and congratulating her. The flight attendant even made an
announcement that a celebrity passenger had just joined us. As she told
everyone about Miss USA, the other passengers clapped and cheered
for her. She took it all in stride and even seemed a bit bashful about
the attention. That impressed me more than her title. A gentle, humble
spirit in the face of such notoriety is something to be admired.

After all the fuss over Miss USA settled down, I started thinking
about the banners we all wear every day. While they may not drape
across our chest and be printed in bold letters that sparkle, we all say
something about who we are just in our countenance and interactions with others. Galatians 5:22-23 describes for us what our banner
should read: love, joy, peace, patience, kindness, goodness, gentleness,
faithfulness, and self-control. The Bible calls these fruits of the Spirit,

which means they're evidence to others that we are a Christian. While others may not applaud us as a celebrity, they will notice the difference it makes to have God's Spirit in us if these fruits characterize our interactions with them.

It's important to understand that exemplifying these fruits is a choice we must make every day. Just as Miss USA must intentionally put her banner on, so must we. We must make the choice moment by moment, interaction by interaction, word by word, step by step, day by day. When I let another driver over into my lane in traffic, when I smile and thank the grocery store clerk, when I let someone go ahead of me in the coffeehouse line, when I give a gracious answer to someone being harsh with me, when I hold the door for an elderly person, or when I carry the groceries of an overwhelmed mom to her car, I am intentionally choosing to exemplify Christ.

While the world may never applaud or crown me with glory, I imagine Jesus beaming and maybe even applauding.

Dear Lord, may the evidence of my love for You be the banner I put on each day. Not so that I may draw attention to myself, but rather to cause other people to want to know what makes me different. I love You, Jesus, and I want to tell the whole world about You, using words only if necessary. In Jesus' name. Amen.

Application Steps

Look for a way to show Jesus to those you come in contact with today. Think about the fruits listed in our verse for today, and let them characterize your interactions with others.

114 In the Shadow

Wendy Pope

HE WHO dwells in the secret place of the Most High shall remain stable and fixed under the shadow of the Almighty [Whose power no foe can withstand].

PSALM 91:1 AMP

I love the way the Lord chooses to illustrate the promises of His Word in my life. When we open our spiritual eyes and ears, God speaks. He speaks very clearly in ways we can understand. Jesus said in John 5:17, "My Father is always at his work to this very day, and I, too, am working." Since Jesus tells us His Father is always working, we must believe it to be true and expect to see His work all around us.

My daughter is not the most athletic young woman in the world. She excels in academics, but when it comes to outside sports, she struggles. We recently installed a basketball hoop. Right away my son, who is almost three years younger than his sister, took to basketball like a fish to water. His success intimidated my daughter to the point where she stopped trying.

One sunny afternoon while my son and I played ball, my daughter decided to join us. She attempted several times to make a basket but missed. With each attempt she became more frustrated. I demonstrated the "granny shot." My demonstration shot went in the basket. With a strong desire to make the shot, my sweet daughter aligned herself within my shadow. She took a deep breath, aimed, and scored. We gave each other a high five and did a victory dance. She was ready to shoot again. She knew exactly where to stand to be successful—in my shadow.

As I stood there, watching her carefully align herself in my shadow again, I heard the sweet voice of my Holy Reminder, "He who dwells in the shelter of the Most High will rest in the shadow of the Almighty."

Right before my eyes and with a whisper in my ear, God made Himself real to me.

Today's verse is taken from the Amplified Bible, and I love the words "remain stable and fixed." I also love the notion of a "secret place," which suggests that only you and the Father know what's there. The original Hebrew describes this shelter as a place of protection. The author of this psalm uses the word "dwells," which means "to inhabit or to be settled." I can almost visualize each of you curling up in this place of secrecy and protection. You go there to find rest and to gain strength and confidence to make the "goal" you are attempting. Bless you today, dear friend, and rest in His perfect shelter of secrecy. Then stand up in faith, align yourself within His shadow, and He will give you success.

Dear Lord, You are indeed God Almighty. You know Your children need a place of rest and protection and have most graciously provided a place in Your shadow. Help me today to make the choice to align myself in Your shadow and not in what the world offers. In Jesus' name. Amen.

Application Steps

Write down several things you are attempting. Pray and determine if these are things God desires for you to do. On the same piece of paper, write today's verse. Memorize this verse. Each time you feel anxious about what you are attempting, recite the verse out loud.

115 Got Rain?

Van Walton

Disaster strikes like a cyclone...but the godly have a lasting foundation.

PROVERBS 10:25 NLT

■ The southwest United States boasts fantastic terrain. Recently, while visiting the desert and driving through the barren yet colorful land, I was reminded that all sunshine with no rain results in a wasteland. Life void of clouds, rain, and yes, even storms, becomes dry.

All the locals agreed that rain was desperately needed. Clouds were a welcome sight. A good old-fashioned gulley washer would be greeted with great joy, for it would bring much needed moisture to trickling streams, dry yards, and withering crops. Everyone was praying for rain.

I began to wonder if there are times in my life when I need to be open to, and even welcome, an emotional storm or two. Could I learn to live anticipating the challenging clouds of life's storms, instead of living in fear and dread of the next tempest? Can I accept that every season of life has its storms? Do I understand that where it doesn't rain, there is no growth? And where there is no moisture, there is no maturing?

I praise God for trial-free days, and thank Him for all my blessings. But, as I consider a cushy life, I can't help but accept the truth that the strength and confidence I have is a result of the emotional and spiritual storms that threatened to drown me.

I also recognize that I take my prayer requests, deep troubles, and challenging trials to those whose lives have been freshened by the downpours of life. These are the friends whose wells are full of sweet and living springs. Their lives run deep because of the rain that has fallen on their parades. I run to my girlfriends whose experience with life's trials has turned them into inviting oases offering real comfort and spiritual refreshment.

I need spiritual rain in order to survive. Downpours bring springs of living water, a necessary ingredient for an abundant and purposeful life. Storms develop strength, confidence, and faith, important traits for spiritual overcomers. Floods create perseverance and trust, two qualities that reflect Christ.

Instead of dreading the gathering clouds of crises or disaster, I hope to stand strong with my face to the wind. With deep confidence and open arms I want to welcome the storms of life that will certainly come and go. I know they bring their own rewards: the fresh scent of rain on the grass, the shimmering clean leaves on the tree, and the babbling water in the brook.

The next time I'm cowardly contemplating an escape route, I want, with God's help, to be able to step confidently into the downpour. I hope to be found dancing in the storm.

Dear Lord, help me appreciate the storms in my life. You don't mean them for destruction. You allow them for development. Teach me to desire the tests instead of forever living in dread of the trouble. In Jesus' name. Amen.

Application Steps

Read about Paul's trials in 2 Corinthians 11:16-31. The storms he experienced at sea obviously developed his character.

116 My Image of God
Renee Swope

The Son is the radiance of God's glory and the exact representation of his being.
HEBREWS 1:3

I love taking pictures. The funny thing is I don't always like seeing the images after they're developed. I always pitch the ones that aren't good. I'm especially quick to get rid of those where eyes are half-closed or a mouth is crooked. And you can just forget about the ones where the camera adds ten pounds. These are not the images I want in my photo album or hanging on my refrigerator.

I was editing digital photos and began to wonder if God sees the way I picture Him and wants to edit or delete a few of my images. There have been many times when my image of God didn't accurately portray who He is—times when my image of God conjured feelings of fear and condemnation instead of protection and assurance.

My childhood experiences shaped my earliest images of God. Growing up, we went to church on and off, but God wasn't talked about at home. He seemed distant and unapproachable. I thought if I wanted to talk to Him I needed to go to someone who knew Him a little better, like a church leader. We had religion, but not really a relationship with God.

I remember wanting to please God so He wouldn't get mad at me. This was the same reason I performed well at school and at home—so people wouldn't reject me. I feared punishment and wondered what I could do to make God happy.

I also thought God expressed love the same way my father did. My dad showed love by taking me shopping and giving me hugs. If God brought good things in my life, such as recognition at school or tangible blessings like a trophy for cheerleading, I felt His love. When life was hard and I was lonely, I wondered where God was and what I had done wrong.

I basically saw God on the sidelines of life keeping score. I had created Him in my image, and some photos needed restoration. A few images even needed to be deleted permanently.

If God were looking at your images of Him, would He want them hanging on your refrigerator for friends and family to see? Today's verse tells us, "The Son is the radiance of God's glory and the exact representation of his being."

I've found this verse to be powerfully true. The more I get to know Jesus by spending time with Him, the more I know the heart of God and the truth about His heart toward me. If you really want to get to know God—if you really want to know what He looks like—spend time with Jesus, His Son. Everything about them is exactly the same.

Dear Lord, I want to know You. Please look at my images of You and show me which ones are distorted. Help me get to know Jesus better so I can know Your heart and the truth about Your heart toward me. In Jesus' name. Amen.

Application Steps

Close your eyes and think about God. Journal what you see and feel about Him. Is He approachable and loving, or distant and demanding? Do you run to Him when you're hurting or wait until you're composed to approach His throne? Read the Gospel of John, (re)defining your image of God through portraits of Jesus.

117 Hearing the Coach's Voice

Melissa Taylor

*Come here and listen to me! I'll pour out the
spirit of wisdom upon you and make you wise.*

PROVERBS 1:23 NLT

I was recently attending my son Hayden's soccer game. He liked to
play offense in hopes of scoring a goal, but on this day his coach had
him on defense. The coach knew that even though Hayden was good
at playing offense, he was better at defense. The game was close and
our team was down by one.

Everyone was excited and the parents were very vocal. I noticed the
coach shouting to Hayden, "Back up and play your position." Another
adult shouted, "Kick the ball and follow through." Another said, "Come
on, number nine. Chase that ball and go for the goal!" The coach said,
"Come on, Hayden! Listen to me!" I saw a look of frustration on my
son's face. When the game ended, I asked Hayden what was wrong.
He said, "Mom, I couldn't figure out who to listen to! I couldn't tell
which one was the coach's voice."

I explained to my son that in order to discern the coach's voice, he
needed to stop and look at his coach. He had to listen to that voice
only and learn it so he could always recognize it. The others meant
well, but it was his coach who he needed to listen to and obey. Then
he would be a wiser and better player.

I am also guilty of not listening to my Coach's voice. In the book
of Proverbs, we are told to "come here and listen to me! I'll pour out
the spirit of wisdom upon you and make you wise." So often I get
busy...too busy to stop and "come here and listen" to the voice of my
Coach. Just like Hayden, when I don't slow down and focus, I hear a
lot of voices. Friends, family, books, TV, and others that mean well can
never take the place of God. The Bible says we must listen *very carefully*

to the truth we have heard, or we may drift away from it (Hebrews 2:1). In order to listen very carefully, I must silence everything around me. Then I can determine the voice of my Coach.

This situation proved to be an important lesson for Hayden and me. I shared with him what I had learned too. I confessed that I had been too busy. God was calling me to slow down so that I could hear His voice. The next step was for me to show what I had learned by actually obeying God. I needed to guard my quiet time with Him, read my Bible, and be still enough to hear what He had to say. I had to listen, learn, and obey.

Hayden's soccer coach called him to listen, learn, and obey. As a mom, I call my kids to do this. God is calling us to do this too. It begins by discerning the Coach's voice. As we do, we'll learn who He is and what He is saying so we can obey. "Come here and listen to me! I'll pour out my spirit of wisdom upon you and make you wise."

Dear Lord, slow me down when I get too busy to hear Your voice. Help me to listen, learn, and obey Your Word. In Jesus' name. Amen.

Application Steps

Spend some quiet time with God daily. Take time to be still so you can hear His voice. Then take the time to share with your children what God is doing in your life.

118 False Advertising

Susanne Scheppmann

When Jesus saw Nathanael approaching,
he said of him, "Here is a true Israelite,
in whom there is nothing false."

JOHN 1:47

A small car sped along side my van. Hundreds of money-green dollar signs were painted across the car's white exterior. I noticed the name of a local bank displayed prominently between the dollar insignias. What a clever way to advertise, I thought.

As I slowed to a stop at a red light, I spied very small black writing on the car. The fine print read, "Warning: This car carries no money, only documents." The thought struck me, *With all those dollars signs everywhere, I think that might be classified as false advertising.* The promise of money was on the outside, but it held no reality on the inside.

This made me reflect on my own life. How often do I display false advertising to those around me? Let me reveal three of my most common fraudulent appearances:

1. I argue with my husband all the way to church. Then as my car door opens to our church friends, I paste a big toothy smile on my face. My grin implies, "My marriage is perfect."

2. I bump into an acquaintance at the grocery store. I ask, "How are you?" (I really don't care and just want to get on with my day.) My pretense of being a caring friend falls flat when I glance at my watch as she begins to tell me her woes.

3. I recite Scripture, attend a Bible study, and exhibit the outward behavior of a model Christian woman.

However, on the inside I detect ungodly attitudes that mock me when I look in the mirror.

I know this isn't how Christ wants me to function. He desires authenticity in every area of my life. Although I know I will never be perfect this side of heaven, I do want to rid myself of false advertising. I long for an inward attitude that matches my outward sponsorship of the Christian life.

The following verse reminds me to sweep clean my life of falsity. "Clean house! Make a clean sweep of malice and pretense, envy and hurtful talk. You've had a taste of God. Now, like infants at the breast, drink deep of God's pure kindness. Then you'll grow up mature and whole in God" (1 Peter 2:1-3 MSG).

Each phrase of these verses motivates me. I need to examine myself for symptoms of malice, pretense, envy, and hurtful talk. I need to stay close to God and become a mature Christian in His eyes—and an authentic Christian in the eyes of others. I also want to see authenticity when I look in the mirror.

Let's take these verses to heart today. Let's wipe false advertising from our exteriors. Then Jesus will exclaim, "Look at her! There is nothing false about her!"

Dear Lord, I want to please You in all I say and do. Teach me to be authentic. Reveal to me where I rely on false advertising when I am around other people. Help me to be like Your friend Nathanael. In Jesus' name. Amen.

Application Steps

Write John 1:47 on an index card. Write your first name in the place of Nathanael and position the card on your mirror. You will have a daily reminder to rid yourself of any false advertising that you might be tempted to display. Ask God each morning for authenticity in your daily encounters with others.

119 Seeking Shade

Marybeth Whalen

The LORD watches over you—the LORD is your shade at your right hand; the sun will not harm you by day, nor the moon by night.

PSALM 121:5-6

You may be familiar with the story of Jonah running from God and then being swallowed by a great fish in the beginning of the book of Jonah, but have you ever paid attention to the ending of the book? After finally obeying God and preaching a message of repentance to the Ninevites, Jonah goes to see what will happen to Nineveh. Because he does not think Nineveh deserves God's mercy, he is hoping for the destruction of the city and wants a ringside seat.

Jonah 4:5 says, "Jonah went out and sat down at a place east of the city. There he *made himself a shelter,* sat in its shade and waited to see what would happen to the city" (emphasis added). He was clearly trying to rest, but he was resting under shade of his own creation. Jonah 4:6 says, "Then the LORD God provided a vine and made it grow up over Jonah to give shade for his head to ease his discomfort, and Jonah was very happy about the vine."

It was time for God to teach Jonah yet another lesson. In the very next verse, God sends a worm to kill the vine. The heat blazes down on Jonah because the vine is gone. The Scripture says that Jonah grew faint and wanted to die. This scene shows us that Jonah has not learned his lesson from his experience with the great fish and is quick to revert to his old ways. Instead of totally resting in God and God's plan, he wants things to be his way, and he tries to seek out his own resolutions.

I'm a lot like Jonah. I allow my limited view to taint the bigger picture that only God can see. I allow my negative feelings to sabotage the good works God has in store for me. Most of all, I let God down by building my own forms of shelter. My shelter might be material possessions, a well-appointed home, or money in the bank. I love the story of Jonah and the vine because it so clearly illustrates how foolhardy it is to rely on such things. God showed Jonah that He could provide a much better shelter. He also showed him how quickly He could remove that shelter when Jonah's heart was far from Him.

God wants to be our shelter—a place of rest and shade. He wants us to come to Him when we are hurting and pour out our feelings to Him. When we do this, He will provide a shelter from injustices, misunderstandings, and hurts. He will cause the resolution we seek to spring up overnight, just like the vine. May we all demolish the pitiful, substandard, human forms of shelter we have tried to erect, and find the real shade our souls are longing for by learning to totally rest in God.

Dear Lord, please help me to seek Your shelter when I am upset and not to rely on shelters of my own design. Please help me to wait on You "to grow up" the perfect place for me to rest. In Jesus' name. Amen.

Application Steps

Read the book of Jonah. Then write down any forms of shelter you have erected in your life that God is showing you today. Ask Him to help you tear those down and replace them with a shelter from Him. Thank Him for being a living, active God who is at work in your life each day.

120 Feeding Black Clouds
Rachel Olsen

Jesus said, "Don't let your hearts be troubled.
Trust in God and trust in me."
JOHN 14:1 NCV

Does your outlook sometimes grow gloomy? Ever feel like a little black cloud follows you around—hovering over you and blocking out your sunshine?

For Sarah, it literally did. Sarah is a school bus driver by trade. For 12 years she fed the crows that sometimes gathered in the bus parking lot where she worked. After more than a decade of feeding them, 30 to 40 crows follow her around everywhere she goes.

The school district warned Sarah to stop feeding the birds. While she ceased feeding them on school property, she continued to feed them elsewhere. Therefore, the cloud of black crows continually hovered over her and her bus—causing a spectacle, leaving a mess, and damaging the paint. Soon she was suspended from her bus driving job.

What strikes me in this true story—besides the mental picture of a yellow school bus going down the road swarming with black crows—is that Sarah continued feeding the birds that threatened her livelihood. Why would anyone keep encouraging the swarm despite the negative effects it brought?

Perhaps I shouldn't be so surprised. We all encourage our black clouds from time to time. We may have never fed crows, per se, but we've fed our own personal swarms of fear, pity, anxiety, or doubt. We've dwelled on the past. We've refused to forgive ourselves. We've been pessimistic. We've pushed the love or help of others away. We've refused to forgive someone. We've doubted God's ability to deliver us. In short, we've nourished our own black crows.

Have you been spending too much time "bird-watching" lately? If so, trade in your birdseed for the truth of Scripture. Let God's Word be your scarecrow:

- "Forget the former things; do not dwell on the past. See, I am doing a new thing! Now it springs up; do you not perceive it? I am making a way in the desert and streams in the wasteland" (Isaiah 43:18-19).
- "God is able to make all grace abound to you, so that in all things at all times, having all that you need, you will abound in every good work" (2 Corinthians 9:8).
- "Jesus said, 'Don't let your hearts be troubled. Trust in God, and trust in me'" (John 14:1 NCV).

As we read through Scripture, taking it into our heart with hopeful faith, the swarm will clear and we will again see the light of truth. Jesus is fully trustworthy and fully able to brighten our day.

Dear Lord, I regret feeding those joy-stealing, peace-robbing, light-blocking crows. I purpose to seek the hope that is found in You and Your Word. Help me to keep my spiritual skies sunny, despite my circumstances here on the ground, by keeping my focus on You. In Jesus' name. Amen.

Application Steps

Look around and see what crows you may be feeding with your attitude. Then look beyond the swarm to the Word of God to renew your mind. Read a little of the Bible each day.

121 A Father's Love

Micca Campbell

We love Him because He first loved us.

1 JOHN 4:19 NKJV

After my husband died, I knew that if I remarried, it would have to be someone special because I came with a three-year-old son. You might say it was a "buy one, get one free" kind of deal.

While not just anyone could be the recipient of such an exclusive package, I began asking God to protect me from the wrong person until the right person came along.

Quickly I knew there was something different about Pat. Whenever he invited me out, it was always a family affair. My son was included. Pat wanted to get to know us both. Right way, this caught my attention.

Eventually, we married. I had a new husband and my son had a new daddy. Still, I wondered. Since Pat was not Mitch's biological father, would their relationship develop like a father and son's should?

As I watched Pat parent Mitch, I realized that anyone can "father" a child, but a real daddy is one who's around to wipe the nose—and the other end too! A daddy is eager to play in the living room floor after a long, hard day at work. He's the guy who gives up his golfing hobby to coach little league baseball, and who carries the child to bed after he's fallen asleep. A true dad also cares enough to discipline his son.

I don't recall what Mitch did, but I do remember on this occasion his reaction to his dad's discipline was unlike anytime before.

"You're not my dad!" Mitch screamed with rage. "I hate you, I hate you!" he added between sobs.

I was shocked as I watched the two of them. I had never seen my son like that. He was completely out of control and overwhelmed with anger, fear, and pain.

Pat fell to his knees and embraced our son. Mitch fought back. Without letting go of him, Pat began to calm Mitch's worries.

"You can hate me if you want, but I will always love you," Pat said, struggling to keep his arms around Mitch as he tried to pull loose. "You're my son. I will never leave you."

Every word Pat whispered into Mitch's ear began to melt away his fears, and he returned his father's embrace. In that moment, Mitch began to believe in the love of his father. He not only accepted it; he loved Pat back. Not because he was someone to play with, or someone who filled a certain role in his life, but because he fully felt Pat's love.

Pat's enduring Godlike affections enabled Mitch to receive and return his love. Likewise, we love our heavenly Father *only* because He first loved us. Without the love of God being poured out upon us, we would never be devoted to God or others on our own. It's just not in us. For that reason, God doesn't wait on our affections. We love because we've first been loved.

Dear Lord, thank You for loving and accepting me just as I am. Fill my heart with Your love so that I may love You and others as You have loved me. In Jesus' name. Amen.

Applications Steps

Thank God for His love by finding a way to express your gratitude. You might do that through prayer, singing Him a song, writing a poem, or sharing His love with someone else.

122 Clothed in Prayer
Luann Prater

*She opens her arms to the poor and extends
her hands to the needy.*

PROVERBS 31:20

"I'll drive. You pray." These words, forever etched in my children's
memories, have roots in an average day of doing laundry. After washing,
drying, and folding, I discovered putting away was getting to be the
toughest job of all. I pushed and shoved the last sweatshirt into submission and forced the drawer shut. Whew! Finally, everything was
in its place.

As I plopped onto the couch to take a five-minute recess, I leafed
through the mail to find piles of advertisements reminding me Christmas
was just around the corner. Christmas—my favorite time of year. It
brings family together, cards from old friends, and gifts we don't need.
After spending the last several hours laundering our abundance, I realized my kids needed a lesson in giving this year, not receiving.

That afternoon, as my children gathered around the table for their
after-school snack, I threw out a radical idea—"This year let's ask God
to help us give." Puzzled faces told me I needed to explain. "Let's pray,"
I said, "and ask God to use our excess to help someone else. When
you are done with your snack, go to your room, put everything you
don't play with or wear into a trash bag, and bring it to the living
room." They all agreed to do so and ran off to complete the task. I
was amazed as the bundles poured into the room. Panting and puffing,
the four-year-old pulled the last bag to the end of the pile, making a
grand total of 15 bags.

We loaded up the van and I told them, "I'll drive. You pray and
ask God to lead us." Calmness fell as they bowed in prayer. In unison

they said, "Go straight. Turn right." This pattern continued until we were deep in the heart of the inner city.

Suddenly they shouted, "Stop! That's it back there!" A row of rundown duplex townhouses lined the street. I went to the door and knocked. Two women came out onto the porch. I shared that the children had been praying for God to lead us to someone who needed our extras. They both began to weep and then called into the house for the others to come to the door. Half-clothed children began to emerge with no shoes on their feet, no coats, no sweaters, and no pants. Only the thinnest garments covered their skinny little bodies. My children jumped from the van and formed an assembly line with the other children. They worked side by side to move the bags into the house. The women were praising and thanking God for answering prayers.

Prayer is the thread that weaves our lives into submission and joins us together in God's plan. I challenge you to teach the lesson of giving and allow God to create a tapestry of answered prayer in your world.

> *Dear Lord, people in our world are praying for something specific. Will You help us to find them and fill their needs? Allow us to reflect Your love. In Jesus' name. Amen.*

Application Steps

Pray for God to reveal a need. Discover who is sick, has lost a job, or needs something you can provide. Equip yourself and tend to their need. Go to them, tell them God sent you, meet the need, and leave.

123 Stumbling Blocks

Charlene Kidd

Don't condemn each other anymore. Decide instead to live in such a way that you will not put an obstacle in another Christian's path.

Romans 14:13 nlt

The truth of this verse got under my skin the other day. We had recently become friends with a new family. We had lots in common. The mother and I even began to watch each others' children, providing date opportunities with our husbands or an afternoon to catch up on chores. It was a great blessing.

Then some challenges arose. The children didn't always get along and soon accusations were flying. Things became tense, even hurtful. I knew I'd need to walk an uneasy road of forgiveness and perhaps take blame because of who I say I am (a follower of Christ). I was willing because I wanted to reflect Christ's willingness to turn the other cheek and forgive.

Things did not resolve as fast as I thought they should, and soon I found myself airing my frustrations with another neighbor. I fell into the snare of gossip. When I read today's verse from Romans 14:13, I realized by not giving the situation completely in prayer to God, but talking with another person about it, I could very easily be putting a stumbling block in another Christian's path.

Before I became a Christian, airing a frustration about someone with someone else would not have bothered me. Now, however, my spirit was unsettled; I knew it was wrong. First Peter 1:14-15 says: "Obey God because you are his children. Don't slip back into your old ways of doing evil; you didn't know any better then."

That night while I was reading the book *The Adventures of the Itty Bitty Spider and the Itty Bitty Mouse* to our three-year-old, I was struck by a statement: "We all do things that sometimes we should not do, but if we are wise enough to fix them, then we always shine through." I knew I had to confess to God and ask forgiveness of my neighbor. I did and now we are on a better path again. But I wonder how many other places I have put up stumbling blocks...blocking someone's good reputation, blocking someone's obedience to God, or blocking someone from seeing Christ in me. Have you been a stumbling block lately?

Dear Lord, I thank You for Your words of caution and correction. Help us to see ourselves clearly and repent so that we may not cause another believer to stumble. In Jesus' name. Amen.

Application Steps

Is there a relationship you are having struggles or frustrations with? If so, take an inventory of how you are handling it. Turn it over to God, and do not fall into the trap of either gossip or condemnation.

124 The Marks of Love

Glynnis Whitwer

See, I have engraved you on the palms of my hands.
Isaiah 49:16

As a sign of her undying love and faithfulness, a certain celebrity permanently tattooed the name of her beloved on her arm. This act of affection was "permanent"...until she and he broke up. Then the tattoo was removed and another's name was tattooed in its place. So much for everlasting love.

Unfaithfulness abounds. The world is littered with broken hearts and shattered dreams left in the wake of deceit and rejection. Selfishness defines our society, which counts relationships as an expendable part of life.

When someone we love turns away from us, we're left wondering how a love that seemed so true turned into such a lie. And how did we *not* see it coming? Rejection spawns a downward spiral into grief and despair that leads us to more lies telling us we are worthless and unlovable. It's a dangerous cycle in which many find themselves.

At the depth of our pain, in the darkest moment of the night, God speaks words of truth into our hearts: "Never will I leave you; never will I forsake you" (Hebrews 13:5).

Though others may forget their promises to us, God will not. To make sure we know He is serious, God made two eternally permanent marks of His faithful love. First, in Isaiah 49:16 God tells us, "See, I have engraved you on the palms of my hands."

We're not written in a black, semipermanent henna tattoo that wears off, or a "permanent" color tattoo that can be removed with lasers. God has *engraved* us on His palm. That's a mark that cannot be erased.

Then, God made His second mark of faithfulness with the blood of Jesus. Ephesians 2:13: "Now in Christ Jesus you who once were far away have been brought near through the blood of Christ." We are covered in this crimson blood that washes us white as snow. The cross is our reminder of that love.

Although people may fail you, God will not. You are cherished and loved by the Almighty God. Today He holds your sweet face in His hands, hands that are engraved with your name, and reminds you that He chose you and He will never turn away.

> *Dear Lord, You are faithful and true. Thank You for never changing and for loving me with an eternal love. Help me to love others with the same type of love. Forgive my selfishness and the times I have not modeled Your love. In Jesus' name. Amen.*

Application Steps

Think about someone who has lied to you. Now think about our God who never lies. Worship God for His faithfulness. Offer forgiveness to the one who has lied.

125 Dealing with the Yuckies

Lysa TerKeurst

Rejoice in the Lord always. I will say it again: Rejoice!
Let your gentleness be evident to all. The Lord is near.
Do not be anxious about anything, but in everything,
by prayer and petition, with thanksgiving,
present your requests to God. And the peace of God,
which transcends all understanding,
will guard your hearts and minds in Christ Jesus.
PHILIPPIANS 4:4-7

My youngest daughter, Brooke, had just been struck by what I call the "yuckies"—sick to her stomach and throwing up over and over again. Looking up at me she said, "Mommy, I've prayed God would make me stop throwing up, but He's not answering my prayer."

"Oh, sweetheart," I replied. "God wants all the yuckies to get out of your tummy so your body can be healthy again. He'll help you stop throwing up as soon as the yuckies are gone. Why don't we pray together right now?"

With her little raspy voice she said, "Lord, thank You for this most wonderful day. Please help me to stop being sick. But most of all, thank You for this most wonderful day."

I learned a valuable lesson from my six-year-old that day. In the middle of life's yuck, I want to still be able to see God's goodness and thank Him for each wonderful day. How often I get caught up in the emotional waves of life's ups and downs, losing sight of God's goodness. When this happens I cease operating in His peace. Today's verse outlines a few steps for walking in God's peace.

Rejoice. Verbalize God's goodness. In times of stress, we often verbalize our complaints, frustrations, and anxiety. If, however, I make the choice to rejoice in the Lord's ability to handle what I can't, I invite God's peace to invade that moment.

Be gentle. When we're gentle even when life is harsh, we show that God is real. People meet the reality of God in us when our spirit reflects His character rather than our natural reactions.

Remember that He is near. Do we really believe God is near? When I come to God, I declare that He has the ability to help me. Because I know He can help me in every situation, I don't have to be anxious about anything big or small.

Pray. The last half of today's verse says it all. Prayer is good. But prayer *with* thanksgiving is even more powerful. When we present our requests to God through thankful prayers, God's peace will fill us and protect us. It will guard us from allowing Satan to sweep us away in a sea of overwhelming discouragement because he is thwarted the minute we call on the power of the Lord.

> *Dear Lord, thank You for this most wonderful day. God, will You rid my heart of the yuckies of doubt, discouragement, and stress and help me be filled with You? But most of all thank You for this most wonderful day. In Jesus' name. Amen.*

Application Steps

1. Instead of verbalizing your frustrations, practice verbalizing pleasure about the blessings of God in your life.

2. In moments where harsh words seem to fit the scenario, practice the discipline of asking the Holy Spirit for His gentle touch so you can portray a gentle response.

3. Instead of becoming bitter because of unpleasant circumstances, press into Him, trusting that He is near, and ready to help you.

4. Press into God through prayer. Instead of getting stressed, let His peace sweep over you as you rejoice in all He is capable of doing.

126 Spring-Cleaning
Susanne Scheppmann

Jesus called the crowd to him and said,
"Listen to me, everyone, and understand this.
Nothing outside a man can make him 'unclean' by going into him.
Rather, it is what comes out of a man that makes him 'unclean.'"
MARK 7:14-15

Dust bunnies run under the bed. Spidery cobwebs dangle from the ceiling. Handprints point the way to the bedrooms. Filmy windows play hide-and-seek with the bright sunshine. It's time for spring-cleaning!

I begin to deep clean my home when the air warms and the sun shines brightly. I heave furniture so I can vacuum underneath it. I teeter on a ladder as I stretch to remove telltale signs of fall and winter from my home.

Spring-cleaning began thousands of years ago in the Middle East. It began when God issued the decree to the Hebrews to eat the Passover meal and celebrate it for generations to come. One of the requirements in commemorating Passover was to remove any type of yeast or leaven from their homes.

So what's the big deal with yeast? In the New Testament, we are told that yeast represents various types of sin. Many times Jesus warned His disciples, "Watch out for the yeast of the Pharisees." He didn't want the disciples to be influenced by the cold legalism of the religious teachers.

The apostle Paul elaborated on yeast a bit more. He wrote, "Get rid of the old yeast that you may be a new batch without yeast—as you really are. For Christ, our Passover lamb, has been sacrificed. Therefore let us keep the Festival, not with the old yeast, the yeast of malice and wickedness, but with bread without yeast, the bread of sincerity and truth" (1 Corinthians 5:7-8). Paul points out what our verse for today indicates. It's the junk inside of us that makes us unclean, not what's on the outside.

Even as I scrub my house, I consider spring-cleaning my soul. Should I remove a few sullied attitudes? Do I need to shine up my life with sincerity and truth?

Just as my home gathers dust, dirt, and smudges over time, so does my soul. I need to get the tarnish of yeasty sinful attitudes out and allow God to polish me to shine for His kingdom. Ephesians 5:26 tells me what type of cleanser to use: "Cleansing her by the washing with water through the word." The Word of God holds the power to wash us clean.

On that note, I think I will quit vacuuming the drapes. Spring-cleaning my soul sounds much more compelling. I am going to enjoy the warmth of this beautiful day. I'm off to the backyard with my Bible in hand to begin spring-cleaning myself from the inside out. How about you? Do you have a few cobwebs that need attention?

Dear Lord, I thank You for the power of Your Word. As I study its truth, reveal to me the attitudes, thoughts, and behaviors You desire to cleanse in me. Polish me to shine for Your kingdom. In Jesus' name. Amen.

Application Steps

Stroll through your house and decide what needs spring-cleaning. Closets? Drawers? Make a list of what you would like to accomplish in your home and tackle one project a week. Now take a spiritual inventory. What needs to be cleansed within you? Bitterness? Unforgiveness? Lack of love? Using your Bible's concordance look up verses to memorize that will aid in your spiritual spring-cleaning.

127 Believing Is Seeing

Micca Campbell

O Lord, open his eyes so he may see.
2 Kings 6:17

Discouragement is a normal emotion when we've experienced loss or when we are waiting on God to do something in our life. It may be that we are waiting on God to find our mate, begin a family, provide a job, cure an illness, or help us achieve a dream. Yet when we have unaccomplished goals or unfulfilled dreams due to circumstances beyond our control, it's easy to feel disappointed with God.

Waiting is the hard part. It's living in the unknown that we don't like. We wonder, *What is God up to? When is He going to do something? Does He hear my cries?* I can answer with a confident yes! God knows your pain, He hears your cry, and He is at work on your behalf whether or not you see Him working.

I have learned that while we are waiting, peace comes by trusting God. To help increase my faith, I often pray what God has promised me in His Word. *Lord, I trust that You are with me. I know that You will never leave me nor forsake me. I am not alone. You care for me. You are my provider, and You have a perfect plan just for me. I do not have to be afraid, for You are faithful.*

Then I ask God to open my eyes so that I can see what I have professed with my mouth. God did that for Elisha's servant, and He'll do it for you and me too.

It happened like this. King Aram was at war with Israel. During this time, the prophet Elisha would spy on King Aram and then report his strategy to the king of Israel. When King Aram found out Elisha was the one blowing his cover to Israel, he sent horsemen and chariots by night to surrounded Elisha's camp and capture him.

When Elisha and his servant awoke and saw that they were encircled by the enemy, the servant cried out in terror, "What shall we do?" Elisha said to him, "Do not be afraid. For those who are with us are more than them." Then Elisha called to the Lord, "Open his eyes so that he may see." Suddenly, the servant saw chariots of fire from God all around.

Do chariots marked with doubt, fear, and discouragement have you surrounded? Are you afraid they will conquer you? Are you crying out like Elisha's servant, "What am I going to do?" Instead, ask God, "What are *You* going to do?" God is greater than your anxiety. Perhaps it's time to ask God to open your eyes so that you can see His power and love working together to fight your battle. Seeing the truth will help you overcome your discouragement and fear while you're waiting for God to claim your victory.

Dear Lord, open my eyes so that I can see You and Your power at work on my behalf. Conquer my fears and replace them with trust in You alone. In Jesus' name. Amen.

Application Steps

Stop looking at what you can do and look to God. Recognize Him at work in your everyday occurrences.

128 The Shame of It All

Wendy Pope

As they ate it, suddenly they became aware of their nakedness, and were embarrassed. So they strung fig leaves together to cover themselves around the hips.

Genesis 3:7 TLB

My little boy is a man's man. He loves any project involving tools. I was sanding some spots on walls that had been spackled, preparing them to be painted. Griffin, of course, had to have his own bit of sandpaper. At first we worked together, but he was doing such a great job that I went to work in another area.

As I pulled the couch from the wall, I noticed a piece of broken red plastic. Because Griffin was so busy, I decided not to distract him with questions about my discovery. Pulling the couch out further from the wall, I saw Griffin's fireman's mask, broken. I had to ask him about it. "Griffin," I said, "your fireman's mask is broken." He answered without looking at me, "Yeah, I know." I couldn't believe his reaction. This was one of his favorite toys. But since he didn't want to discuss it, I decided to let it go. We continued to work.

A few minutes later the Holy Spirit prompted me with the word "shame." I realized my Griffin had broken his mask and hidden it from me. I had him crawl up in my lap to talk about what had happened. Without looking in my eyes, he confessed that he had broken the mask. I asked him why he put the mask under the couch. He said, "Because I did not want you to see it." He had done something wrong and was ashamed. I assured him that he could always come to me when he had done something wrong.

I didn't have to teach my son shame. He was born with it, just like you and me. But we don't have to be victims anymore. Praise God! The penalty that Jesus paid on the cross assures of this: Shame doesn't have to define us or bind us. God sent His Son so that we might have a life of abundance and freedom. Second Peter 1:3 says: "His divine power has given us everything we need for life and godliness through our knowledge of him who called us by his own glory and goodness." The key to our freedom is knowledge of Him. Our knowledge of Him gives us power, and this power helps us choose to not live in the bondage of shame.

Just like Griffin, you don't have to be ashamed of what you have done. You never have to hide the truth from God in fear that He will not love you anymore or that He will not forgive you. Crawl up in His lap, experience His tender loving care, and accept His forgiveness.

Dear Lord, I come now, asking You to forgive me for the time I have wasted living in shame when You paid such a high price for my freedom. Today, I am going to believe I am free and live like I am free. Help me to be disciplined enough to spend time growing in the knowledge of Your Word, which gives me everything that I need for life and godliness. In Jesus' name. Amen.

Application Steps

Write 2 Peter 1:3 on an index card, personalizing it with your name. Place the card in a place you will see every day. Recite the verse each time you see it. Keep a copy in your purse for emergencies.

129 Lessons from an Ostrich

Rachel Olsen

The wings of the ostrich wave proudly;
but are they the pinions and plumage of love?
Job 39:13 WEB

My feather duster is made of gorgeous, decadent ostrich feathers, which are tops at attracting and holding dust. Who would have guessed an African bird could make housecleaning a little easier?

It is a myth that these curious birds bury their heads in the sand when afraid. In fact, there is very little the ostrich need fear. The ostrich grows to a size of about eight feet and weighs as much as 300 pounds. Large and heavy, the ostrich cannot fly—but it holds the distinction of being the fastest running creature on two legs. A giant bird that doesn't fly, but can outrun you and me—I think God has a sense of humor.

There is one thing, however, the ostrich should fear—her own carelessness around her nest. Job 39:13-17 reads:

> The wings of the ostrich flap joyfully, but they cannot compare with the pinions and feathers of the stork. She lays her eggs on the ground and lets them warm in the sand, unmindful that a foot may crush them, that some wild animal may trample them. She treats her young harshly, as if they were not hers; she cares not that her labor was in vain, for God did not endow her with wisdom or give her a share of good sense.

Looking at the ostrich, it's easy to be awed by her majestic size, her unparalleled speed, and her beautiful plumes. I sometimes look at other women and become enamored with their God-given attributes, their stunning beauty, or their noteworthy accomplishments. However, this small passage in God's conversation with Job reveals that a better measure of a woman can be found in how she cares for her loved ones, particularly her young.

Although God did not endow the ostrich with wisdom, Proverbs 2:7 reveals that "He grants a treasure of good sense to the godly" (NLT). In fact, anytime you or I are in need of wisdom, all we have to do is ask God. "If any of you lacks wisdom, let him ask God, who gives generously to all without reproach, and it will be given him" (James 1:5 ESV).

Let's wisely stop to consider if we're flapping our wings proudly or running through life at ostrich-speed. Sure we may accomplish a lot—we may even garner the admiration of others—but we often wind up stepping on our eggs, endangering our nest, and treating our young harshly. Perhaps we should slow down and shift our focus to displaying the feathers and plumage of love.

Dear Lord, thank You for granting me a treasure of good sense, and giving me wisdom when I ask. Help me to slow down and focus on what You deem important. Help me to care for my loved ones in a way that honors both You and them. In Jesus' name. Amen.

Application Steps

Get out your calendar, schedule, and to-do list. Decide what is most important and what can be postponed or skipped all together. Plan time to enjoy and nurture your family.

130 The Dreaded Relationship
Sharon Glasgow

My brethren, count it all joy when you fall into various trials,
knowing that the testing of your faith produces patience.
But let patience have its perfect work, that you may be perfect
and complete, lacking nothing.

JAMES 1:2-4 NKJV

Life was busy. I wanted to be a part of a group Bible study without the burden of getting to know anyone, so I came in late and left early each week. It worked out wonderfully until one week when the leader passed around a basket and asked everyone to put their name in it for a prayer partner exchange.

I was perturbed that they were forcing me to do something I didn't want to do, so I stood my ground, and when the basket was passed I simply handed it to the next person without putting my name in it. After the names were counted, the leader announced that there was a name missing—possibly it had fallen out of the basket—and she asked that everyone look around the floor to see if they could find it.

Reluctantly I announced that it was my name that was missing. I explained why it was impossible to have a prayer partner with my lack of time. They giggled and put my name in the basket. The names were passed and, being the last person to get the basket, only one name was left for me. There, written before my eyes, was the name of a lady everybody disliked. I wasn't even sure she was a Christian by the way she conducted herself. She was argumentative, confrontational, and rude.

We met at the end of the study to decide on a day and time for our prayer meetings. The first night came and I quickly realized this wasn't going to work. We were as compatible as two pit bulls locked in a cage.

Each meeting was grueling. I felt trapped. One week I called her to tell her I couldn't make it. She wouldn't stand for it. We were going to keep our commitment at any cost! With an attitude, I hopped into my car and went down the road to tell her this was the end—no more prayer partners for us. I walked up to her house, ready to do battle, when all of a sudden she opened the door and I melted. A peace came over me. I humbly walked in and said, "Let's get on our knees and pray." The Holy Spirit filled both of us, and when we opened our eyes we looked at each other differently. We hugged and cried and felt intoxicated by His Spirit!

Soon she wasn't argumentative anymore. She even started neighborhood Bible studies in her home. We prayed together for many years and are still friends. God taught me things I would never have known without the time I spent with her.

Our agenda isn't always God's agenda. His plans are so much higher than ours. The last thing I wanted to do was to be stuck with a negative person, but the Lord had greater things in mind than my comfort. He wanted us to grow. Like sandpaper grinding against wood, gradually the rough places in our personalities were smoothed out.

Dear Lord, give me the ability to cope and minister when I'm faced with hard relationships. Open my eyes to the condition of each person's soul, that I might love them as You do. In Jesus' name. Amen.

Application Steps

Reach beyond your comfort zone of friends.

131 Close to You
Marybeth Whalen

Love GOD, all you saints; GOD takes care of all who stay close to him, But he pays back in full those arrogant enough to go it alone.
PSALM 31:23 MSG

I have often wondered if it is possible to be close to God in the midst of a busy, demanding life. Is it realistic to be still and know that He is God (Psalm 46:10) when everything else in life is calling out for my attention? Oh, how I long to be close to You, God!

I have a few practical suggestions that have helped me to draw close to God in spite of my busy life:

1. Commit to getting up just 15 minutes earlier each day to spend time with God. This short amount of time will not drastically affect your sleep, yet it will drastically improve your habit of spending time with Him. Increase this time as you are able.

2. Think of God as your friend (John 15:15). How do you spend time with your friends? You talk to them and carve out time for them regularly—otherwise the friendship would grow stale.

3. Find a quiet place in your home to be your prayer closet. For me, this is the shower! The pounding of the water drowns out the noises in the rest of my home so that I can focus my attention on Him.

4. Start a prayer journal or spiritual journal to document particular Scriptures that speak to you, prayer requests, and answered prayers. Document your children's or grandchildren's spiritual growth and questions.

5. Don't know what to study? Do word searches in your concordance on words that are coming up in your own life—words like "joy," "peace," or "faith." Get your Bible out and read the Scriptures mentioned in these devotions each day. Read the whole passage and not just the one verse.

6. Play praise music in your home. I find it beneficial for us to crank up the local Christian radio station about lunchtime each day. This helps me to refocus my day and my attitude.

7. Be intentional about drawing close to God. Learn to listen for His voice, follow His leading, and respond accordingly.

8. Forgive yourself when you can't or don't do these things. Try again the next day.

Closeness with God is not "one size fits all." It will vary according to each individual person. The most exciting thing is that when you draw close to Him, He will draw close to you (James 4:8). Take comfort in this and feel the wonder of being close to Him no matter what other demands are pressing in on you today.

Dear Lord, help me to find ways to be close to You amid all I have to do each day. Help me to not get caught up in my busyness and forget You in the process. Thank You for wanting to be close to me in return. In Jesus' name. Amen.

Application Steps

Pick a few of the suggestions that particularly speak to you and commit to trying them this week.

132 Wanting What I Have

Renee Swope

*Keep your lives free from the love of money
and be content with what you have.*

HEBREWS 13:5

Frantically searching for the doll her daughter had to have, my friend Janet drove all over town looking for Generation Girl Barbie. She couldn't believe how desperately she wanted to find this one-of-a-kind doll. She tracked down Generation Girl days before Christmas. Janet couldn't wait to see her daughter Ali's excitement when she opened the box and played with her new friend for days on end.

A week into the new year, Janet was cleaning house when she stumbled over Ali's Barbies. Funny how they all look alike wearing no clothes! Generation Girl had ended up with the rest of her glamorous friends in a loss-of-identity crisis. Janet laughed out loud when she realized her efforts to accumulate the perfect collection had brought her nothing but a bucket of naked Barbies!

Do you have your own "bucket of naked Barbies"—things you *had* to have that don't really matter anymore? In our quest for contentment, isn't it easy to accumulate things that promise to fill voids in our lives yet leave us feeling empty, wanting for more? Historian Arthur Schlesinger observes that our society is marked by an "inextinguishable discontent."

For many of us, discontent has become a way of life. Often I wonder if it's possible to be content with what we have instead of always wanting more. There was a time when I doubted it. Then I learned an important lesson—contentment doesn't mean I get what I want. Author Linda Dillow explains, "Happiness is getting what I want. Contentment is *wanting* what I have." The difference is determined by whether I focus on what I have or what I want.

When my heart wrestles with discontent, I've learned to ask God to give me a "want" for what I have. Simple prayers change my indifference to desire: "Lord, thank You for the gifts I have: my family, friendships, church, home, health, and time. Thank You for the favor of Your grace, the freedom of Your forgiveness, the unconditional love, and acceptance I long for and find in You. Thank You even for things I don't want—track marks on the carpet reminding me of those who live here, never-ending laundry reminding me how You provide for us, high power bills reminding me I have a warm home, taxes to be filed because we have income, and exhaustion at the end of the day because I'm alive and active. Please give me contentment that is separate from my circumstances and my stuff."

As we seek to have a heart filled with contentment, let's seek the Lord, not with a list of what we want, but with a *want* for all we have.

Dear Lord, I want contentment in the depth of my soul, but I fall into the trap of believing things will make me happy. Then I feel frustrated and confused. Show me areas of my life I am trying to fill with something or someone other than You. I want lasting contentment that comes from knowing and being loved by You. Help me recognize and want all I have in Christ. In Jesus' name. Amen.

Application Steps

Refrain from buying anything you do not *need* for one week. Write Hebrews 13:5 on the cover of a notebook and start a gratitude journal. For one week, list three different things you're thankful for each day. Continue by listing things daily or weekly and watch your contentment grow.

133 A Legacy

Susanne Scheppmann

*I remember the days of long ago; I meditate on all your
works and consider what your hands have done.*

Psalm 143:5

The dust scatters as I lift a long forgotten box from the closet shelf.
Sneezing, I peek curiously into the cardboard container. Ahh! My
children's memory boxes! Crayon-colored cards, plaster molds of tiny
hands, and report cards all whisper of childhoods long past. Precious
reminiscences flood my mind as bittersweet tears flood my eyes.

Sifting through the priceless cache, I feel the Lord nudge my heart
with these questions, "What treasures are *you* leaving for your children
to remember? Are you leaving a legacy for them to follow?" Scripture
leaps into my thoughts, "Take to heart all the words I have given you
today. Pass them on as a command to your children so they will obey
every word of this law. These instructions are not mere words—they are
your life! By obeying them you will enjoy a long life in the land you are
crossing the Jordan River to occupy" (Deuteronomy 32:46-47 NLT).

Suddenly a new resolution springs to my mind. I want my children
to find a legacy of faith when they divide my belongings after I am
gone. Turning from their cluttered closet, I march to my own jumbled
bedroom closet. Reaching to the top shelf, I grab down dusty volumes
of my history with God. I begin to gather the spiritual souvenirs that
will guide my children through my walk of faith. I dig out my old
completed Bible studies, tear-stained and joy-filled prayer journals,
dog-eared inspirational books, and dilapidated Bibles. These records
of my faith will reveal many struggles of doubt and heartaches. More
important, however, they will chart years of God's faithfulness. They
will provide an accurate and enduring map of my journey of learning
to trust Jesus, even in the most difficult moments of my life.

Out of the corner of my eye I spy a cedar chest tucked in the back of the closet. It holds old blankets. Hmm…I decide this piece of furniture will now become the safety-deposit box that will guard the heritage my children will someday inherit. As I carefully place my collectibles of faith into the chest, I pray that my life will become a living inheritance to the goodness of God to all those who come after me.

Dear Lord, let me remember I am leaving a legacy for all those who come behind me. Jesus, I pray that my life will encourage others to trust in You not only now, but in the coming days. Let my legacy of faith inspire my children, my grandchildren, and others who come behind me on this journey. In Jesus' name. Amen.

Application Steps

Think about what legacy of faith your life can provide. Begin to collect the various treasures of your faith. Keep them in a place where you can review them to encourage yourself and others.

134 Fearfully and Wonderfully Made

Melissa Taylor

*I praise you because I am fearfully and wonderfully made;
your works are wonderful, I know that full well.*

PSALM 139:14

If you were asked to describe yourself, what would you say? Most of us would probably be modest and humble in our response, answering something like, "I'm five foot four and have blondish-brown hair," "I'm just a mom," "I'm tall with dry skin," or something like that. It's hard for most, including myself, to accept a compliment. Just yesterday my neighbor told me how good my hair looked. Instead of thanking her, I replied, "Do you think? It's a frizzy mess in all this rain!" Why do we do this? Why not respond with a hearty "Thank you" and accept the compliment?

I've noticed when I give someone a compliment, often I get a response that negates the compliment I just gave. Not so with my four-year-old daughter. I'll tell her, "Hayley Grace, you look beautiful today." She'll say back, "I know, Mommy. I am blutiful." Then I'll ask, "How did you get so beautiful?" Every time she says, "Because God made me that way." She believes it too. When do we lose the belief that God made us beautiful? Do you believe that about yourself? Did you ever?

Hayley Grace believes that because that's what her mommy and daddy told her. There's no reason for her to believe any different. She trusts us. How I pray she'll always believe that. Realistically, though, I know that won't be easy. Once she begins comparing herself to others, she'll question whether she really is beautiful. I know because I struggle with this daily.

Hayley Grace recently brought home a picture she made at preschool. To me, it looked like a baked potato with legs and a smile. I asked her to tell me about this lovely creation she made. She said in a very proud voice, "It's a picture of you, Mommy. Isn't it blutiful?" I replied, "Yes, it is." This picture that I viewed questionably was viewed by its maker as a masterpiece. She was so proud of it.

Our Maker views us the same way, as a masterpiece. He didn't goof up when He made us. What we may view as flawed, He views as fearfully and wonderfully made.

You want to know the honest truth about yourself? Don't ask someone else, and don't ask yourself. Ask the One who made you. You are "fearfully and wonderfully made," my blutiful sister. Let's not ever forget it.

> *Dear Lord, thank You for loving me and making me for Your unique and special reason. I know I serve a great purpose in Your kingdom because You made me. Forgive me when I forget that and forgive me for listening to what others think of me. Help me to feel Your love today and equip me to give that love to all those I come in contact with. In Jesus' name. Amen.*

Application Steps

The next time someone gives you a compliment, accept it by saying "Thank you." Then thank God for making you just the way you are.

135 Brain Blips, Mishaps, and Feelings of Failure

Lysa TerKeurst

Everyone who hears these words of mine and puts them into practice is like a wise man who built his house on the rock. The rain came down, the streams rose, and the winds blew and beat against that house; yet it did not fall, because it had its foundation on the rock. But everyone who hears these words of mine and does not put them into practice is like a foolish man who built his house on sand. The rain came down, the streams rose, and the winds blew and beat against that house, and it fell with a great crash.

MATTHEW 7:24-27

Do you know what amazes me about these verses? The person doing right and the person doing wrong experienced hard times. In both cases the rains came, the streams rose, and the wind blew and beat against the house.

Living out God's principles for life does not mean we won't face difficult circumstances, but being a Christian determines how difficulties affect us. If we are hearing and heeding God through our prayer time and reading His Word, then we will be able to stand strong in the storms of life. Our faith will not be shaken, and our identity will not be rattled.

I once heard my pastor lament to my husband that sometimes he only feels as good as his last sermon. I can identify with his comment because as a friend, wife, and mother, sometimes I only feel as good as my last interaction with someone close to me. A friend tells me I hurt her feelings, and suddenly I feel like a bad friend. I forget to take the cookies I signed up to bring to the church nursery, and suddenly

I feel unreliable and disorganized. My husband asks me where our passports are, and when I can't find the file, suddenly I feel like a wife who can't be trusted.

The passport thing is still fresh on my mind because it just happened yesterday. My normal reaction would have been to become frustrated, short-tempered, and beat myself up while tearing the house apart looking for it. But God's Spirit knocked on the door to my heart and said, "Let Me invade your natural reaction. Call your husband and pray about the passports instead of getting angry." So Art and I prayed. I went from defining myself as a failure of a wife to being a godly wife who faces hardships in a godly way. The frustration was diffused, and we determined to look at this from God's perspective. If we find the passports, we'll praise God! If we don't find them, we'll see this as God's protection not to go on a planned trip later this month, and we'll still praise God.

When hard times come and beat against our stability, we must be determined to hear God's words and put them into practice. Then nothing can topple our peace, security, or true identity.

Dear Lord, thank You that my identity doesn't have to be determined by the circumstances of my life. Help me to hear Your words, put them into practice, and stand firm on Your truth. In Jesus' name. Amen.

Application Steps

Write down something you've been mentally beating yourself up over. Find three Scripture verses that deal with this issue and commit to praying these Scriptures into your situation. Stand firm on God's solid truth that you are a godly woman who will face this circumstance in a godly way.

136 Hang On
Glynnis Whitwer

We wait in hope for the LORD; he is our help and our shield.
In him our hearts rejoice, for we trust in his holy name.
PSALM 33:20-21

I told my first grade son, Robbie, that I would bring him a special treat for lunch that day. He was overjoyed. He knew that several times a month for the past few years I had been joining his older brothers for lunch at school, and now it was his turn. He got to pick his favorite fast-food meal and sit at a special table with Mom.

I left the house with just enough time to pick up the food, but I didn't anticipate a short-staffed restaurant. I waited my turn as the minutes ticked by, anxiously checking my watch every 30 seconds. If I could have jumped behind the counter to help, I would have.

The school schedule is exact, and so I knew when Robbie would be walking from his classroom to the cafeteria. I knew when he would be sitting at a table, staring at the door, willing me to walk through it. Unfortunately, at that moment I was still in line.

I could have cried knowing my little boy was waiting and wondering where I was. I'm sure he was wondering things like: *Is she coming? Did she forget? Did something happen to her? Should I try and eat something from the cafeteria?*

Hang on, Robbie, I thought. *I'm coming as fast as I can.*

I arrived at the school about five minutes late, which is an eternity when you are six. I raced into the cafeteria to find him sitting alone, with his little arms crossed on the table, and his head resting on his arms. As I called his name, he looked up and his big brown eyes shimmered with brimming tears. But that quickly changed to joy when he saw the Happy Meal bag (oh, and me, of course).

I wish I could have erased the anguish Robbie felt during that wait. God must feel that way too.

Although God's delays are never because of poor planning, sometimes we must wait upon His perfect timing. He knows He's just around the corner with something even better than the Happy Meal we've asked for. He knows we often wring our hands, wondering if this time He'll forget. But the truth is, He never forgets. He watches us and knows our anxious thoughts. Although I couldn't comfort my son when I was delayed, God has sent the Holy Spirit to be our Comforter.

Waiting is never easy, but we can trust Him while we wait. We can rest in the knowledge that He never forgets, He never is late, and His plans for us surpass our fondest hopes.

Dear Lord, I praise You for Your faithfulness. Help me to trust You, even when I can't see what You are doing. Help me wait with anticipation as You reveal Your plan for my life. Thank You for Your steadfast love. In Jesus' name. Amen.

Application Steps

Remember a time you had to wait for God to answer one or more of your prayers. Can you see how His timing was better than yours? Describe it in a prayer journal.

137 Pillow Talk
Rachel Olsen

[God] grants sleep to those he loves.
PSALM 127:2

I love to sleep. In fact, I earned the nickname "Sleeping Beauty" in college. Did I mention I also love to nap?

Despite my affinity for snoozing, I am not very good at falling asleep. I'm a classic night owl. My body temperature rises in the evenings, and I gain energy as the sun sets. I find evenings are prime time for getting stuff done, particularly after the kids are in bed. Once I head to bed, thoughts of the day, concerns for tomorrow, and hopes for the future often race through my mind. Ever wish for a switch you could flip to "off" when you were in need of some rest?

If any man should have had trouble falling asleep, it would have been King David. David was a man after God's own heart, but he was also a man with many enemies. His own son Absalom rebelled against him and gathered as many as 10,000 soldiers to kill him. In Psalm 3:5 David said, "I lie down and sleep; I wake again, because the LORD sustains me." The king echoes this thought in Psalm 4:8 when he says, "I will lie down and sleep in peace, for you alone, O LORD, make me dwell in safety." With so many men seeking his harm, David had left his palace for the cover of the wilderness. There in the wild, David declared his life to be in the hands of the Lord, and then he lay down and slept like a baby.

It's not likely you or I will ever be on the run from soldiers seeking to take our life, but it's likely this very day that we are pursued by stress and strife seeking to sap our quality of life. Like David, we should look to the Lord as our source of life, peace, and rest.

Jesus told us how we can find rest. He said, "Come to me, all you who are weary and burdened, and I will give you rest. Take my yoke upon you and learn from me, for I am gentle and humble in heart, and you will find rest for your souls" (Matthew 11:28-29).

Sleep is like the reset button for the body. It helps us recover from the day's events. While we sleep our bodies repair themselves at the cellular level and we regain our strength. Coming to Jesus with our burdens is like hitting the reset button for our souls. It too will help us recover from each day's events. While we pray, the Holy Spirit repairs us at the spiritual level and we regain strength of mind and heart.

Paul advised in Philippians 4:6-7, "Do not be anxious about anything, but in everything, by prayer and petition, with thanksgiving, present your requests to God. And the peace of God, which transcends all understanding, will guard your hearts and your minds in Christ Jesus." No sleeping pill is a better prescription for rest than spending some pillow talk prayer time with Jesus, the Lover of your soul. Sweet dreams.

> *Dear Lord, teach me to lay my burdens at Your feet. Show me I can trust in Your loving care. Grant me the nourishing blessing of rest and peaceful sleep. In Jesus' name. Amen.*

Application Steps

Spend some time alone with God before drifting off to sleep. Thank Him for all that went well today and release to Him all that did not. Ask Him for a restorative night's rest.

138 The Narrow Way

Micca Campbell

Enter by the narrow gate; for wide is the gate and broad is the way that leads to destruction, and there are many who go in by it. Because narrow is the gate and difficult is the way which leads to life, and there are few who find it.

Matthew 7:13-14 NKJV

In an emergency you often only have a split second to make the right decision. There is no time to think it over, list the pros and cons, or discuss it with an expert. You have to make a choice and then live with the result.

Hundreds of people in South Asia had only moments to make a life-saving decision when a horrifying tsunami hit with its devastating rage. From my television set, I watched in sorrow as some had time to escape death while others, not so fortunate, were sent to a watery grave.

As the death toll continued to rise, it was comforting to hear from those who had survived. Each testimony reminded me of God's faithfulness and provision amid the tragedy. One man's story stuck in my mind.

He began sharing with the journalist how the people scattered like frantic mice, running in every direction, when the giant wave hit. "Most of the people took the broad road, pushing and shoving one another, as they tried to escape. It appeared to be the logical choice," he humbly testified. "I was about to join them when I noticed one man running in the opposite direction. He was a native. Something from inside told me to follow him. Instantly, I called to my family, and we escaped by the narrow road."

With only a moment to decide, the man chose to follow the road less traveled. By taking the narrow path, he and his entire family were saved.

Like this man, the Bible speaks of two different roads. Whether we are conscience of it or not, each of us chooses the road we will travel in life. You and I will either follow the broad way or the narrow way.

The wide road seems the most favorable. It's considered "easy street." You'll find an abundance of company on this route as it seems to be the most pleasurable path. The disadvantage, however, is that it leads to destruction.

The other road is narrow, often difficult, and sometimes lonely. Taking it is the first step toward total dependence on God. The advantage of this road is that it leads to life, both now and forever.

If you look closely, you can see a man, God's Son, standing on the narrow path faithfully calling, "Follow Me. I am the way."

Today, as waves of sin and guilt attempt to drown you, the Lord is there providing a way of escape. Two roads lie before you. Time is short. You need to make a decision. As long as you stay on the wide road, destruction will follow. Choosing the narrow path leads to life. Today is the day. Now is the time. Which path will you choose—life or death?

Dear Lord, I've traveled the broad way too long. Today, I choose the path of life. I'm not sure what's ahead, but I trust You are leading me. In Jesus' name. Amen.

Application Steps

Write down everything that kept you on the broad road. List the benefit of each. Did anything on your list provide peace or purpose? If not, trade them for the path to life.

139 Dressed for Success
Zoë Elmore

As God's chosen people, holy and dearly loved,
clothe yourselves with compassion, kindness, humility,
gentleness and patience. Bear with each other and forgive
whatever grievances you may have against one another.
Forgive as the Lord forgave you. And over all these virtues
put on love, which binds them all together in perfect unity.
Colossians 3:12-14

In my job I am required to wear a uniform. Each morning I don a white lab coat over my black slacks and blouse. I never really appreciated the freedom in wearing the same thing each day until I began this job. Gone are the mornings filled with frustration as I hunted through my overflowing closet, only to find nothing to wear. Now I experience freedom to focus on my job instead of myself as I wear what is required. Of course, even my uniform looks its best when I wear the right undergarments.

Just as my physical job requires me to wear a uniform, the life I lead as a believer requires me to wear a spiritual uniform. Before we can put on this new spiritual uniform, we must remove the filthy rags of our old sinful nature and put those behaviors to death. Then we are encouraged to put on the seven virtuous undergarments of this spiritual uniform.

The first virtuous undergarment is living in the reality that as a believer in Christ we are chosen, holy, and dearly loved. Secondly, we are to clothe ourselves with compassion, as we enter into the suffering of others. Third, we put on acts of kindness, which thwarts evil in the lives of others. The fourth undergarment is humility, as we live our lives in awareness of God's grace. The fifth undergarment is gentleness, as we are gracious toward others. The last two undergarments are patience and forgiveness. God is so patient with me and is faithful to forgive my confessed sins, so in turn I must be willing to extend patience to others, even those who are difficult to deal with. I must be willing to forgive those who have harmed me, even if they never apologize or ask for forgiveness.

As we put on these seven virtuous undergarments, we will create the perfect foundation for the outer garment of love, which binds all of the seven undergarments in perfect unity. This outer garment of love identifies us with the one we follow, Christ.

If you want your life to show others that you follow Christ, I encourage you to take a look at your spiritual closet. Is it filled with outdated attitudes and behaviors that just don't fit your life as a believer? Get rid of them. Are there bad habits hidden in the dark recesses of your spiritual closet that need to be discarded? Get rid of them. Perhaps the unflattering accessories of impatience and unforgiveness need to be removed and destroyed. Get rid of them. I want to encourage you to get rid of anything and everything that doesn't fit your life as a believer and then experience the freedom that comes from wearing the correct undergarments with the outer garment of love.

Dear Lord, reveal the sinful areas in my life that need to be removed and destroyed. Help me to clothe myself in the garments spelled out in these verses. In Jesus' name. Amen.

Application Steps

Clean out your spiritual undergarment drawer. As you do, ask the Holy Spirit to remove any patterns that keep you in bondage to your former ways and to replace them with God's virtuous clothing.

140 Our Provider

Susanne Scheppmann

Abraham called that place The LORD Will Provide.
And to this day it is said, "On the mountain of the LORD
it will be provided."

GENESIS 22:14

Death, doom, and depression stalked a dear friend of mine. She had just moved to Las Vegas, Nevada. (Not many women really want to move here.) She knew no one. Her children were scattered across the United States. The desert landscape depressed her. The summer heat of 110 degrees moved her to tears. Her faithful dog died of cancer shortly after the move. It seemed as though things couldn't get much worse.

Yet they did. Her beloved husband of 40 years developed terminal cancer. My friend felt like Job of the Old Testament. Although a Christian for most of her life, she felt completely abandoned by God. She questioned God's trustworthiness in her life. Her heart cried out to Him...

"My face is red with weeping,
deep shadows ring my eyes" (Job 16:16).

"Why do you hide your face
and consider me your enemy?" (Job 13:24).

Even as her faith stumbled, God heard her and the answers were on the way. Just as Scripture assures us, "Before they call I will answer; while they are still speaking I will hear" (Isaiah 65:24), the Lord responded.

She happened to drop by a Bible study I was teaching on the names of God. The day's lesson was on Jehovah-Jireh, which translates "God will provide." I read:

Abraham lifted up his eyes, and looked, and behold behind him a ram caught in a thicket by his horns: and Abraham went and took the ram, and offered him up for a burnt offering in the stead of his son. And Abraham called the name of that place Jehovah-jireh: as it is said to this day, in the mount of the LORD it shall be seen (Genesis 22:13-14 KJV).

Although familiar with the Bible, she listened carefully as I talked about the Lord as our Provider. God whispered comfort to her aching heart, "I will be Jehovah-Jireh to you. I will provide for *you*."

After that, God confirmed His message to my friend. Within a week, she received a postcard from a local card store inviting her to come and select a gift. As she approached the designated gift table, she could tell most of the offerings were junk: broken candles and mismatched cups and saucers. Her eyes swept the table expecting to find nothing she would bother taking home, and then her eyes landed on a small devotional book titled *Jehovah-Jireh*. Aha! A token of love sent straight from heaven through a retailer's promotion. On that day she realized that although her troubles abounded, God knew all the details and He cared for her. She acknowledged her need to simply rest in His love and His plan for her life.

Indeed, sometimes it's hard to trust God, especially when everything seems to go wrong. But God is faithful even when we *feel* otherwise. My friend learned that God would provide for her every need.

Dear Lord, help me to trust You when I do not understand my circumstances. Open my eyes to Your love and care even in the small details of life. Reveal Yourself to me as my Jehovah-Jireh. In Jesus' name. Amen.

Application Steps

On a piece of paper, list the areas that you have the most difficulty in trusting God and then pray for Jehovah-Jireh to provide for you in those areas.

141 The Pull of Home
Rachel Olsen

He's just the carpenter, the son of Mary and brother of James, Joseph, Judas, and Simon. And his sisters live right here among us.
MARK 6:3 NLT

Though many Jews considered Nazareth a godforsaken place (see John 1:45-46), nothing was further from the truth. It was the God-chosen spot for the Son of Man to grow, study the Scriptures, and prepare for His world-changing ministry. After being baptized in the Jordan River and tested by Satan in the desert, Jesus made this region of Galilee His ministry "base camp."

Many of the people of Jesus' region had a hard time accepting Him as the Messiah. In Mark 3:20-25, Jesus heals a man on the Sabbath and the religious leaders accuse Him of working for the devil. Jesus then left the region and traveled about preaching, performing miracles, and being mobbed by crowds.

After raising a girl from the dead, Jesus returned home to Nazareth with His disciples. The people there were "deeply offended and refused to believe in him" (Mark 6:3 NLT). Though He taught with uncommon wisdom, they replied, "He's just the carpenter, the son of Mary and brother of James, Joseph, Judas, and Simon. And his sisters live right here among us" (Mark 6:3). Jesus replied, "A prophet is honored everywhere except in his own hometown and among his relatives and his own family" (Mark 6:4). The Scriptures say Jesus was surprised by their degree of unbelief, and because of it His ministry there was limited.

Do you come from a small, could-anything-good-possibly-come-from-there kind of town? Have you ever felt that your own family or friends can't see past your "humanness" to recognize your God-given potential? Has their unbelief in you limited your ministry or life in any way? Jesus can surely relate to your frustration.

After His death and resurrection, where do you think He went? Besides His disciples and friends, whom do you think He purposed to appear before in His resurrected glory? Was it the Gentiles who didn't know Him? Was it the Jerusalem Jews who had condemned Him? Was it the Roman centurions who had crucified Him? Was it the Pharisees who had opposed His every move? No, it was the people of His homeland—the people who in many ways knew Him best, yet still didn't believe. The risen Christ headed straight for Galilee, going to His earthly home before ascending to His heavenly one.

The pull of home is strong—even for the Lord. Jesus was surely disappointed that the people of His hometown rejected Him, as did the synagogue leaders, whose job it was to recognize Him. Ultimately, however, Jesus' identity, worth, and power came from the heavenly Father and not from the validation of any earthly being. The same is true for us today.

Dear Lord, help me to always look to my Creator for my identity, purpose, and strength. In Jesus' name. Amen.

Application Steps

Copy the first chapter of the book of Ephesians. As you do, insert your own name, or the pronoun "me" as the person to whom these words were written. Then read it aloud each day for a week.

142 Hats Off

Wendy Pope

God made him who had no sin to be sin for us,
so that in him we might become the righteousness of God.

2 Corinthians 5:21

I love hats. Unfortunately, I don't have a head that looks good in any kind of hat, not even a ball cap. I admire the ladies who still wear hats to church with outfits that aren't complete unless the shoes and purse match. We listen to fashion gurus to learn whether "hats are in" or "hats are out." In the church where I grew up, we had a sweet lady who wore a hat every Sunday no matter what the fashion guru had to say on the subject.

Recently a friend said to me, "Just once I wish I could take off all the hats I wear and be me." It made me think of all the hats women try to wear all at once. We are wives, mothers, teachers, nurses, counselors, chauffeurs, coaches, chefs, and housekeepers. We sometimes lose sight of who we are because of all our hats. We need to slow down and look in the mirror and determine which hats we should be wearing.

I fell in love with today's verse while I was wearing one of my hats—teacher. I was preparing to teach by reviewing the seven principles of a "Proverbs 31 Woman" in the book *A Woman's Secret to a Balanced Life. Lord,* I wondered, *how can I be all of these well?* Opening my Bible, suddenly the last part of today's verse became alive to me. Read it again.

Christ died for us "so that we might become the righteousness of God." Did you catch the word "become"? Becoming is a process that takes time. It takes determination. It takes a willingness to leave the past in the past and press toward the hope of a new way of being. We don't have to "be someone" because we are becoming—perhaps slowly but surely—the righteousness of God. Doesn't that bring a sense of relief to your weary spirit? I know it does to mine each time I read it.

I realized that if I made my relationship with Jesus Christ my number one priority, I would indeed be all I needed to be to my family, friends, and coworkers while becoming the righteousness of God. And that thrills my soul, because I can look forward to one day looking good in hats designed specifically for me.

> *Dear Lord, I want You to help me evaluate the activities and commitments in my life. I need Your guidance to know which commitments to lay down and which to continue to be involved in. It's my desire to do only that which is part of Your plan for my life, and to do it in the righteousness of God. In Jesus' name. Amen.*

Application Steps

Make a list of all the "hats" you are currently wearing. Pray faithfully every day, asking God to show you which hats you should focus on for today, or even take off altogether.

143 Disabled

Luann Prater

*I tell you the truth, whatever you did not do for one
of the least of these, you did not do for me.*

MATTHEW 25:45

Pulling into a parking lot, I noticed an elderly woman getting out of her car with a cane in hand. She had chosen not to park in the handicap spot, but instead left that for someone in greater need. I slowed down as I approached because her feeble legs couldn't sprint across the pavement, as I'm sure they once did. Slowly and methodically, she placed the cane one step ahead of her as she shuffled in front of me. Her fluffy white hair reminded me of my own mom, and I smiled patiently as I waited for her to pass by.

Suddenly a car sped up behind her. The driver slammed on the brakes and wildly began blasting the horn. A red-faced woman was about to explode in her sleek silver Honda. Luckily, it was a hot day, so her windows were up. The air-conditioning was blowing her stiff locks, and we were all spared the obvious obscenities she was spouting at this poor grandmother now close to a cardiac arrest.

Try as she might, her body just wouldn't move any faster. Without mercy, the red-faced maniac continued to lay on her horn and jut forward as if she was considering running the little old lady down. I was horrified! Just as she lifted her frail foot to the sidewalk, this hot-tempered driver squealed right into the space marked "Handicapped." She slipped her handicap sign onto her rearview mirror, jumped out of the car, and leaped into the nail salon five steps away.

We all have disabilities; some are just more visible than others. The red-faced woman had a disabled heart. She couldn't see past her own wants, needs, and desires. She is an extreme example of each one of us—looking past the needs of others and focusing on our own little world. There are hurting people all around us that God is expecting us to see, and yet we pass them by. Maybe we don't run them over, but we try hard not to notice.

It is so inconvenient to care. Oh, we may care about our family, our friends, and our church, but what about that neighbor who just keeps to herself, or that irritating child who is left alone after school? Look around—people around you are hurting. Zig Ziglar says, "Pretend everyone you meet is wearing a sign around their neck that says, 'I'm hurting,' and nine times out of ten, you'll be right." We live in a fallen world full of "the least of these."

Even the red-faced maniac was hurting. You can't act that nasty without having a deep hurt somewhere inside. When you know the Savior, you have a healing balm that binds the wounds of this world. Will you reach out to someone in need today? Will you take time to notice the "least of these"?

> Dear Lord, we live in a fallen world with so many hurting hearts. You have appointed one of those hearts to me today. Help me to see who needs healing. Give me words that care, hands that share, and shoulders to help bear the burdens of those around me. Teach me that this day is not about me; it's about You. In Jesus' name. Amen.

Application Steps

Read Matthew 25:31-46. Ask God to reveal a special hurting heart to you today. God is working. See the opportunity He gives you.

144 Crime Scene
Van Walton

For you are my lamp, O LORD, and my
God lightens my darkness.
2 SAMUEL 22:29 ESV

We pulled into our motel at 4:00 a.m. after passing through a dead-to-the-world town. It seemed strange to be up, traveling, and checking into a place to "spend the night" when the world around us would be waking in a couple hours. Turning the corner into the parking lot, we noticed strange lights moving around in a field overgrown with weeds and shrubs.

What's happening out there at this time of the morning? A moment later, a police officer with a searchlight emerged and walked toward his patrol car.

I can't believe he's alone and out there in the dark. Anyone or any beast could be hiding under cover in those weeds! I hoped all my wild thoughts would remain just that—concerns and not reality. My fears calmed when another police officer emerged. The two conversed and then both disappeared again into the underbrush. Relieved there were two and not one, we parked our car and carried our overnight bags into the lit up and strangely-cheery-for-this-time-of-day hotel lobby.

Hours later in the light of day, we curiously drove past the crime scene wondering what had happened there last night. It dawned on me that I live in a crime scene. You do too! The Bible says the world in which we live is filled with terror, battles, pestilence, and destruction (Psalm 91:5-6). There is a criminal of all criminals, who plots to destroy us (1 Peter 5:9).

Like smart police officers and savvy detectives, we aren't to walk the beat alone. In fact, God tells us that He patrols with us saying, "Wait for Me...for the day when I rise up...I am going to deal at that time with all your oppressors" (Zephaniah 3:8,19 NASB).

Before approaching any scene, it's wise to collaborate with someone who will watch your back. Jesus is always on duty and always available. He walks with us in the midst of darkness and evil. He is the light we need. I know Him to be a trustworthy partner—He placed Himself in harm's way before by giving His life on the cross to save me.

> *Lord, You know I am a coward by nature. I should not be stepping into perilous circumstances alone. I panic and make crazy decisions. It gives me great comfort and confidence to know that I don't have to face anything by myself. I have a Partner whose strong right arm protects me. Help me to stick close to You. In Jesus' name. Amen.*

Application Steps

Talk with God before stepping into your day. Ask Him to open your eyes and make you observant of your surroundings. Invite Him to partner with you as you investigate the possibilities of life.

145 Beloved
Rachel Olsen

I will call them My people, who were not My people,
and her beloved, who was not beloved.

ROMANS 9:25 NKJV

"Beloved" is what the Lord calls you and me. This term takes my breath away as I ponder the fact that God doesn't just love me in some perfunctory way, but really LOVES me.

You know the difference. I love chocolate ice cream (a lot, actually), but I really LOVE my husband. I love our pediatrician, but I LOVE my two children so much more. While the Lord loves the sweet-songed sparrows He created, He really LOVES you and me. "Are not two sparrows sold for a penny? Yet not one of them will fall to the ground apart from your Father. And even the hairs of your head are all counted. So do not be afraid; you are of more value than many sparrows" (Matthew 10:29-31 NRSV).

Someone who is beloved is loved to a great extent. Do you realize the great extent to which the holy One loves you? It was demonstrated on the cross where God sacrificed His perfect Son in order to gain you and me as daughters. Romans 5:8 says: "God showed his great love for us by sending Christ to die for us while we were still sinners" (NLT).

I know I am a flawed and selfish human being, so I can't fully comprehend why God loves me so dearly that He desired to draw me to Him and cleanse me of my sin. Though we may have a hard time understanding how God could love us despite our flaws, our inability to comprehend makes it no less true.

Some synonyms for the term "beloved" are: much-loved, dearly loved, adored, favorite, darling, and highly thought of. This is the image God holds of you. Is this the image you hold of yourself? Say this out loud: "I am wholly and dearly loved by the holy God Almighty." Do you experience any hesitation or doubt saying or believing that?

Henri Nouwen said, "Self-rejection is the greatest enemy of the spiritual life because it contradicts the sacred voice that calls us the 'Beloved.' Being beloved constitutes the truth of our existence." How different could our lives be if we agreed with the Sacred voice, rather than the condemning voice? We have to choose each day, sometimes hour by hour or minute by minute, which voice we will listen to: the Sacred voice of God, or the lying, condemning voice of Satan. Romans 8:1 assures us that "there is no condemnation for those who belong to Christ Jesus" (NLT).

Paul says in Romans 8:38, "I am convinced that nothing can ever separate us from his love" (NLT). You, my friend, are beloved—highly thought of and adored. Rejoice today, beloved, because you will always hold that status in your heavenly Father's heart.

Dear Lord, I'm awed by Your great love for me. May I listen to Your Sacred voice today and always. In Jesus' name. Amen.

Application Steps

Read Psalm 103:11 and Romans 8:38-39 and take a few minutes to contemplate the heights and depths of God's love for you. Go ahead and wallow in it!

146 Anxiety

Melissa Taylor

Don't worry about anything; instead, pray about everything.
Tell God what you need, and thank him for all he has done.
Philippians 4:6 NLT

I am experiencing more anxiety in my life than ever before. I don't know why. While the world around me seems to spin out of control, I feel as though I'm drowning, gasping for air, and fighting my way out.

How can this be happening? I love God. I believe His Word. I'm active in my church. I'm a speaker and a writer. I'm a mother of four and the wife of a terrific husband. I live in a comfortable home in a nice neighborhood. I have great friends. So what is wrong with me?

I suspect the main reason anxiety takes over is due to what I'm focusing on. My mind dwells on problems that are usually beyond my control. That leads to fretting. Fretting leads to anxiety.

Sometimes I go looking for comfort: a hug from my husband, a call to a friend, or a piece of chocolate cake. The relief proves to be temporary. Only one thing seems to have the power to really assure me that I will be fine—the Word of God.

Have you ever had times in your life when you needed a hug from God? I know I have. There have been days when nothing else would do but for Jesus to wrap His loving arms around me. "Peace I leave with you; my peace I give you. I do not give to you as the world gives. Do not let your hearts be troubled and do not be afraid" (John 14:27). "In this world you will have trouble," Jesus warned. "But I have overcome the world" (John 16:33).

The next time you are feeling anxious, go to the Lord and allow Him to take care of you. Let's make it a daily practice to give Him our burdens. We need to be intentional about trusting Him to solve the problems surrounding us.

Our enemy, Satan, would love nothing more than to hold us captive by keeping our minds set on that which makes us anxious. Then he knows we aren't focusing on or listening to God. Dwelling and fretting are strongholds on our mind. Use the power of God in you to knock out anxiety.

Dear Lord, how I need You each and every minute of my life! I need Your guidance, direction, and assurance that everything will be okay. I know You are in control. I know You will provide for all my needs. I know You will take care of me. Help me to trust You and not to dwell and fret. Lead me along each day with total faith in You. In Jesus' name. Amen.

Application Steps

Rather than worrying, pray about your troubles. If you find yourself unable to quit thinking about your problems, seek Christian counseling for help or join a Bible study group where you can get the encouragement and support you need.

147 Everybody Gets to Play

Glynnis Whitwer

Now you are the body of Christ,
and each one of you is a part of it.

1 CORINTHIANS 12:27

I grew up a freckle-faced brunette in a neighborhood of blonds—13 of them. Not just any blond, but the light, almost white kind of blond. To say I stood out in the crowd was an understatement. Normally it didn't matter to any of us, except when we played *The Big Valley.*

In the late '60s, *The Big Valley* was a popular television show. For those of you over 40, you're humming the theme song right now…"The big valley, the big valley…" (Okay, I know there weren't words.) As little kids, we would reenact various episodes, and inevitably there was an argument over who would get to play Audra Barkley.

Audra was the beautiful, long-haired daughter, who was fussed over by her mama and pampered by her three handsome brothers. As much as I would have liked to play Audra, that was never an option. Audra had blond hair. With my brown hair, I wasn't even considered. I did, however, get a part. I was Nick, the hotheaded, troublemaking brother. When I didn't play Nick, I (gulp) played a horse.

Although I write that tongue-in-cheek, it hurts to be left out or relegated to a role that doesn't fit you whatever your age. What I love about God's kingdom here on earth is that everybody gets to play! And we get to play a part specifically designed for us.

Each of us is called to serve God in a wonderfully unique way. He gives us skills and talents at birth, and then He calls us into service. Once we say yes, God fine-tunes our skills and increases them according to our faithfulness in using them. Yet many Christians never fully discover their gifts.

There's nothing more frustrating than an underused Christian. I wonder what would happen if every believer served God according to his or her gifts and talents—and not based on where there's a vacancy in Sunday school or on a committee.

My challenge is to discover my God-given gifts and talents and surrender them to God and His purposes. If my gift is teaching, then I need to be somewhere I can teach. If I have financial skills, then I should be working with money. If I love to pray for the sick, then I should be praying for the sick. It would be nice if someone identified my skills and asked me to serve accordingly, but the responsibility for using my gifts ultimately falls to me.

Although my days of *The Big Valley* and playing Nick are past, I'll never forget feeling out of place and longing to play another role. God's kingdom is big enough for each of us to fulfill the calling God has for us. We need to say no when someone asks us to play Nick, and we need to pursue opportunities to play our own brand of Audra.

Dear Lord, thank You for allowing me to play a part in Your kingdom. Thank You for needing me and for blessing me with gifts and talents. I pray for wisdom to know when and where to say yes and no. I long to honor You in all my ways. In Jesus' name. Amen.

Application Steps

Identify three of your God-given talents. Are you using those in God's service? If not, list three ways you can use those natural gifts and skills.

148 Love the Ones You're With
Renee Swope

Since God so loved us, we also ought to love one another.
1 John 4:11

I have a confession to make. I'm embarrassed to admit it, but there are times when I'm with my family but I'm not really there because my mind is somewhere else, getting something done! What about you? When you're with the ones you love, do you really love the ones you're with?

One night my family was all snuggled on the couch watching a movie. We were spending quality time together, but then I got distracted. I was still there *physically,* but I started returning phone calls and e-mails *mentally.* I glanced at the clock to see how many hours before the kids went to bed and noticed the silhouette of my son's face. He looked so grown up. *How quickly ten years have passed.* I knew it wouldn't be long before he'd be counting down the hours until I go to bed so he can instant message his friends. Suddenly, I recognized the gift of being *with* the ones I love while they're still with me.

Jesus knew His time on earth was limited. He was intentional about loving people with His time and attention. He didn't see their requests as interruptions, but welcomed them as invitations.

Unlike Jesus, I am a type A, get-it-done kind of girl. Just "being" is hard for me. That's why I take my struggle to God almost daily and ask for balance. He wired me this way, so He's the only One who can make me more like Him. When I spend time with God, He challenges me to slow down and spend more time with my husband and children. He knows how important they are to me, but He also knows how I can get tangled up in my to-do list. He's helped me to see my family as my greatest treasure and my time with them as my most important investment.

Focus doesn't always come naturally, so when I get distracted, I do a few things to help me stay focused. First, I look into their faces and remember what they used to look like. That helps me grasp how quickly time passes. Second, I think back to what life was like without them. That jolts my memory and makes me thankful God gave them to me. Third, I imagine the day they won't be with me—the day my children may live in another state with their own family. Then I remind myself that to-do lists will always be here, but the ones I love won't.

What about you? How often are you really with the ones you love... no agendas, no errands, no planning...just being? Let's make a pact today to slow down and really be with the ones we love and love the ones we're with while they are still with us!

> *Dear Lord, thank You for the people You have given me to love. Help me slow down and see them through Your eyes and love them the way You love me. Remind me daily that only two things will last for eternity—my relationship with You and my relationship with others. In Jesus' name. Amen.*

Application Steps

Plan a date with someone you love. Talk about things/people they care about most. Really listen and enjoy them. If you get distracted by things you need to do, imagine this is the last time you'll be with them and make it the best ever!

149 Nobody Likes a Quitter

Susanne Scheppmann

Stay with GOD! Take heart.
Don't quit. I'll say it again: Stay with GOD.
PSALM 27:14 MSG

I never seem to accomplish my admirable goals such as weight loss, exercise, a cleaner home, or more home-cooked meals. I give up. I quit.

Nobody likes quitters, except God the Rejuvenator.

Think about the prophet Elijah. He called down fire from heaven. He prayed for and received a downpour of rain in the midst of a drought. Then he quit. He ran into the desert and sat under a lone scraggly tree. "I have had enough, LORD," he said. "Take my life" (1 Kings 19:4). In other words, "I quit!"

However, God came to rejuvenate Elijah. He refreshed Elijah with food, drink, and rest. Rejuvenated, Elijah went on to finish his ministry.

Nobody likes quitters, except God the Encourager.

Do your recall Jonah? He quit before he got started. God has a way about changing our minds. After Jonah floated around in the stomach of a big fish for a while, God stepped in to encourage him to complete the mission to Nineveh. The Bible states, "God spoke to the fish, and it vomited up Jonah on the seashore" (Jonah 2:10 MSG).

Next, God spoke to Jonah. "'Up on your feet and on your way to the big city of Nineveh! Preach to them. They're in a bad way and I can't ignore it any longer.' This time Jonah started off straight for Nineveh, obeying GOD's orders to the letter" (Jonah 3:2-3 MSG).

Nobody likes quitters, except God the Restorer.

My favorite biblical quitter is John Mark. This young Christian man quit while on a missionary endeavor with Barnabas and Paul. He ran home when the going got tough. His desertion made the apostle Paul furious.

Have you already guessed what happened? You're right! God restored John Mark back to ministry. God restored the relationship between John Mark and Paul. Look at what Paul wrote, "Only Luke is with me. Get [John] Mark and bring him with you, because he is helpful to me in my ministry" (2 Timothy 4:11).

So what about you? Have you ever been tired of ministry, tired of family, or sick and tired of being tired? Do you want to throw in the towel and quit?

Unfortunately, I have quit more times than I like to admit. Yet I know God the Rejuvenator, the Encourager, and the Restorer. He urges me on just as He did with Elijah, Jonah, and John Mark. He whispers in my heart, "Haven't I commanded you? Strength! Courage! Don't be timid; don't get discouraged. GOD, your God, is with you every step you take" (Joshua 1:9 MSG).

Don't quit! Listen to God whisper, "Be strong. Be courageous!" Keep moving on the life path where He has placed you. God sees you as a winner!

Dear Lord, sometimes I feel like quitting. I want to quit being a wife and mom. Some days I would like to quit being me and be someone else. I am asking You to encourage and refresh me on those days. If I quit on something I shouldn't, I ask that You rejuvenate, encourage, and restore me. In Jesus' name. Amen.

Application Steps

Read Joshua 1. Underline in red pencil every time you see the words "Be strong and courageous." List a few things you need to be strong and courageous about in your life. Then ask the Lord to remind you that the Lord your God will be with you wherever you go.

150 Friendship Choices

Lysa TerKeurst

Ruth replied, "Don't urge me to leave you or to turn back from you. Where you go I will go, and where you stay I will stay. Your people will be my people and your God my God."

RUTH 1:16

"I want to quit school!" Oh, such delightful words to hear from my twelve-year-old. Growing up is hard to do, especially in those tween years. It turned out my daughter was having problems with her girlfriends. One of her friends had made plans with Hope and then canceled when a more appealing offer came along from another girl. To me it seemed like a simple sign of immaturity on her friend's part. But to Hope it was devastating. So I hugged her, prayed with her, and gave her some tips on dealing with friends when they hurt your feelings.

A few days later she got in the car after school and said, "Mom, I've decided you have a choice with your friends. You can either deal with their quirks or stop hanging around them."

I replied back, "Hope, that is profound wisdom. If you can remember that piece of relationship advice it will serve you well, not just for the middle school years, but on into your adult friendships as well."

Do you ever find yourself struggling in your friendships and ponder how you can change those things about your friends that annoy you? Well, changing someone else is nearly impossible and very frustrating. Maybe we would do well to take the focus off changing this other person and put it on improving ourselves. Making this subtle shift will allow real progress. Because while you can't change the way someone else acts and reacts, you can control yourself. Make sure that your actions and reactions are honoring to God and reflecting the types of friendship qualities you long for in a friend. After all, if we want a really good friend, we have to be a really good friend.

Once you've determined to make positive changes in yourself, pray for that friend who has qualities that are less than desirable. Chances are she has a lot of great qualities you can choose to focus on. Praise God for her good qualities and mentally hand over each thing that troubles you in your friendship. God will either give you the patience to love her despite your differences, or He will show you how to create a healthy distance that will serve you both well.

> *Dear Lord, thank You for the precious gift of friendship. Help me to see and appreciate my friend's good qualities without getting caught up and frustrated with her negative qualities. Lord, give me wisdom to know when to draw boundaries in my friendships and how to choose my friends wisely. My heart desires friendships that are characterized by Your love. Help me to be the kind of friend I long to have. Thank You for friends with whom I can laugh, learn, and journey through life. In Jesus' name. Amen.*

Application Steps

Ask God to give you a lifetime friend that characterizes your desires in a friendship. If God has already given you this kind of friend, look for ways to bless her and thank her for her friendship. Let her know you will stick by her through thick and thin. Look for ways to grow closer together by growing closer to God through praying, studying God's Word, or doing ministry together. Write her a note today that reminds her that she is loved, and list all the reasons you appreciate her.

151 Surviving the Storm

Micca Campbell

*When he woke up, he rebuked the wind
and said to the water, "Quiet down!"
Suddenly the wind stopped,
and there was a great calm.*

MARK 4:39 NLT

When you're in the midst of a raging storm—whether it's financial, relational, or an unexpected illness—does Christ seem far away and unaware of your situation? While I know that's not true, the weight of my own burdens can often make me feel as if I'm carrying them alone. Even in situations that seem reasonable for me to handle, I frequently find myself saying, "Where are You, God? I need to know You are near."

While the disciples were experienced seamen, they found themselves in a desperate situation that only Jesus could overcome. The angry sea was tossing them about as water filled their boat. Surely they would drown. Where was Jesus? He was asleep in the boat, unaware, or so it seemed.

Unable to save themselves through their own power, the disciples became afraid and anxiously cried out to Jesus. Responding to their cry, Jesus rebuked the wind and calmed the storm. Then He asked, "Why are you so afraid? Do you still not have faith in Me?"

Good question. What comes to the surface when you're in a raging storm—faith or fear? If Jesus promised to never leave us or forsake us, then we have nothing to fear. In order to survive, we must keep our eyes on Him instead of the raging winds of our circumstance.

Even though Jesus was asleep in the boat, He was aware of their situation. The storm didn't wake Him, but the cry of His disciples did, and Jesus took immediate action. Isn't that interesting? The howl of the storm didn't demand Jesus' attention, only the cry of His friends. Jesus is aware and in control of your situation too.

God will answer your cry for help. While it may appear as though Jesus is asleep in the midst of your storm, He may be waiting for you to reach your point of desperation. Though the disciples were experienced fishermen, in this storm they were in over their heads. Sometimes we have to come to the end of our own self-effort before we invite God to work. When we give up and cry out, Jesus will answer our call.

Every one of us is going to face hardship. Only the friend of Jesus has the promise of His presence with them in the midst of a storm. Although Jesus never promised us a life of smooth sailing, He did promise us a safe journey. God will not leave you abandoned in the middle of your hardship. He will see you safely through.

When the waves of trouble come crashing in on you, know that you are not alone. There's no need to fear. Instead, have faith that Jesus is in the boat. With Him, you can survive the storm.

> *Dear Lord, You are my provision in the midst of my storm. Help me to trust You when I can't see land for the rain. Lead me safely through and set my feet on solid ground once more. In Jesus' name. Amen.*

Application Steps

Next time you're in a storm, don't just work relentlessly to survive. Call out to Jesus and allow Him to calm the sea of your troubled heart.

152 My Black Thumb

Marybeth Whalen

Blessed is the man who trusts in the LORD,
whose confidence is in him. He will be like a tree
planted by the water that sends out its roots by the stream.
It does not fear when heat comes; its leaves are always green.
It has no worries in a year of drought
and never fails to bear fruit.

JEREMIAH 17:7-8

I am not a gardener. I seem to have a black thumb—I'm even capable of killing weeds. I admire people whose gardens yield beautiful flowers, lush landscaping, and bountiful harvests. Meanwhile, I have trouble keeping the two ferns on my screened-in porch from turning brown and dropping their leaves. Sad, but true.

I have a friend who is a florist. Recently I was telling her how much I love hydrangeas, and she surprised me with the news that a hydrangea bush will grow a different color of flower depending on the composition of the soil it is planted in. I was impacted by the spiritual implications of this truth.

I thought of the many types of people God created—different in appearances, in temperament, and in talents. Just as the hydrangea bush blooms different hues of flower according to the soil it is planted in, so people grow and bloom according to the foundation in which they are rooted. Sometimes the soil is shallow, rocky, and deficient. Sometimes the soil is rich and lush. Sometimes the soil is highly acidic. And sometimes it's perfectly balanced.

I have six children. I began to ponder what kind of soil I have been providing for my little buds in our greenhouse. Am I providing them with a rich soil that will enable them to grow into vibrantly colored blooms that testify to God's plan for their lives? Or am I making due with rocky, thin soil that does not provide room for their roots to grow deep? I can tend the soil—plowing deeper into their hearts and discovering what God has planted there. I can water and feed the soil—ministering to them with encouraging words. I can fertilize the soil by picking out the unwanted character qualities of sin I see them struggle with. Overall, no matter what kind of soil I begin with, I can allow the Master Gardener—the Creator of all living things—to show me how to maximize the soil's potential and grow big, beautiful flowers that point to Him.

I am thankful that God used the simple hydrangea bush to remind me of my part in allowing these little buds He has placed in my care to blossom to their full potential. I pray that we will all look for ways to enrich the soil of our lives, and produce greenhouses full of beautiful blooms, no matter their color.

Dear Lord, I ask for Your help as I tend the soil of my children's lives so that they can grow to reach their full potential. Thank You for Your plan for their lives, and Your patience with me as I learn to "garden" by Your design. In Jesus' name. Amen.

Application Steps

Post a photo of a hydrangea somewhere visible in your home to remind you each day of the value of cultivating the soil in your home. Then write down some specific actions you can take to provide a rich environment for your children to blossom in.

153 Meet a Joyful Giver

Rachel Olsen

You must each make up your own mind as to how
much you should give. Don't give reluctantly or in response
to pressure. For God loves the person who gives cheerfully.

2 CORINTHIANS 9:7 NLT

I get excited each time the catalogs arrive. Not the L.L. Bean or Sharper Image catalogs, but the Heifer International and Samaritan's Purse catalogs. They are filled with practical gifts of food, medicine, livestock, blankets, and building materials that can be purchased for needy children, families, and villages around the world.

God has certainly done a tremendous work in my heart for me to get a kick out of giving. It's not that I am a coldhearted woman, mind you. I am actually very encouraging. It's just that in my natural state I am rather stingy with my money. I'd spend it like it's going out of style, but I was not interested in handing it over for others to spend. Over the years God has softened this area of my heart as I've prayed for the ability to cheerfully give.

Now I appreciate that my money can make a difference in someone's life I otherwise could not help. The money I'd spend on a restaurant dinner, for example, can train a young believer to tell others about Christ in a remote area of the world. The money I'd spend on a latte can supply a hungry child with a week's supply of milk. I can give up relatively little and provide someone else with so much more. Not only that, but God measures back to me what I have given out (Luke 6:38). Don't you just love God's economy?

I am thrilled to be partly responsible for someone saying: "The LORD is good, a refuge in times of trouble" (Nahum 1:7). I take satisfaction in knowing that I am not only blessing my fellow man, but the very Lord I love.

Jesus, speaking of the future day of judgment, said:

> The King will say to those on the right, "Come, you who are blessed by my Father, inherit the Kingdom prepared for you from the foundation of the world. For I was hungry, and you fed me. I was thirsty, and you gave me a drink. I was a stranger, and you invited me into your home. I was naked, and you gave me clothing. I was sick, and you cared for me. I was in prison, and you visited me." Then these righteous ones will reply, "Lord, when did we ever see you hungry and feed you? Or thirsty and give you something to drink? Or a stranger and show you hospitality? Or naked and give you clothing? When did we ever see you sick or in prison, and visit you?" And the King will tell them, "I assure you, when you did it to one of the least of these my brothers and sisters, you were doing it to me!" (Matthew 25:34-40 NLT).

Dear Lord, thank You for the opportunity to bless others by giving, and for the privilege of giving to You. Cultivate in me a heart that gives cheerfully. In Jesus' name. Amen.

Application Steps

Consider what ways you will reach out to meet the needs of your community or world to show them the love of Jesus.

154 The 9-1-1 Plan
Sharon Glasgow

Be merciful to me, O God, be merciful to me!
For my soul trusts in You; And in the shadow of Your wings
I will make my refuge, until these calamities have passed.
Psalm 57:1-2 NKJV

I slowly hung up the phone, upset by the words of the person on the other end. Everything was going well before the call, and now I felt despair. It was hard to continue on with my day—cleaning, cooking, and paperwork. I didn't want to talk to anyone about it, but I was paralyzed by fear.

I went to my Bible and opened it. I looked in the concordance for verses on peace. I found them and read them out loud, repeating them with urgency and praying for God's power to refresh me through His Word. His response was utterly amazing. It always is. He refreshed me in His supernatural way. My circumstances didn't change and no earthly person had given me counsel. My relief was from the King of the universe through the power of His Word.

I started to cry tears of joy, realizing that God could take such a desperate moment and give me peace. I remembered how Jeremiah felt such despair that he wished he had never been born. Yet in the middle of his despairing thoughts he found God's words and ate them, and they were a joy to Jeremiah's heart. Wow, what power we have access to!

I held my Bible close to my chest as if squeezing it into my soul and praised God for what He had done for me that day. You too can find peace despite your despairing circumstances through he power of His Word. The next time you have a "9-1-1 emotional emergency," you'll know where to go for the rescue.

Dear Lord, thank You for giving us the Bible to strengthen us and deliver us from despair. Make me thirsty for Your instruction. Help me understand what I read within its pages. In Jesus' name. Amen.

Application Steps

Start reading the Bible today for your source of hope tomorrow. Write your thoughts on the side bars of the pages. Highlight God's promises of hope and write them on index cards for easy access in turbulent times. The Bible promises to be the lamp unto your feet when you don't know where else to turn (Psalm 119:105).

155 A Rule Change

Wendy Pope

If ye love me, keep my commandments.
JOHN 14:15 KJV

We had waited so long that summer. It seemed as if we went every other day to see if he met the requirement. The weeks passed slowly; patiently he waited. Then one day it happened. Two weeks before the pool closed for the winter, my son finally met the height requirement allowing him to slide down the big slide. His shouts of joy echoed throughout the pool deck, "Mom, I am finally big enough. I am big enough!" I was so happy for him. This was an important day, one we would long remember.

The following spring, right before the pool opened again for the summer, we received notice that the height requirement for the big slide had changed. With the rule change my son was once again not big enough. I made a call to the director of the Aquatic Center to get more information. Plain and simple: The rule change was necessary for the protection and safety of the pool members. I understood the reason for the rule change, but I was still disappointed for my little boy, who thought he was finally big enough.

The Lord used this situation to remind me of the importance of His law. He prompted me to refresh myself with His commandments. As I did, I realized that, like the change in rule at the pool, God's commandments are necessary for the protection of His children. The commandments were not meant to keep us from having fun and enjoying God's creation, but to give us boundaries that keep us from harm. A fresh look at the Ten Commandments made me praise Him for His consistency and for never changing the rules. Refresh yourself with God's commandments (Deuteronomy 5:7-21):

1. You shall have no other gods before me.
2. You shall not make for yourself an idol.
3. You shall not misuse the name of the LORD your God.
4. Observe the Sabbath day by keeping it holy.
5. Honor your father and your mother.
6. You shall not murder.
7. You shall not commit adultery.
8. You shall not steal.
9. You shall not give false testimony.
10. You shall not covet.

I am reminded of God's precious grace. We all fall short of the glory of God. Maybe you are reading these commandments and feeling convicted. Maybe you are reading these commandments and feeling unworthy. If so, accept God's free gift of forgiveness and live in that forgiveness each day. No one is worthy of relationship with God, but through His grace and mercy we shall become the righteousness of God (2 Corinthians 5:21).

Dear Lord, I acknowledge that I fail to obey Your commandments as I should. I need to experience Your healing peace today. Help me to accept Your forgiveness and move past my sin to enjoy the life You have given me. Thank You for never changing. I praise You because You are the same now and forever. In Jesus' name. Amen.

Application Steps

Choose two commandments that are particularly challenging for you. Write them down. Write a prayer confessing why obeying these commandments is difficult for you and ask God to help you obey them.

156 Telling Our Friends the Truth

Glynnis Whitwer

*Carry each other's burdens, and in this way you
will fulfill the law of Christ.*

GALATIANS 6:2

One summer's day my mother, little sister, and I drove east across the
Arizona desert after visiting California. Lizzie and I were too young to
help drive, so we occupied ourselves by talking and reading comics.

At a stop for gas, Lizzie and I waited in the car while Mom filled
the tank. It was a windy day, and we could see the fronds of a few palm
trees waving wildly. My mother tucked a strand of her long brown
hair behind her ear as she leaned over the gas pump. Within seconds
a strong gust of wind blew through the station and caught the edge of
my mom's wraparound skirt.

Normally, Mom would have worn a slip, but she'd opted for cool
comfort that day. As the wind grabbed her skirt, it flipped over my
mother's back, revealing her behind to the world! Unaware of the spectacle, my mother continued to pump gas.

My sister and I saw the whole thing. One would think kind daughters would have rolled down the window and told their mother to cover
herself! However, Lizzie and I were doubled over in laughter. We were
so consumed with the hilarity of the situation we couldn't even rap on
the window to get her attention.

Mom finished filling the tank, straightened her skirt, and off we
drove—hopefully never to see those gas patrons again. Although we
should have stopped laughing long enough to help our mother, it was
a relatively harmless incident. It illustrates, however, what can happen
when believers hold off bringing concerns about another believer to
their attention.

Galatians 6:2 says, "Carry each other's burdens, and in this way you will fulfill the law of Christ." This verse follows verse 1, which advises believers, "Brothers, if someone is caught in a sin, you who are spiritual should restore him gently. But watch yourself, or you also may be tempted."

As Christian women, we are called to lovingly guard our sisters' backs. When we see a sister in dangerous territory, we are to correct and bring her back into safety. The purpose is not to create spiritual watchdogs, but to "carry each other's burdens."

Telling our friends the truth about their attitudes or behavior is extremely difficult. We don't want to offend or alienate someone we love. However, believers helping believers stay true to their calling is God's design for His church. God's goal is unity and purity (Ephesians 4 and 5)—but we sometimes sacrifice purity for what we think is unity.

Telling a difficult truth involves much prayer, affirmation of a friend's strong points, and a gentle, loving spirit. It's not our job to convict our friend, only to help shoulder her burden and possibly prevent further harm.

It's also a good idea when we see someone's skirt up over her back to stop laughing long enough to tell her to put it back down. (Sorry, Mom.)

> *Dear Lord, I praise You for Your loving-kindness. Thank You for placing people in my life to help me stay true to You. I ask for a spirit of humility to receive their correction. In Jesus' name. Amen.*

Application Steps

Always pray—for both of you—before confronting a sister with difficult truth.

157 A Blessed "Steppie"

Shari Braendel

Her children stand and bless her.

PROVERBS 31:28 NLT

Recently, while visiting my daughter at college, I asked her roommate if her parents were still together. When she said yes, I smiled and told her what a blessing that was in today's society.

What happened next took me by surprise. My daughter Carly piped up with a confident, cheery voice and said, "But life's good with a steppie!" And she meant it. I felt a deep warmth come over me. Carly and her two sisters are my stepdaughters, and "Steppie" is their term of endearment for me.

To say living in a blended family has been easy would be a lie. Stepparenting is the hardest thing I have ever done, but it is also the thing that has kept me closest to Jesus. I had to learn that I was not a replacement for their mom—I couldn't be. What I could be, though, was their cheerleader, encourager, and spiritual mentor.

Somehow in the last ten years of being "Steppie," God has taught me to be "bigger" than I ever wanted to be. Instead of doing things my way, He invited me to follow His Word. I learned instead of screaming and yelling to bite my tongue and be quiet. Trust me, there were more times than I care to admit that I didn't do that. However, as the years went by, I got better at it. God had to change me, not the children. I learned that being quick to listen, slow to speak, and slow to become angry (James 1:19) is a prerequisite for Proverbs 31:28, which says, "Her children arise and call her blessed."

If you are in the middle of living life as a stepmother, I encourage you to daily draw near to the One who gave these "steppies" to you. When you are wondering why in the world God entrusted you with them, remember that they may be the greatest gift you ever receive. One day you might just hear them exclaim, "Life's good with a steppie!"

> *Dear Lord, please help me remember You gave me these precious children because You trusted me with them. May I draw close to You each day and know they are looking to me for an example of Your love. Help me be the kind of mother You are proud of and help me to love them as much as You do. In Jesus' name. Amen.*

Application Steps

The deepest desire of my heart is that my children will call me blessed. If this is your desire, copy James 1:19 on an index card and tape it to your bathroom mirror where you will see it first thing every morning. This will remind you to bite your tongue and listen when this is the last thing you want to do. Then pray for your stepchildren by name and ask God to forgive you for any hurts you may have caused them with your words or actions. Learn to recognize when you are not being loving and fair. Ask God to reveal concrete ways you can show more love and acceptance to them. You'll be amazed at the way He will show up for you on this one.

158 Able and Available

Renee Swope

You have been faithful with a few things;
I will put you in charge of many things.
MATTHEW 25:21

"This is the best thank-you note I've ever read," Janie insisted. "Renee, you have a writing gift and you need to use it." I was confused. It was only a thank-you note. Yet later that day I wondered if God could use me to encourage more than just one friend with my writing. I'd been asking Him for a place to serve in our church.

His answer came while I drove home from a women's dinner that fall. I'd taken notes on a napkin, but I wished I had the message outline to look over. Then I got the craziest idea: *Maybe I could write a study guide for the dinners to give to women who want to go deeper too.* Doubt filtered my idea through reality. Who was I to think I could write something women would want to read?

Several weeks later I told Janie my idea. She was on the women's ministry team and told me they'd prayed for a gift to give women after the dinners. Much to my shock, they asked me to write a study guide! Although I felt unqualified and insecure, with Janie's prayers and prodding I wrote it. More than 1000 copies were given away. I wrote another the next year and then another. I never felt able, but I wanted to be *available.*

I hadn't always been available. I was more like the third servant Jesus described in Matthew 25:14-30. The servant worked for a business manager who was going out of town. He gave each of his three servants individual projects to complete according to their abilities. The first two were given bigger assignments. Maybe they had more experience or were better at multitasking. Both gave their time and talents to serve their boss. He was pleased with them when he returned.

The third servant was given less responsibility, and he neglected his assignment. Perhaps he thought, *Oh, this little project isn't much, why worry about it? My boss will never notice.* I've thought that before.

Were the others given more visible responsibilities? Perhaps envy turned to anger toward his boss, making him apathetic about his assignment. His manager was not pleased. I wonder how God feels when I'm not faithful with what He's assigned to me.

Our Boss is on an out of town assignment. He's asked each of us to oversee something in His kingdom, according to our God-given abilities. With each ability comes an assignment that holds the possibility of reward or the potential of regret. It doesn't matter how much or how little God's given us. What matters is how well we use what we've been given.

It's been several years since I wrote that first study guide. God gave me more eventually, and just as promised He gave me joy I'd never known. It started with a friend who was faithful to encourage and pray. It started with another woman who was simply available, and God made me able to give back what He'd given me.

Dear Lord, what abilities have You given me that I don't see? Show me little things that can make a difference for You and others. I lay down my doubt, my jealousy, and comparison. I want to know the joy of serving You! In Jesus' name. Amen.

Application Steps

Read Matthew 25:14-30. List things you or others think you do well. List steps you can take to be a good steward of the abilities God has given you.

159 Sweet Potato Times

Susanne Scheppmann

There is a time for everything, and a season for every activity under heaven.

ECCLESIASTES 3:1

Another holiday spent with my husband's family. I did not want to go. I begrudged the yearly expectation to show up with a smile and a hot dish. My list of complaints grew each year as to why we shouldn't go. For example:

- The turkey stuffing included raisins.
- The rolls were store-bought.
- The glazed ham with pineapple slices was not to my taste.
- The women mingled in the kitchen; the men hung out in the den.
- The primary side dish was sweet potatoes.

I griped incessantly each year, pressuring my husband to stay home. My husband must have felt the truth of Proverbs 21:19: "Better to live in a tent in the wild than with a cross and petulant spouse" (MSG).

Now the funny thing about it was that I loved his family. However, my independent spirit yearned for my *own* holiday traditions. Any small displeasure validated my excuse not to spend Thanksgiving with them.

Finally one year on the way to the annual event at his parents' home, I snapped. My assigned dish was sweet potatoes. I'm sure you know the recipe that includes lots of brown sugar, marshmallows, and butter spread across the top of the orange squashy vegetable. (I do not like sweet potatoes of any kind.) I wrapped the steamy dish in towels to transport it to dinner. We piled the kids onto the backseat. I plopped down in the front seat and my husband placed the hot pan of syrupy, bubbling goo on my lap. As we rounded the first corner from our house, the pan slid, tipped, and spilled all across my beige pants. My legs burned as my eyes filled with tears. I let all my pent-up frustration break upon my husband as my children sat silently with their eyes looking down. I ruined the day for everyone.

As I look back, I realize how selfishly I acted each year. My heart did not display thankfulness for my husband, my kids, extended family, or the abundance of provision God provided. It was all about me. Even worse, I illustrated a poor example of Christian behavior to primarily unbelieving relatives.

Times change.

Two of my grown children now live out of state. My dear mother-in-law died a year ago. Funny how time alters our feelings. At this moment I would jump at the chance to return to times past. I would watch my children play with their cousins. I would hug my mother-in-law. I would bring that silly marshmallow orange glob and I would eat it with relish. I miss those sweet potato times.

Remember to be grateful for the small things in life. And if you are married, give your husband the opportunity to say, "House and land are handed down from parents, but a congenial spouse comes straight from GOD" (Proverbs 19:14 MSG). Joyfully give thanks to the Father God for the family and friends you have. Because times change and there is a season for everything, even sweet potato times.

> *Dear Lord, remind me that time changes circumstances. Let me display grace and thanksgiving throughout the year. Teach me to exhibit kindness, patience, and joy to my family and friends. In Jesus' name. Amen.*

Application Steps

Make a list of every person you will see at the next family gathering. Write one compliment for each person and share it with them with a grateful heart.

160 A Christmas Miracle

Micca Campbell

I have told you these things, so that in me you
may have peace. In this world you will have trouble.
But take heart! I have overcome the world.

JOHN 16:33

For me Christmas was always a time of celebration and joy. That year, it would be different. We were consumed in grief over our nephew, a troubled kid. Our sadness robbed the sacred holiday of its awe and wonder. So I began to pray. "Please, God, don't let us miss Christmas."

Tradition in our home is that family and friends join us for Christmas dinner. This year was no different. The house was full of those who had come to celebrate.

The house glittered with lights and tinsel, inside and out. The presents were sorted into piles according to name tags that were tucked beneath the bows. Aromas of holiday foods cooking in the kitchen made our mouths water with anticipation. Outwardly, all seemed right, yet for my family no celebration or sweet treat could comfort our hearts. Again, I prayed. "Lord, please don't let us miss Christmas."

As the evening drew to a close, Cory put on his coat. "Merry Christmas," he said, waving goodbye with his hand high in the air.

Cory, a friend of our son, had joined the Marines and was due to report after graduation. He fiddled with his jacket as if he was hesitating. "Are you excited about the Marines?" I asked.

"I wish I had never joined. I'm told the only way to get out of it is not to graduate. So I'm not going to finish school," Cory said as he shuffled his feet back and forth.

I sighed and began sharing with Cory what I needed to hear myself.

"Peace comes in impossible situations when we rely on God and trust Him with our future, whatever that may be."

Stunned, Cory asked, "In order to trust and rely on God, don't I first have to…what's the word? Get saved?"

"You've never trusted Christ to be your personal Lord and Savior?" I asked.

"No, ma'am, I haven't." Cory said, shaking his head back and forth.

"Well, we can fix that right now if you'd like."

My niece and I escorted Cory into a quiet room where we explained about the love and forgiveness of Jesus Christ. Cory accepted the peace of God and his countenance changed right in front of our face.

With excitement, Cory announced to our guests, "Guess what, everybody? I just gave my heart and life to Jesus!" Cheers filled the house and the true celebration of Christmas had finally begun! It was a Christmas miracle I'll never forget.

God had heard my prayer. He hadn't let us miss Christmas at all. In fact, as we looked to Christ for Cody's sake, He was birthed anew in all our hearts. Isn't that why we celebrate Christmas each year? To refocus on the One who offers hope for the hurting, sick, and lost, and fills us with lasting peace?

We often need reminding to rejoice in the truth that no matter what we face on earth, Jesus has overcome the world. Gazing on Christ helps us to see that if we have Jesus, we have everything we need.

> *Dear Lord, thank You for the Savior of the world, who brings peace all year long. In Jesus' name. Amen.*

Application Steps

To receive God's peace, confess your sinful nature to Christ and invite Jesus to become your Savior and Lord. Be ready to help others do so as well.

161 Trusting God in All Things

Melissa Taylor

*Trust in the LORD with all your heart and
lean not on your own understanding; in all your ways
acknowledge him, and he will make your paths straight.*

PROVERBS 3:5-6

Lately, my faith has been challenged. Am I following God's will for my life? Will my children ever quit being sick? Will there always be some problem to deal with? Am I going to cry again today? God, are You there?

While my words may seem as though they come from someone who lacks hope, faith, and trust, I bet you can relate. I am overwhelmed with concerns for those closest to me, my children. One is having problems in school. One won't sleep through the night. One seems so down on himself. One is having health issues we just can't seem to solve. Each time the phone rings, my heart pounds because I worry it is yet another problem that will be out of my control.

The truth is, many of my problems are out of my control, but I do have faith and hope. They don't come from doctors, teachers, counselors, or even my pastor. They come from the Lord, and I have to ask for them daily.

In James we are told that if we want wisdom, we need to ask for it. I have found that in order for me to have peace, I need to go to God for that daily too. I can't just ask for it once and then depend on it every day. I have to meet with Him. Then I have to acknowledge that He is in control and put my trust in Him. I am always amazed at the strength I am filled with after spending time with the Lord. I am always amazed that I can be filled with faith, hope, and peace even in the worst of circumstances. I know this filling is from Him. It's not possible any other way.

Are you feeling empty? It may be because you are pouring out your life to others daily and doing it all in your own strength. Go to God, who knows you best. Go to God and ask, just as Jesus did, for your daily bread. "Trust in the Lord with all your heart, and lean not on your own understanding; in all your ways acknowledge him, and he will make your paths straight" (Proverbs 3:5-6).

And remember to do it every day.

> *Dear Lord, You know how I need You today. I confess that I cannot live today without You. I give You every area of my life and ask that You would fill me with spiritual wisdom. I trust You with my life and the lives of those around me. In Jesus' name. Amen.*

Application Steps

Read Colossians 1:9-12 as a personal prayer for yourself. Then read it as a prayer for others in your life. Journal these prayers.

162 An Unexpected Gift

Rachel Olsen

Every good and perfect gift is from above,
coming down from the Father of the heavenly lights,
who does not change like shifting shadows.

JAMES 1:17

I watched with amazement as beautiful package after package was carried to the stage for a door prize giveaway at the Christmas event where I was invited to speak. The prizes ran the gamut...specialty coffees, bath and body products, scrapbooking supplies, and gift certificates to local restaurants. Then a small box was held up for the final drawing: a pair of genuine diamond stud earrings donated by a jeweler from the congregation. One fortunate woman went home with some extra bling that evening!

I always love to watch women's faces light up with anticipation when it's door prize time. I've spoken at events where the door prizes were many and grand, and also where they were simple and few. No matter the scale or cost, everybody enjoys receiving an unexpected gift.

Several years ago I was deep in the trenches of daily life with two children under the age of four. I counted it a good day if I managed a shower and a supper plan. It was difficult for me to see beyond the next meal, much less the next week, month, or year. During this time I received an unexpected gift: A pretty note card arrived in my mailbox, sent anonymously. The card contained $40 in cash and a few handwritten words encouraging me to invest the money in my talents and calling.

I remember wondering exactly what my talents and callings were; however, it was a powerful encouragement to know that someone out there—I still don't know who—saw potential in me. It was a seed planted; a small but generous gift of money and encouragement that has paid great dividends in my life and in the kingdom of God.

This gift confirmed to me that my Father has good plans in store for my future (Ephesians 2:10). The fact that my benefactor chose to remain anonymous made her gift, and the affirmation it brought, all the more compelling. I don't know if she remembers sending that card, but it was an unexpected gift I will never forget.

Now—as a speaker, writer, and editor of this devotional—I seek to give others the blessings my benefactor gave to me: encouragement for today, hope for tomorrow, and a sense of godly worth. These are the very same gifts our Lord so lovingly wrapped up for us at the cross of Calvary. Share these gifts with someone today.

Dear Lord, thank You for the gift of Your Son, Jesus, who both arrived and departed this earth in most unexpected ways. I praise You that we don't need a raffle ticket, or to win some spiritual lottery, to receive Your gifts of mercy and love. We need only to trust You with the very soul we already possess. In Jesus' name. Amen.

Application Steps

Look with the Lord's eyes today and see who around you needs hope, validation, or encouragement. Find a way to bestow it upon them—anonymously.

163 The Marriage I've Always Wanted

Lysa TerKeurst

What God has joined together, let man not separate.
MARK 10:9

■ If you were to describe your ideal marriage, what are some things you would include? Engaging conversations, romantic dates, fun adventures, shared responsibilities, financial security, passionate intimacy, and a partner to pursue my dreams with would be some of mine. As I walked down the aisle on my wedding day and mindlessly repeated the vows the pastor instructed us to say, I toted with me all these expectations of my ideal marriage. I thought our marriage would just have these things built in and all this would naturally come as part of the package.

But I soon discovered that a marriage is like that wonderful toy that you get on Christmas morning. You rip open the attractive packaging and go straight for the "on" button. When nothing happens, you feel confused and very disappointed. You were so sure that getting the toy would result in instant happiness, so when it failed to meet your expectations, you set it aside and moved on to something else. If only I'd taken just a moment to read the instructions I would have discovered three little words that could have made all the difference: batteries not included.

Had I read the instructions I would have realized that I can only get the toy to meet my expectations when I take the time to put energy into it. Having a great marriage is a matter of choice, not chance. Leaving it up to chance is saying, "Well, I just hope we'll have good communication, great sex, romantic dates, and share the responsibilities of life." But the realities of life don't lend themselves naturally to these things.

We get busy, stressed, and distracted, and before we know it, we've neglected our marriage for years. We keep pushing the "on" button hoping to get more from our marriage, but if we don't put in the batteries, we'll never really experience all that it can be.

I don't want to leave my marriage up to chance. I want to make the choice each day to invest wisely in it. If I want good communication, then I have to set the scene for times that my husband and I can really talk. Not just debriefing about the events of the day, but taking time to dream together, plan together, laugh together, and grow together. If I want romantic dates, then I have to educate my husband on what this means and discover things we can enjoy doing together. If I want my husband to long to come home at night, then I have to ask him to define the word "haven" and make sure our home reflects that.

When I invest energy into my marriage, suddenly it starts working the way it's supposed to. And I must also remember the real power source for my marriage comes from getting into God's Word and letting His Word get into me. God's Word is the ultimate marriage instruction manual!

Dear Lord, help me to put aside my pride so I can hear You whisper to my heart things I can do to improve my marriage. In Jesus' name. Amen.

Application Steps

- Set a date for you and your husband to go out and have time to really talk.
- Ask your husband to define what a haven is to him.
- Identify the areas of marriage you are struggling with and look up verses in God's Word that address each.
- Commit to memorizing these verses and refer to them often.

164 God's Rx for a Restful Life

Zoë Elmore

Come to me, all you who are weary and burdened,
and I will give you rest. Take my yoke upon you and
learn from me, for I am gentle and humble in heart,
and you will find rest for your souls.

MATTHEW 11:28-29

I don't know about you, but my life seems to be getting busier and more complicated with each passing day. I'm finding it difficult to balance all of my responsibilities and still find time to be refreshed, renewed, or even rested. I've heard it said that you can't give away what you don't have, and these days I'm feeling pretty empty.

Every day I see people typing away on their BlackBerries during conversations and talking on cell phones while eating, driving, or walking their dogs. We have become a society that is attached to some type of technological gismo every waking minute, yet most of my friends and coworkers will tell you that with all of this technology available to make our lives easier, they are wiped out. They feel as if they have nothing left to give their families at the end of each day. In all honesty I have to admit that lately my life resembles what I've just described.

How did I allow myself to fall into this exhausting lifestyle, and where can I find the rest I desperately need? I believe I've discovered the answer to both questions in Matthew 11:28-29. In part the answer lies in the fact that I have been relying on my own strength as I pursue "spiritual activity" instead of pursuing "active spirituality."

Once again I seem to have it backward. I forgot that the Lord isn't interested in or impressed with the number of spiritual activities I'm involved with. Instead, the Lord is interested in my pursuit of ever-increasing spirituality. As I spend time reading God's Word and praying each morning, I am able to identify the activities He is calling me to be involved with. Being obedient to His calling and laying extraneous activities aside, I can once again experience His renewed strength, refreshment, and rest.

If life's activities leave you wiped out, worn out, and exhausted, I want to encourage you to leave "spiritual activity" behind and to pursue "active spirituality."

> *Dear Lord, I confess I have relied on my own strength for too long as I have chased after activities in order to be successful or appear spiritual. I lay them all down at the foot of Your cross and await Your plans and purposes for my life. Thank You for uncovering the answer to a life of refreshment, renewal, and rest. In Jesus' name. Amen.*

Application Steps

Surrender your plans and agenda to the Lord daily. Commit yourself to a life of active spirituality and rest. Journal about the differences you feel as you experience regular rest in Him.

165 Of His Dreams

Sharon Glasgow

Who can find a virtuous wife? For her worth is far above rubies.
The heart of her husband safely trusts her; so he will have no lack
of gain. She does him good and not evil all the days of her life.
PROVERBS 31:10-12 NKJV

My dad left our family when I was young, so I lacked the example of a godly marriage. Being the oldest child, I naturally became independent. These two factors added together equaled a negative value in my tendencies toward marriage. My learning curve took years.

I loved my husband, but I didn't respect all of his ideas. I had my own ideas of how things should be, and naturally, I thought I was right. Overall we had a good marriage, but it wasn't what it should be until one day, after reading the Bible, God led me to make a decision that tamed my independent mind-set. I decided to submit to Dale's role as the leader in our home and to respect his thoughts and opinions no matter how much I might disagree.

Our marriage started changing after that day. When Dale would share what he thought the kids needed to do about school or church, my first impulse was to say, "Are you kidding? No way!" Instead, I said nothing. I would bite my tongue, receive his words, and follow his leading. Amazingly, good things started to happen. Dale was making decisions that led us in the right direction! Why—because he cares about our family. Dale doesn't rule over us with an iron fist. He lovingly considers our needs, opinions, and dreams.

Since I yielded to my husband's right to lead, I haven't always agreed with his decisions. Nevertheless, I stood firm in my commitment and followed Dale anyway. The outcome has always been positive and a sure sign that God is leading him. I am honored to follow such a man of God.

Now I find myself in awe of my husband. He is everything I could ever dream of. It is my desire to be everything he dreams of too! If he wakes me up before the alarm with kisses, then I pray that God will give me the ability to be what he needs. I actually enjoy making his favorite meals, dressing the way he likes, and sharing the same interests and hobbies he does.

Sometimes when Dale walks by me, my heart will skip a beat. You know what I mean? We are two people passionately in love—now more than ever. When you and I honor our husbands in every way—at home, in public, and in our conversations with others—God will pour out His passionate love, and we will be swept away by it.

Make a conscious decision to honor your husband. Allow him to love and care for you as Christ loved the church and watch your passion for him grow. You will become the woman of your husband's dreams, and this legacy will live on in your children's marriages for generations to come.

Dear Lord, help me to honor my husband in everything I do and say. Help me to bless him by lavishing him with passionate love. In Jesus' name. Amen.

Application Steps

Seek God's help in honoring your husband with your words and actions. Be wise and loving in all your transactions with him.

166 Out of Control
Marybeth Whalen

Peace I leave with you; my peace I give you.
I do not give to you as the world gives.
Do not let your hearts be troubled and do not be afraid.
JOHN 14:27

Peace. The very word settles down in my soul and sits quietly there, hopeful and waiting. How I long for peace to well up to a point of overflow within me. Instead, I search in vain for this elusive part of God's promise. Didn't Jesus say He was leaving us with peace when He ascended into heaven? Then where is my peace? Can I have my peace now?

I often make the mistake of seeking peace by trying to control my life—my circumstances and the people I love. Surely if I can exercise control over what happens to me, then peace will be a by-product of the perfection that I orchestrate. Right?

I know I am not the only woman who struggles with the desire to control my life. I think that it's in our nature to want to control things. When Adam and Eve were cursed by God, He told Eve, "Your desire will be for your husband, and he will rule over you" (Genesis 3:16). God was telling Eve that her desire for control would be a struggle for the rest of her life. She would want to be in charge, yet that was not God's assignment for her. She and all women after her have been struggling with this ever since.

In my search for peace, I found that peace was not a product of control, but the very opposite of it. When I surrender control, then I find peace. When I say to God, "I can't," I feel the absolute serenity of knowing that He can. I have found that being out of control is actually a very peaceful state of mind. When I am out of control, God is certainly in control.

To help myself remember this valuable lesson, I developed an acronym for "Peace" that I want to share with you:

P urposefully

E mbracing

A ll

C ircumstances

E very day

I don't have control and never will. When I purposefully embrace all the circumstances God allows to come into my life, and accept that He has allowed them according to His perfect plan to accomplish His purposes, then I can experience the peace He intends me to have.

Try peace God's way today. It may not be what you expected, but I can testify that His peace truly is perfect peace.

> *Dear Lord, help me to embrace everything You allow in my life. Help me to surrender the control I have tried to have and to trust You instead. Thank You for giving me perfect peace as You promised. In Jesus' name. Amen.*

Application Steps

Write down the acronym for PEACE and John 14:27 on an index card, and carry it with you throughout your day. Ask God to help you surrender control and submit to His plans for you. When you feel yourself starting to wrestle back control, reflect on the acronym and the verse on your card.

167 Lost in the Crowd

Susanne Scheppmann

When he saw the crowds, he had compassion on them, because they were harassed and helpless, like sheep without a shepherd. Then he said to his disciples, "The harvest is plentiful but the workers are few. Ask the Lord of the harvest, therefore, to send out workers into his harvest field."

MATTHEW 9:36-38

Stacey sprawled across my family room floor in the midst of our small group for high school girls. Her waist-length blond hair wrapped across her bared midriff. Her pose struck me as seductive, and I wondered where she would land in life.

Although not a regular member of the youth group, Stacey visited occasionally. Other nights she drank vast amounts of alcohol and flirted with drugs. She told us she had been sexually active since she was 14. She attempted to shock us, but regardless, the girls chose to accept her into the group.

One evening Stacey rang the doorbell. We gasped in surprise. Her beautiful Rapunzel-like hair was chopped off and dyed jet black. Her eyes were red and swollen. She told us her father had became enraged at her. For punishment, he had cut her hair. In teenage retaliation, she dyed it black.

We tried to comfort her, but a new, bitter hardness peered out from her blue eyes. Once again, she felt lost even in the crowded room of girls. She came to our meetings more sporadically. As the adult leader, I counseled with her over the next several weeks, but I could feel her withdrawing.

I told Stacey that Jesus loved her. He wouldn't condemn her for her behavior. Unlike her father, He had compassion. She wouldn't or couldn't believe it. Her home life continued to worsen, as did her destructive behaviors.

The last time I saw Stacey, she had run away from home. She was living on the streets lost in a crowd of runaway teens who were looking for unconditional love. She called to see if I could bring her some food. I gathered some sandwiches, chips, and cookies. She met me on a corner. As her thin arm reached eagerly for the sack lunch, my heart ached. I attempted to coax her to come home with me. She vowed she could live on her own. Sadly, I left her to cope with life as a runaway.

In our verse today, we saw that Jesus had compassion on the crowds. It didn't matter to Him that they were dirty, uncouth, and sinful. His heart longed to be the Shepherd who would guide and care for them. Today let's ask Jesus to give us love and compassion for those who do not fit into the image of perfect people. Let's step out of our safety bubble into the crowds of lost people who filter through our lives.

And if you happen to meet a young woman named Stacey from Las Vegas, would you tell her Jesus loves her and offer her something to eat?

Dear Lord, grant me the ability to love those who are helpless. Give me a heart of compassion so that I can point the lost to You, the Good Shepherd. Teach me to step out of my comfort zone to those lost in the crowd. In Jesus' name. Amen.

Application Steps

Read Matthew 9. List all of the different types of people Jesus helped that day. Make a second list of people you know who could use your compassion and love to help point them to the Good Shepherd. Then make an effort to contact them with the love of Jesus Christ.

168 The Nod of a Sinner

Glynnis Whitwer

He said, "Jesus, remember me when you come into your kingdom." Jesus answered him, "I tell you the truth, today you will be with me in paradise."

Luke 23:42-43

My dad's health was failing fast. He'd been admitted to ICU with severe dehydration and aspirated pneumonia. When the ICU nurse started asking us hard questions about my dad's last wishes, we knew the outlook was grim.

A scientist and biology teacher all his life, my father was practical about matters of life and death. The downside of his pragmatic mind was a resistance to anything spiritual. For years he watched my mother faithfully take my sister and me to church, yet any attempt at a discussion of faith was met with an annoyed change of subject.

Now critically ill, able to respond only in nods, my dad's need for Jesus was never more obvious. Our prayers over him grew bolder with each passing hour.

One night my mother and I stood talking with the nurse in charge, while my 12-year-old son Dylan was in with his grandpa. After ten minutes, Dylan came out, we said our goodbyes to my dad, and left the hospital.

On the ride home, Dylan was unusually quiet. He finally spoke and said, "Mom, I think Grandpa accepted Jesus tonight. I told him he needed Jesus and I told him why, then I waited a few minutes and asked if he wanted to accept Jesus into his heart, and Grandpa nodded yes."

There wasn't a doubt in my mind that at the invitation of a child, and with a nod, my father was immediately adopted into the family of God. Even though Dad couldn't speak, I believe that nod was enough.

In Jesus' final hours, He displayed the grace of God toward a broken sinner. Without saying the sinner's prayer, the thief dying next to Jesus rasped, "Jesus, remember me when you come into your kingdom." With an answer that rings hope into my heart, Jesus said, "I tell you the truth, today you will be with me in paradise."

The grace of God reached out to that thief on the cross. And the grace of God met my father at his point of greatest need. The incredible news is that God's amazing grace is there for anyone who admits their need for Jesus and invites Him into their lives, no matter what point they are in their living...or dying.

Unfortunately, we weren't able to have a conversation with my father about his faith because he got progressively worse and died a week later. As I reflect on the goodness of God, I'm in awe that His grace extended to a gentle old scientist who'd rejected God for years and was unable to feed himself or speak. I imagine God looking from heaven, His heart filled with love, saying, "Just nod, Richard. I know that's all you can do right now, and that's all it will take."

Dear Lord, I worship You because of Your goodness and the undeserved grace You offer. Thank You for Your love that accepts us as we are. Open my eyes to those who need You and increase my boldness to witness for You. In Jesus' name. Amen.

Application Steps

Identify someone who has rejected Jesus for years. Begin to pray boldly for an opportunity to talk about Jesus with her. If she is closed to hearing from you, pray for God to bring someone else into her life.

169 Strolling on the Water

Rachel Olsen

"Come," he said. Then Peter got down out of the boat, walked on the water and came toward Jesus.

MATTHEW 14:29

I live in a town by the sea and love to spend time on its shore. I'll often see people paddling in the waves by the pier, attempting to walk on water with surfboards. I've tried it, and it's hard—it requires a lot of strength. It takes strong arms to repeatedly paddle out against the current, strong legs to get you up standing on the board, and strong abs to hold your balance as the water flows beneath you. It's a lot of work, but the few moments you are standing up there are exhilarating.

A certain young man took a very exhilarating walk on the water. At the end of Matthew 14, Peter and the other disciples found themselves in a boat, at night, a considerable distance from shore with violent winds kicking up the waves. Already unnerved by the storm, they were frightened when they looked out past the boat's deck and saw a figure coming toward them on the water. They assumed it was a ghost until the figure spoke with a familiar voice saying, "Take courage! It is I. Don't be afraid." "Lord, if it is you," Peter replied, "tell me to come to you on the water." "Come," the figure said. Then Peter got down out of the boat and walked on the water toward Jesus.

Just like that Peter skimmed across the stormy water with no surfboard, water skis, wet suit, or life jacket to aid him. He had not spent hours at the gym strengthening his muscles for this moment. He did, however, spend a lot of time with the Son of God, and he believed that whatever Jesus commanded to happen, would happen. The only muscles Peter needed for this thrilling feat were the spiritual muscles of faith and focus.

Interestingly, walking on the water was Peter's idea. He displayed mind-bending faith when he told Jesus to speak forth his ability to do so. Then he added action to this faith by climbing over the edge of the boat when Jesus said, "Come." Author John Ortberg wrote, "Getting out of the boat was Peter's greatest gift to Jesus; the experience of walking on water was Jesus' greatest gift to Peter."

Once out of the boat on the shifting waves, Peter kept his eyes on Christ. As long as his attention was on the Lord, his faith remained strong enough for the task. He placed one human foot after the other on common, liquid water and walked nearer to the heart of God. Sadly, when Peter looked away from Jesus to the winds whipping all around him, his faith faltered and he sank into the waves.

I've learned that when my focus is on the Lord, I can walk in my calling and accomplish my dreams. When I take my eyes off Jesus and place them on myself, my circumstances, or other people, I sink neck-deep in pride, fear, or envy. I much prefer strolling on the water.

Dear Lord, I want to walk in faith, and focus on You today. Increase my faith. In Jesus' name. Amen.

Application Steps

Read Matthew 14:13-33. Begin exercising your faith and focusing your sight on Christ.

170 The Fear Factor

Micca Campbell

You should not be like cowering, fearful slaves.
You should behave instead like God's very own children,
adopted into his family—calling him "Father, dear Father."
For his Holy Spirit speaks to us deep in our hearts
and tells us that we are God's children.

ROMANS 8:15-16 NLT

My husband and I are opposites. He's conservative, while I'm more free-spirited. I love, however, that he takes care of everything from grooming the dog to life insurance, which he keeps in a lockbox at the bank in case there's a house fire.

One summer, while vacationing, my husband attempted his first daring feat! Joined by friends, we ventured with the kids to a water park. They had every kind of water slide imaginable.

The most adventurous slide was one that dropped straight down, providing the thrill of free falling. This slide was for the brave and daring only.

Challenged by family and friends, Pat slowly climbed the tall stairs of the giant slide, looking back every so often as if he were going off to war. Our son went down first followed by our friend. Now it was Pat's turn. He peered over the top of the slide and then took a few steps back.

"You can do it, Dad," our son yelled. Pat still didn't get into position.

"Hey!" I called. "Just in case, where did you say the key to the lockbox is?"

That did it. He sat down, crossed his arms in front of his chest, leaned back, and away he flew! He made it and lived to tell about it too.

348

The only dreadful thing that happened was his bathing suit ended up around his neck, but it was worth it to have conquered his fear.

The Bible says that God does not give us the spirit of fear. Fear was introduced to the human race by a satanic lie that says we can be our own god.

The truth is we were made to live under the love and protection of the one and only God. But because of our fallen nature, we desire to be in charge and live according to our own rules. As a result, we feel as if everything depends on us. We sense that we are not enough, and it scares us. We know it, but we don't want to admit we are weak and out of control.

Letting go and living in childlike faith is the cure for our fears. You will never experience the peace of God until you admit that your fears are the result of believing in yourself instead of trusting Him.

If you want to slide through life free from fear, then stop peering over the edge as if letting go will result in death. Splash into the pool of God's love and protection. It's an adventure worth experiencing.

> *Dear Lord, I don't want to carry the burden anymore. I confess that I'm not enough. I lay it all down at Your feet. Take control of my life. In Jesus' name. Amen.*

Application Steps

Give God your fear as many times as you need to until victory over it is yours.

171 Lead Me Not into Temptation

Wendy Pope

Don't let us yield to temptation.
MATTHEW 6:13 NLT

Each day the enemy has a plan for you. The plan is to tempt you or persuade you to do or say something you know is not the result of a life yielded to the Holy Spirit. He looks at your weakness and preys on your past mistakes.

What tempts you? Is it food? Could it be the 30 percent off coupons for your favorite store that come via e-mail? Maybe it is the handsome new coworker in your office? I love the New Living Translation of today's verse. "Don't let us yield to temptation." Many times we ask the Lord to forgive us when we are weak regarding temptation, but we forget to ask for help saying no to the temptation in the first place.

God clearly defined through my son what He meant by not yielding to temptation. Our family was away for the weekend for a little rest and relaxation. Part of the rest and relaxation was riding a two-seater John Deere Mule through the bumpy mountainous terrain of the 200-plus-acre farm where we were staying. After spending most of the day driving around with his father, my six-year-old son was determined to drive the Mule himself. He came up with great reasons why he could drive the ATV. He even demonstrated his ability to start the engine, but no amount of reasoning was going to convince his father to let him drive.

My husband was ready for a little real rest, so he parked the Mule in front of the cabin. My son, however, wouldn't give it a rest. He insisted he would only drive around in the circle of the driveway and assured his father once again of his skills as a driver. Once again, his dad said no. With a pout and some mutters under his breath, he slammed the door. In a few moments, he returned with the key to the Mule. As he handed it to his father he said, "Here, Dad. This is so I won't drive."

Wow, I thought. *How profound!* At the age of six, my son recognized his temptation and removed it by taking the key to his father. Isn't that exactly what we are supposed to do with our temptations? In the moment we are tempted, we need to take the temptation to our heavenly Father. We have the power to overcome the temptation through the Holy Spirit. He has given us the power of self-discipline. The next time the enemy brings you face-to-face with your weakness, place what is tempting you in the hands of God Almighty. Experience victory!

Dear Lord, I acknowledge that I am weak but You are strong. Help me to recognize temptation and to overcome it. Thank You for supplying all I need to overcome temptation. I look forward to celebrating each and every victory. In Jesus' name. Amen.

Application Steps

Identify what tempts you. Pray daily for deliverance from that temptation. Look up Scripture that deals with this type of temptation. Write these verses in a journal. Keep the journal with you to record each temptation and then pray the verse that addresses it.

172 Don't Send Me to Africa

Lysa TerKeurst

The eyes of the LORD range throughout the earth to strengthen those whose hearts are fully committed to him.

2 CHRONICLES 16:9

Since I was a little girl I've had a heart for the people of Africa. To be honest, though, I didn't want to be a missionary who lived in a hut, ate grubs fried on an open flame, and wore tribal headdresses. What a limited view of Africa I had. So while I prayed for the people of Africa, I would always throw in, "But, Lord, don't send me." I can just imagine God smiling and looking back at me saying, "Really, princess? You don't want to go to Africa...fine. Then I'll send Africa to you."

And that's exactly what He did. One night while attending a concert by the Liberian Boys Choir, God clearly spoke to my heart and told me that two of those boys were mine. I tried to ignore Him, but to no avail. At the end of the concert, two of the boys walked straight up to me, wrapped their arms around me, and called me Mom. After months of prayer and piles of paperwork, we went to pick up our two sons, Mark and Jackson. Africa had come to our home.

No longer was the plight of the starving orphans in Africa a nameless face on TV; they were precious children who deserved a second chance. Not only did we think so, but other people in my church soon felt moved to also adopt children from Liberia. Today, as I walk up to church on Sunday mornings, I am always moved by the precious sight I see. A little white hand holding a little black hand, a brother and sister skipping and laughing together! And something in my heart just knows this is the way it's supposed to be.

This is the way the body of Christ is supposed to work. God speaks, we listen; He confirms, we obey; He gives us the strength to do amazing things, we watch miracles come out of our lives. I love 2 Chronicles

16:9 because it brings a picture to my mind of God standing in front of a crowd of people asking, "Who is willing to do an amazing assignment for Me?"

Many shrug and make excuses. But one little girl jumps up and in complete abandon says, "Me, Lord! Me! Pick me! I am willing!" Then God smiles, scoops her up, brings her into His loving embrace, and whispers back, "Well done, My child. I am so pleased. You have made the good choice. I will give you the strength to do this. Do not be afraid. I will be with you."

> *Dear Lord, let me always be that little girl with the up-stretched arm and obedient heart. Give me the wisdom to know Your voice and the courage to say yes to whatever You ask of me. My greatest desire is to walk with You all the days of my life. I don't want to settle for the good life. I want the great life, where I live the adventure You created my soul to live. In Jesus' name. Amen.*

Application Steps

Look for an opportunity to say yes to God today. It might be as simple as writing an encouraging note to a friend or paying for the food of the person behind you in the drive-through. Or maybe it will be the start of something big. Either way, start training your heart to recognize God's divine appointments, and discover the thrill of saying yes.

173 What Caused My Fire to Lose Its Glow?

Melissa Taylor

Be satisfied with what you have. For God has said,
"I will never fail you. I will never forsake you."
HEBREWS 13:5 NLT

If asked to describe my faith, for years I would have told you I was on fire for the Lord. My relationship with God was intimate and joyful. I was passionate for His Word. No matter what my circumstances, I seemed to be able to draw peace and joy that could only come from knowing Jesus. I trusted God completely.

Why then did that fire I had in my heart suddenly start decreasing? What was causing my fire to lose its glow? I didn't love God any less. I hadn't lost faith in His power. I still believed every bit of His Word. Why was I not "feeling" renewed, excited, joyful, and peaceful the way I always had before? Was my fire burning out? The truth is, I was burned out.

I never thought my life or those around me were in my control, but I was beginning to feel helpless in many areas of my life. I was being pulled in many directions. Where I ordinarily relied on God for guidance through the tough times, I couldn't feel His presence anymore. The worst part of this for me was that I couldn't pinpoint why.

I thought I was doing all the right things. I searched my Bible for answers. I prayed. I cried out for help. I confided in my closest friends. I was lost and felt abandoned by God without a reason. My passion and fire had fizzled. My flame had reduced to a spark.

All my life, I've been an encourager and someone who naturally had a smile to share. What happened to that person?

I began to feel better over the next few months. I wish I could tell you the way that the spark became a flame again. I hesitated even to write this story because I didn't have an answer to the question, "What caused my fire to lose its glow?" What I can tell you is that I never gave up on God. Even though I couldn't feel His presence in my life, I knew He was there. I knew it because I knew His Word, and I believed it. Second Corinthians 5:7 says that we are to believe in what we can't see. I also had to learn to believe in what I couldn't feel.

If you are in a place where you don't "feel" God, don't give up. Don't despair or worry. Hang on to what you know is true, and that is the Word of God. Trust Him to remain faithful, loving, and in control just as it says. He will never abandon you, just as He never abandoned me. God is true to His Word no matter how we are feeling. He is true to His Word today, tomorrow, and forever.

> *Dear Lord, today I want to thank You for Your Word. Give me the desire to read it, know it, and live it. In Jesus' name. Amen.*

Application Steps

If you are struggling to feel God near, surround yourself with truth from His Word. Place verses around your home, car, office, and purse to remind you that God is still with you.

174 Choose to Grow

Luann Prater

He who gathers money little by little makes it grow.
Proverbs 13:11

She wanted a job. She had goals she wanted to attain, and they were going to require money. And she didn't want just any job; it had to be Chick-fil-A. They were closed on Sundays, and working Sundays was not an option. Her desire to be in church was greater than her desire for money. One thing stood in her way: She was 15 and their hiring age was 16. In her mind that was just a detail.

After picking out the perfect outfit, brushing every tooth, and wearing her radiant smile, she bounced into the restaurant. With a firm handshake she introduced herself to the owner, filled out the application, and reassured him that her age would not limit her ability to do a great job. The next day she called him to see if he had any further questions or references he would like. He was so impressed with her attitude that he took a chance and hired her. At orientation he told her these were the rules for making sure she had a successful work life: keep God first, family second, school third, after school activities fourth, and then Chick-fil-A. "But when you are here," he said, "give us all you got."

For the next five years her job worked around every school play, mission trip, and wedding my daughter attended. Unlike many of her friends, she socked her four-hour paychecks away in the bank. Rarely would she pry open her purse strings. She had a goal.

Little by little her account grew. She came home from college during holiday breaks and went right back to the drive-through. One day she announced she was accepted to a study abroad program in Argentina, and she would be leaving in the fall. My husband and I were thrilled but a bit anxious about the expense. She said, "Don't worry, Mom. I've been saving my entire work life for such a time as this."

When you look at the Proverbs 31 woman, you'll find she is a faithful steward of her time and money. My daughter taught me volumes with her technique. First, she kept Christ at the top of her priority list while she sought a job that fit her life demands. Then she collected every little paycheck and saved to achieve a great big dream.

In this fast-paced life we often forget that we have choices. We choose if God comes first. We choose how we spend our time. We choose how we spend or save our money. Let's make wise choices and live richly.

> *Dear Lord, today make me keenly aware of how I'm choosing to spend my time and resources. Help me gather little by little and make it grow. Help me to make better choices that will give me the ability to live out the dreams You've laid in my heart. In Jesus' name. Amen.*

Application Steps

Examine your spending habits. Do you have a budget? Are you saving? Do you have a dream you want to save for? Are you giving to God? A good rule of thumb is "give, save, spend," in that order.

175 His Compassions Never Fail

Renee Swope

Because of the LORD's great love we are not consumed,
for his compassions never fail. They are new every morning;
great is your faithfulness.

LAMENTATIONS 3:22-23

I walked through the small consignment store looking for maternity clothes while Joshua, my then two-year-old, played in the children's area. Making my way through the clothes racks, I was startled when Joshua came running to my side with tears in his eyes. He pulled my hand and led me to the back of the store to show me his injured friend, the clothes mannequin. As we came to her side, Joshua lifted her dress. I blushed as I looked around, hoping no one noticed my son looking up a woman's skirt, even if she was plastic. "Look, Mommy," Joshua cried as he pointed to the metal rod shooting up her back for support. With a tear running down his cheek, he whispered, "Ouch, that hurts."

I was overwhelmed by Joshua's compassion and almost started crying as I knelt in front of him to explain that his friend was okay. She just needed a little extra support.

Joshua's tender mercy was such a picture of God's love that day—love that is full of compassion; love that shows concern, not just with words but with actions. Joshua saw someone who was hurting, or so he thought, and he wanted to ease her pain. He reminded me of a lesson Jesus taught about love and compassion.

A man was traveling down the road one day and noticed an injured pedestrian who had been robbed, stripped of his clothing, and left for dead. Unlike others who ignored him as they passed by earlier, this Samaritan saw the injured victim and was moved with compassion. He bandaged his wounds, took him to an inn, and got him the care he needed.

Jesus told this story to show what compassion—*love in action*—looks like. True to His nature, Jesus didn't just tell us to love; He showed us how to love. He loved first. He said, "Love sacrificially." Then He showed us by sacrificing His life for ours. It was His never-failing compassion that moved His heart to act on our behalf, to come to our rescue and redeem us.

Just like a Good Samaritan, Jesus comes to our side. With an aching awareness of our injured hearts, our sin-wrecked lives, and our need for His forgiveness, He bends down and with outstretched hands He offers to bandage our wounds and give us the care we need.

The same compassion that moved God's heart more than 2000 years ago moves His heart toward you today. No matter where you are or what you need, He offers healing for your hurts, comfort for your concerns, and rest for your wearied soul. Remember that His compassions never fail. They are new every morning!

> *Dear Lord, thank You for seeing my greatest needs. When I fail or feel let down by others, remind this heart of mine that Your compassions never fail me. Thank You for loving me with Your Words and Your actions. Help me do the same—to love You and others with my life. In Jesus' name. Amen.*

Application Steps

Tell God the areas of your life that are hurting (marriage, work relationships, parenting, financial stress). Ask Him to draw near and care for your needs the way the Samaritan did for the injured man. As you experience God's compassion, look for ways to let it flow into the lives of those who are hurting around you.

Index

Principle #1—The Proverbs 31 Woman reveres Jesus Christ as Lord of her life and pursues an ongoing, personal relationship with Him.

"Whosoever" by Micca Campbell, p. 14

"The Difference a Faith-Full Woman Can Make" by Marybeth Whalen, p. 22

"If Only" by Luann Prater, p. 24

"Do I Want Change?" by Melissa Taylor, p. 28

"Shattered and Scattered" by Van Walton, p. 32

"Knowing God" by Micca Campbell, p. 34

"You're Just Like that Little Girl" by Zoë Elmore, p. 40

"Burned-Out and Calling Out" by Wendy Pope, p. 42

"Do You See Me?" by Marybeth Whalen, p. 44

"Plan a Great Date" by Renee Swope, p. 46

"Going Astray" by Luann Prater, p. 50

"Who's Got the Whole World?" by Melissa Taylor, p. 54

"Mirror, Mirror on the Wall" by Charlene Kidd, p. 58

"It Is Enough" by Wendy Pope, p. 64

"Crossroads" by Susanne Scheppmann, p. 68

"Plate Spinner" by Luann Prater, p. 70

"God's Arms" by Marybeth Whalen, p. 72

"Dreams Come True" by Rachel Olsen, p. 76

"Crucified" by Micca Campbell, p. 80

"Learning Contentment" by Glynnis Whitwer, p. 82

"Fill 'er Up" by Luann Prater, p. 90

"Taste and See" by Rachel Olsen, p. 94

"I've Been Scammed" by Glynnis Whitwer, p. 96

"Confidence in Chaos" by Zoë Elmore, p. 98

"Coming Home" by Micca Campbell, p. 100

"Satan Yells, God Whispers" by Marybeth Whalen, p. 104

"No More Shame" by Lysa TerKeurst, p. 110

"Meter Reader" by Wendy Pope, p. 114

"Spend Some Time with Me" by Melissa Taylor, p. 118

"A Cheerful Heart" by Susanne Scheppmann, p. 120

"The Joy of Being a Disciple" by Micca Campbell, p. 122

"My Morning Renewal" by Susanne Scheppmann, p. 126

"Sanctuary" by Van Walton, p. 128

"Facing a Phobia" by Rachel Olsen, p. 130

"Living in the Hear and Now" by Renee Swope, p. 136

"Pardon Me?" by Wendy Pope, p. 138

"Encouragement in a Bottle" by Susanne Scheppmann, p. 142

"Better Late than Never" by Glynnis Whitwer, p. 144

"Finding Sure Footing in a Slippery World" by Rachel Olsen, p. 148

"I'm Not…I Am" by Melissa Taylor, p. 150

"He's Still God" by Micca Campbell, p. 152

"Don't Look Down" by Marybeth Whalen, p. 154

"Letting Go" by Luann Prater, p. 156

"Fear and Love" by Rachel Olsen, p. 164

"Choosing Forgiveness" by Zoë Elmore, p. 166

"And They Were Amazed" by Glynnis Whitwer, p. 168

"On Guard" by Micca Campbell, p. 172

"Look, I Made God Smile" by Wendy Pope, p. 174

"You're the One I Want" by Renee Swope, p. 176

"Conversation Hearts" by Susanne Scheppmann, p. 180

"Bridezilla" by Rachel Olsen, p. 182

"The Pineapple Principle" by Lysa TerKeurst, p. 184

"A Promise Kept" by Glynnis Whitwer, p. 190

"The Pumpkin Patch" by Sharon Glasgow, p. 192

"Fluffy Deception" by Luann Prater, p. 196

"Hallelujah" by Rachel Olsen, p. 198

"Grandpa" by Micca Campbell, p. 200

"A Surprising Answer" by Susanne Scheppmann, p. 204

"Overcoming Our Enemies of Doubt and Fear" by Renee Swope, p. 206

"Born to Be" by Marybeth Whalen, p. 208

"Daddy, Do You Love Me?" by Lysa TerKeurst, p. 210

"Don't Give Up" by Rachel Olsen, p. 214

"The Haircut" by Melissa Taylor, p. 216

"Specks" by Susanne Scheppmann, p. 220

"Toppled" by the Pressure" by Zoë Elmore, p. 222

"Right or Left Thinking" by Marybeth Whalen, p. 226

"I Don't Want to Tell You" by Rachel Olsen, p. 230

"His Banner over Me" by Lysa TerKeurst, p. 234

"In the Shadow" by Wendy Pope, p. 236

"Got Rain?" by Van Walton, p. 238

"My Image of God" by Renee Swope, p. 240

"Hearing the Coach's Voice" by Melissa Taylor, p. 242

"False Advertising" by Susanne Scheppmann, p. 244

"Seeking Shade" by Marybeth Whalen, p. 246

"Feeding Black Clouds" by Rachel Olsen, p. 248

"A Father's Love" by Micca Campbell, p. 250

"The Marks of Love" by Glynnis Whitwer, p. 256

"Dealing with the Yuckies" by Lysa TerKeurst, p. 258

"Spring-Cleaning" by Susanne Scheppmann, p. 260

"Believing Is Seeing" by Micca Campbell, p. 262

"The Shame of It All" by Wendy Pope, p. 264

"Close to You" by Marybeth Whalen, p. 270

"Wanting What I Have" by Renee Swope, p. 272

"Fearfully and Wonderfully Made" by Melissa Taylor, p. 276

"Hang On" by Glynnis Whitwer, p. 280

"Pillow Talk" by Rachel Olsen, p. 282

"The Narrow Way" by Micca Campbell, p. 284

"Dressed for Success" by Zoë Elmore, p. 286

"Our Provider" by Susanne Scheppmann, p. 288

"The Pull of Home" by Rachel Olsen, p. 290

"Hats Off" by Wendy Pope, p. 292

"Disabled" by Luann Prater, p. 294

"Crime Scene" by Van Walton, p. 296

"Beloved" by Rachel Olsen, p. 298

"Anxiety" by Melissa Taylor, p. 300

"Nobody Likes a Quitter" by Susanne Scheppmann, p. 306

"Surviving the Storm" by Micca Campbell, p. 310

"The 9-1-1 Plan" by Sharon Glasgow, p. 316

"A Rule Change" by Wendy Pope, p. 318

"A Christmas Miracle" by Micca Campbell, p. 328

"Trusting God in All Things" by Melissa Taylor, p. 330

"God's Rx for a Restful Life" by Zoë Elmore, p. 336

"Out of Control" by Marybeth Whalen, p. 340

"The Nod of a Sinner" by Glynnis Whitwer, p. 344

"Strolling on the Water" by Rachel Olsen, p. 346

"The Fear Factor" by Micca Campbell, p. 348

"Lead Me Not into Temptation" by Wendy Pope, p. 350

"What Caused My Fire to Lose Its Glow?" by Melissa Taylor, p. 354

Principle #2, The Proverbs 31 Woman loves, honors, and respects her husband as the leader of the home.

"Victoria's Little Secret" by p. 30

"Ice Princess" by Rachel Olsen, p. 38

"Beep-Beep" by Micca Campbell, p. 60

"Spouse!" by Susanne Scheppmann, p. 88

"The Duet" by Rachel Olsen, p. 112

"I Don't Love My Husband Anymore" by Lysa TerKeurst, p. 158

"Expressions of Joy" by Micca Campbell, p. 178

"You Deplete Me" by Luann Prater, p. 224

"The Marriage I've Always Wanted" by Lysa TerKeurst, p. 334

"Of His Dreams" by Sharon Glasgow, p. 338

Principle # 3, The Proverbs 31 Woman nurtures her children and believes that motherhood is a high calling with the responsibility of shaping and molding the children who will one day define who we are as a community and a nation.

"My Septic Heart" by Wendy Pope, p. 18

"Can-Do Kids" by Renee Swope, p. 74

"The DMV of Life" by Van Walton, p. 78

"Before I Fly Off the Handle Again" by Lysa TerKeurst, p. 84

"Pretending" by Shari Braendel, p. 92

"Mother's Trust" by Sharon Glasgow, p. 106

"Thank God for Smelly Shoes" by Lysa TerKeurst, p. 134

"Mother of the Year" by Micca Campbell, p. 140

"Dylan's First Day" by Melissa Taylor, p. 188

"A Legacy" by Susanne Scheppmann, p. 274

"Love the Ones You're With" by Renee Swope, p. 304

"My Black Thumb" by Marybeth Whalen, p. 312

"A Blessed "Steppie"" by Shari Braendel, p. 322

Principle #4, The Proverbs 31 Woman is a disciplined and industrious keeper of the home who creates a warm and loving environment for her family and friends.

"Be There" by Lysa TerKeurst, p. 10

"He Knows the Plans" by Renee Swope, p. 102

"You've Got Charisma" by Luann Prater, p. 124

"Summer Vacations" by Sharon Glasgow, p. 232

"Lessons from an Ostrich" by Rachel Olsen, p. 266

"Sweet Potato Times" by Susanne Scheppmann, p. 326

Principle #5, The Proverbs 31 Woman contributes to the financial well-being of her household by being a faithful steward of the time and money God has entrusted to her.

"Affluenza" by Rachel Olsen, p. 56

"What's in Your Closet?" by Susanne Scheppmann, p. 108

"Being Faithful with Little" by Glynnis Whitwer, p. 116

"Money Lessons" by Sharon Glasgow, p. 146

"Confessions of a Recovering Shopaholic" by Wendy Pope, p. 202

"Finding Balance in a Tilted World" by Glynnis Whitwer, p. 212

"Meet a Joyful Giver" by Rachel Olsen, p. 314

"Able and Available" by Renee Swope, p. 324

"Choose to Grow" by Luann Prater, p. 356

Principle #6, The Proverbs 31 Woman speaks with wisdom and faithful instruction as she mentors and supports other women and develops godly friendships.

"Competition or Mission?" by Rachel Olsen, p. 12

"Mentoring—Moments or Meetings?" by Renee Swope, p.16

"Loving Irregular Dads" by Sharon Glasgow, p. 36

"A Fool's Tongue" by Susanne Scheppmann, p. 48

"My Fab 5" by Melissa Taylor, p. 86

"The Power of the Word" by Marybeth Whalen, p. 132

"Growing Friendships" by Van Walton, p. 170

"Stumbling Blocks" by Charlene Kidd, p. 254

"The Dreaded Relationship" by Sharon Glasgow, p. 268

"Brain Blips, Mishaps, and Feelings of Failure" by Lysa TerKeurst, p. 278

"Friendship Choices" by Lysa TerKeurst, p. 308

"Telling Our Friends the Truth" by Glynnis Whitwer, p. 320

"An Unexpected Gift" by Rachel Olsen, p. 332

Principle #7, The Proverbs 31 Woman shares the love of Christ" by extending her hand to help with the needs of the community.

"Pass It On" by Susanne Scheppmann, p. 20

"The Ministry of Interruptions" by Glynnis Whitwer, p. 26

"Worth Dying For" by Glynnis Whitwer, p. 52

"My Friend the Atheist" by Lysa TerKeurst, p. 62

"Ready to Quit" by Sharon Glasgow, p. 66

"Don't Waste It" by Micca Campbell, p. 160

"Empty Nesting" by Susanne Scheppmann, p. 162

"God's Promptings" by Marybeth Whalen, p. 186

"Are You a Salt Lick?" by Susanne Scheppmann, p. 194

"Behold the Body of Christ" by Micca Campbell, p. 218

"For Those Who Love Him" by Glynnis Whitwer, p. 228

"Clothed in Prayer" by Luann Prater, p. 252

"Everybody Gets to Play" by Glynnis Whitwer, p. 302

"Lost in the Crowd" by Susanne Scheppmann, p. 342

"Don't Send Me to Africa" by Lysa TerKeurst, p. 352

"His Compassions Never Fail" by Renee Swope, p. 358

Proverbs 31 Ministries

We're so glad you've shared your devotional time with us through the pages of this book. If you've enjoyed these devotions and desire more, simply log onto our website at www.proverbs31.org and sign up to receive our daily devotion electronically. It's free—and what woman doesn't like free!

While you're there, take some time to look around our website. You'll find lots of articles and helpful information. If you'd like to purchase other books from our authors, just look through the resources section of the website where you'll find many offerings.

Each of the writers contributing to *God's Purpose for Every Woman* is also a trained and gifted speaker. If you are interested in having one or more of them speak at your next event or retreat, call us toll free at 1-877-P31-HOME to find out how. Or visit the speaking ministry section of our website at www.proverbs31.org.

The Proverbs 31 woman is not perfect. She experiences good days, bad days, blessings, challenges, failings, and victories. The key characteristic of this special woman, however, is that she trusts in God for her peace, perspective, and purpose. That's why this ministry exists—to bring that hopeful truth to women everywhere.

Proverbs 31 Ministries
616-G Matthews-Mint Hill Road
Matthews, NC 28105

877-P31-HOME (877-731-4663)
704-849-2270

www.proverbs31.org

Meet the Contributors

Shari Braendel is a nationally known speaker, contributing author for *Proverbs 31 Ministries* magazine, and happily married with four children. Shari's passion is helping women and teens realize, develop, and celebrate their God-given beauty, inside and out. She is abundantly blessed with the gift of encouragement and converts women's fashion fears to tears of laughter.

Micca Campbell is a nationally known speaker who has touched and transformed the lives of thousands across the United States. She serves as director of outreach with Proverbs 31 Ministries, is a former Mother of the Year, and is a contributing author to *For the Write Reason*. Micca also writes regularly for the ministry's online devotional, "Encouragement for Today."

Zoë Elmore is happily married to Tom Elmore and is the mother of two sons. She makes her home in Charlotte, North Carolina. Zoë has six years of training with Bible Study Fellowship International as a small group leader and three years as assistant teaching leader. Zoë travels throughout the United States encouraging women with her passion of obedience to God's call in their lives.

Sharon Glasgow is a wife and mother of five daughters ranging from 12 to 24 years old. She has been writing and speaking professionally for 15 years. Sharon is internationally known for her popular topic, "The Sloboholic Superwoman." She energetically motivates her audiences by applying biblical truths to our current cultural needs in an engaging storytelling manner.

Charlene Kidd is a wife and mother of four who helps her husband run a home-based business in York, South Carolina. She is a graduate of CLASS and a speaker with Proverbs 31 Ministries. She is passionate about empowering women to walk in the power of the Holy Spirit, and she also teaches marriage retreats with her husband, Allan.

Rachel Olsen is a married mother of two, author, editor, university teacher, and national women's speaker with a master's degree in communication. She serves as senior editor for Proverbs 31 Ministries' online devotions and is on the editorial board of *P31 Woman* magazine. Rachel is also a contributing writer to *Experiencing God's Power in Your Ministry.* Her passion is to draw women closer to Christ and to one another.

Wendy Pope is the author of *Out of the Mouths of Babes.* Wendy also writes for "Encouragement for Today," the online daily devotionals from Proverbs 31 Ministries. Her devotions have been featured on Crosswalk.com. Wendy is a speaker with a heart's desire to know Christ intimately and to stir the same desire in other women.

Luann Prater is a mother of three, friend of two stepdaughters, and grandmother to six. She runs a small business and is active in her church. Luann loves life, and her zest for living is contagious. From stained tragedies to the brilliant glow of grace, she allows God to use her struggles to portray a picture of hope and encouragement to others.

Susanne Scheppmann is a coast-to-coast speaker. She combines her passion for Jesus, her love for women, and her knowledge of God's Word with creative appeal. Susanne's sense of humor, engaging storytelling abilities, and creative parable teachings help relate biblical principles to her audiences. Susanne's Bible study, *Perplexing Proverbs,* is now available. Her next book, *Wild Child: Whispers from a Mother's Heart,* will be released in 2008.

Renee Swope is married to her best friend, J.J. They call North Carolina home with their sons, Joshua and Andrew. Renee is a national speaker, author, and cohost of Proverbs 31 Ministries' international daily radio show. Through personal stories of life, love, and laughter, Renee connects with women around the world, challenging them, encouraging them, and helping them discover the heart of God in everyday moments.

Melissa Taylor is a wife, mother of four, and a speaker with Proverbs 31 Ministries. She has a passion for leading women to discover their true identity in Christ and not in the temporary things of this world. She is a teacher and speaker for Christian women's events and lives with her family in Charlotte, North Carolina.

Lysa TerKeurst is a wife, mom, speaker, and author of 11 books. She's been featured on *Focus on the Family, Good Morning America, The Oprah Winfrey Show,* and *O, The Oprah Magazine.* She cofounded Proverbs 31 Ministries, but to those who know her best she is simply a carpooling mom who loves Jesus and struggles like the rest of us with junk drawers and cellulite.

Van Walton's childhood experiences in the South American jungles exposed her to mission work and foreign cultures, introducing her to Jesus' great commission: Love God and your neighbor. Today she pursues God's purpose for her life through writing and speaking. She also teaches Bible and parenting classes to Latina women. Van rejoices in her marriage of 35 years and the wondrous adventure of parenting two sons.

Marybeth Whalen is the wife of Curt and mom of six children, ranging in age from 15 to 2. She is the author of *For the Write Reason* and a speaker for Proverbs 31 Ministries.

Glynnis Whitwer is on staff with Proverbs 31 Ministries as the senior editor of the *P31 Woman* magazine. She is the author of *work@home: A Practical Guide for Women Who Want to Work from Home,* and coauthor of a Bible studies series entitled *Kingdom Living.* Glynnis and her husband, Tod, run a home-based business, have five children, and live in Glendale, Arizona.

Bible Credits